D0394251

THE CONTEMPORARY GREEK CINEMA

by

MEL SCHUSTER

The Scarecrow Press, Inc.

Metuchen, N.J. & London

1979

Library of Congress Cataloging in Publication Data

Schuster, Mel.
   The contemporary Greek cinema.

   Bibliography: p.
   Includes index.
     1. Moving-pictures--Greece, Modern. I. Title.
PN1993.5.G75S38 1979   791.43'09495   78-20969
ISBN 0-8108-1196-0

FOREWORD AND DEDICATION

In 1975, I spent six weeks in Greece as a guest of
film critic Mirella Georgiadou.   Since I would rather be in
some dark movie theater dealing with the reality of film
images than enjoying the sunny, sometimes unreality of
Greece's famous beaches, this visit became the start of a
logical course of events which led to this book.

That visit provided an introduction to the work of directors for whom my hostess had admiration and rightly adjudged my subsequently shared enthusiasm.   Returning to
Greece for six months in 1976 and five weeks in 1977, it
was an eager choice to pick up where I had left off; the time
was spent in happy immersion in the current provocative and
unique Greek cinema.

I am in awe of the accomplishments of the young
Greek directors.   If some of their works fail to elevate me,
knowledge of their disregard of the impossible provides a
subjective cushion to ease the disappointment of a seemingly
misguided vision.   The commitment, egomania, blindness,
and love which are required of the 1970s Greek film director
inspire an admixture of professional admiration, personal respect and affection, and frank questioning of their sanity!   It
is to these marvelous, talented, and crazy artists that this
book is dedicated in gratitude for the great pleasure they
have given me in sharing their time, their thoughts and their
films.

I could not have met any of them, seen their work,
or been enriched by the experiences without the selfless and
endless aid and guidance of Mirella Georgiadou, to whom this
book is also dedicated in unbounded gratitude and affection.
She plotted my course of action, but never my destination of
reactions and conclusions.

New York City
January 1978   793411

ACKNOWLEDGMENTS

To name each person who cooperated and contributed to this book would be practically a repetition of the index. Most of the people discussed in this book gave of their time for interviews and follow-up correspondence. They donated photographs to be used. They showed their films, often renting a screening room at their own expense. Without their generous contributions and receptivity to this project, it simply could not have been realized, for which very sincere gratitude is felt and offered.

There are those to be thanked who contributed assistance beyond the scope of their personal involvement with the project. Dimitris Koliodemos gathered much of the factual information for the Who's Who section. Thanassis Rentzis became an essential clearinghouse, moving problems presented to him toward their solutions. George Tsemberopoulos translated material as well as contributing valuable suggestions for expanding the scope of coverage and correcting some factual inaccuracies. Panos Ghristopoulos gathered much information by phone when the language barrier became insurmountable. The staff of The Athenian cheerfully gave access to the complete run of that informative magazine. Gert Heller, Richard Trupp, and Wayne Hazeltine gave time and attention to business and financial problems which left me free to continue work on the book. Bob Lehrer proved once again to be not only an understanding employer, but a steadfast friend. There are, no doubt, many people who made contributions unknown to me, as a result of a request from Mirella Georgiadou who constantly eased the logistical problems as well as serving as liaison between myself and most of the people essential to the evolvement of this book. And whatever intuitive perception, analytical ability, and love may be apparent in this book is due largely to Yvonne Youst, who contributed so much to the awakening and development of those faculties within me.

TABLE OF CONTENTS

INTRODUCTION

This is not a history of the Greek film industry because, 1) I don't know enough to tackle such a concept, * and
2) there is no current Greek film industry. Rather, it is
intended as an introduction to what has happened to Greek
films since approximately 1970, aimed at a non-Greek reader
likely to know little about this phenomenon, fascinating on its
individual terms, but in many respects typical of national
film industries throughout the world.

In the late 1960s, the then-existing Greek film industry had hit a whirling peak of formula production comparable
to that of few countries (with the notable exception of India).
It was difficult to tell last week's movie from this week's,
the entire output melding into an anonymous repetition of
stories, stars, and directors. With the advent of television,
the bottom fell out of the whole feverish system, and there
was no longer a film industry.

Since then, filmmaking has limped along, beleaguered
by no money, limited schools at which to learn the craft of
making films, no audience for the handful of films that do
miraculously get made, and no distribution channels leading
to a possible international market. That there is a film output in Greece at all is completely to the credit of a small
number of determined and very nearly martyred filmmakers.
It is to them and their problems and rewards that this study
addresses itself.

My knowledge of Greek films exists as a result of a
nine-month, tightly compressed learning period which included

---

*The films produced during the onslaught of the commercial
cinema are numerous. It would be a formidable task for an
outsider to tackle such a study. An evaluation of this aspect
of cinematic history will, one hopes, emerge from the memory and conclusions of someone who actually lived through
that cinematic experience.

a vast number of hours viewing films, time spent with the filmmakers, and a considerable amount of analyzing of thoughts, feelings and reactions to those films and the people who made them.

In no way, therefore, does this study pretend to be definitive. The title of the book is not only intended to reflect the reader's introduction to contemporary Greek cinema, but is an account and summation of my own. As there have not been all that many films made in Greece during the 1970s, a comprehensive introduction is possible, but it remains just that.

It is often a highly personal account. Interviews frequently began formally, but just as frequently ended with warm and friendly conversation which often led to social exchanges devoid of film talk. Of the people given major attention in this collection, there isn't one for whom I do not feel utmost respect and genuine affection. A few have become close, corresponding friends with lifetime potentiality of remaining so.

It was difficult to prevent my response to them as people from oversensitizing my reaction to their films. In an effort to make adjustments to this subjective probability, films were seen before meeting the directors. This resulted in many surprises. Thodoros Angelopoulos is a physically small man who presented himself guardedly, yet his major opus, THE TRAVELLING PLAYERS, is an epic film of vast, expansive proportions. Tasos Psarras' two films are opinionated and preachy; he displayed a gentle, probing personality not visible at all in his films. The very human and warm Costas Sfikas has produced two methodical, cerebral films. In fact, each proved quite different from his films with the major exception of Pandelis Voulgaris, whose films and personal presentation are very intimate; and most exceptional of all, Nicos Panayotopoulos, whose admixture of humor and seriousness is the same heady concoction in personality as in his three-to-one, properly chilled martini of a film, THE COLORS OF IRIS.

To tell the story of the current Greek cinema is to forego a chronological historical approach; its past is not clearly seeded, its present is ill-defined and its future is definitely unsure. It is more like a modern movie where scenes occur seemingly independent from one another, with episodes juxtaposed in time, meaning and development. It is only at the end that one can unravel and reconstruct with a sense of storyline flow. Thus it is with the film world in Greece in the 1970s. There is little to tie it all together. Each individual goes on his own way, sometimes imitating, sometimes joining in the current "trend." But trends are short-lived and surface without apparent cohesiveness: 1974 was a year of consistently high-quality films, but divergent in subject emphasis; 1975 was nearly universally political; 1976 could most accurately be characterized as pretentious. Angelopoulos and Voulgaris are the leaders, except that no one follows. Each filmmaker moves along on his own dictates and the meeting of the ways is an exception, and, as the Thessaloniki Festival sometimes reveals, a phenomenon.

Since there is nothing to tie them all together--no industry, no producers, no distributors, minimal cinematic external or even internal influence, it becomes necessary to view each element of the Greek film world as a separate entity. As the elements are diluted, it becomes clear that a few filmmakers functioning against fantastic odds are the backbone, or rather, the entire skeleton of Greek films. And so by examining each of them, listening to them talk, responding to them as people and artists, a view of the whole has emerged. They are the pieces which, when put together, comprise the entire picture.

In 1976, only eight feature films were submitted to the annual film festival. This fact should be kept in mind throughout when reading generalizations or conclusions. Such opinions are based on very minimal quantitative data, but since that's all there is, each filmmaker and his work becomes a microcosm of a complete segment of filmmaking. There are entire books on experimental filmmakers in the United States. Experimental film in Greece means the work of Thanassis Rentzis and Costas Sfikas. Major studies are done on genre movies. In Greece, currently, social consciousness is the forté of Tasos Psarras. Propaganda means Thodoros Maranghos. Comedy belongs to Nicos Panayotopoulos. But this categorizing is ridiculous; one film does not a genre make. In fact, the entire Greek film "industry" means the work of 20 or so men and women who somehow manage to find a way to their art where, in the final analysis, no way exists.

Chapter 1

THE GREEK CINEMA--A BRIEF HISTORY

The earliest known Greek film is a 1906 documentary about the revival of the Olympic Games. Despite this early entry into the cinema world, progress has been slow, being severely hampered by wars and internal political strife.

Italian films were highly popular during the early years of cinema in Greece, resulting in film production imitative of those successful imported films. The first comedy made, for instance, was a spoof of the then fashionable Biblical epic QUO VADIS (1912), made by the stage comic Spiros Dimitracopoulos.

One of the early pioneers in Greek cinema was the Hungarian, Joseph Hepp, a cameraman who produced his own documentaries about local life in general and later about the struggle during the Italian conflict, the Second World War and the ensuing Civil War. George Procopiou was the first Greek of importance to follow Hepp in the documentary field. His reputation rests on a film concerning the 1921 military campaign against the Turks.

Costas Bahatoris made the first "serious" Greek film in 1912. GOLFO was based on a popular, idyllic story by Spiros Peressiadis and employed a heavily theatrical technique, a mode which continued, inhibiting the development of cinematic vocabulary. [1]

As of 1940, a total of 47 feature films had been produced in Greece. [2] "But with the possible exception of the work of producer-director-writer Dimitris Gaziadis, nothing of real distinction had been produced, "[3] other than for its historical value.

Despite the post-World War II struggle and the civil war which followed, a steady growth in film production occurred during the 1940s. That decade saw the production of

4

40 films, nearly as many as the entire output of Greek cinema history to that point. Film studios had been built, production companies founded, and their output had found a profitable audience. "Sentimental comedies, popular melodrama and social satires characterized the period."

The 1950s brought a sudden upsurge in production. The 11 films produced in 1950 were the highest number ever in any given year in the history of Greek cinema. That figure was instantly eclipsed, and annual production rose each year during the 1950s until its 1959 peak of 58 films. In addition to this quantitative leap forward, the 1950s began to herald a qualitative difference in Greek films. "Portraying situations, events, feelings and behavior very similar to those experienced by Greek people during the German occupation and the liberation, Italian neo-realism had a considerable impact on the Greek cinema, and its influence can be traced to this day." In essence, Greek cinema had begun to establish its own personality, adapting an external style to suit an internal need.

Although easy film entertainment was readily available during the 1950s, there emerged a small number of filmmakers who established themselves as independent artists. Grigoris Grigoriou, Stelios Tatasopoulos, Greg Talas, Nicos Koundouros, and Michael Cacoyannis all emerged in the 1950s, giving Greek films a tone of personal artistry, despite the fact the studio system was only incidentally supportive of such individual efforts and accomplishments. The studios, however, had not yet succumbed to a big business frenzy in which the sole motivation for making films was box-office receipts, and were therefore still willing to support occasional personal films whose financial prospects were uncertain. Unfortunately, as the industry moved into the 1960s, this situation reversed itself. The big studios like Caryannis-Caratzopoulos and Finos Films had over-extended themselves, and were burdened with a large weekly payroll of steady employees.

From 1960 to approximately 1968, a fantastic upsurge in filmmaking in Greece occurred. Over 100 films a year were literally ground out, most indistinguishable one from the other. A formula had emerged; audiences had clearly indicated interest in Cinderella-type stories which frequently suited the talents of Aliki Vouyouklaki, an actress who enjoyed phenomenal popularity during the reign of the commercial cinema. Anestis Vlahos, a talented and popular actor

during the 1960s, reportedly went from one set to another
all day, appearing in as many as six films every day. "He
didn't know what he was doing. He wouldn't even know the
stories, but they made good money."[4] Not only were the
stories nearly identical, but sets, decor, and actors blended
to produce one long movie that took from 1960 to 1968 to
complete.

There was a vast audience for this product, because
going to the movies was the least expensive form of entertainment available and the average Greek family had little
money. Not only was Greece producing over 100 films a
year, but an additional 700 from other countries were imported. Considering that Greece's total population is less
than that of the city of New York, a veritable orgy of films
must have been indulged in nightly by practically the entire
population.

The Thessaloniki Domestic Film Festival had been
established in 1960 and quickly became the pulse of Greek
cinema. The 1966 festival is still remembered as one of
the most important, not only for its singular quality, but
also because it signalled a potential change of direction for
Greek cinema. A few independents managed to make state-
ments--a welcome treat for the serious filmgoer. If the
commercial cinema felt no threat from these touted independents, they were less casual about the threat of television
introduced in Greece in 1966. But television was slow to
gain a grasp in the villages because of transmission difficulties, and the rural population continued to support the cinema.

Independent filmmakers emerging at this time had envisioned some assistance from the system, much as their
1950s counterparts had received, but before they could gain
the hoped-for support of the commercial cinema, the bottom
fell out, the industry collapsed, and there simply was no
longer a Greek film industry. The studios had over-reached.
They were now into color, and failed to take into consideration a natural economic escalation. The cinema audience
was being chipped away by television, especially in the urban
areas, and, in fact, attendance for foreign films had fallen
in equal proportions.

The junta government takeover in 1967 played a role
in the final demise of the commercial cinema: less films
were made--1968 saw a plunge in film production from 130

to 95, and of those a sizable percentage was porno production or films propagandizing the government's message. The
ensuing heavy censorship resulted in the departure from
Greece of most of its influential and talented artists.

People appeared to have more money during the junta
period, but in actuality there was much paper money in cir-
culation without solid backing. This fact further strangled
the cinema since people bought cars, giving them physical
access to places other than the neighborhood cinema. In an
overall atmosphere of insecurity, they went out to dinner,
and in general partook of more luxurious entertainments.
Since the money in their pockets might indeed be worthless
tomorrow, there was no incentive to save and there were few
investment opportunities which promised much stability.

Meanwhile television was slowly working its way into
the provinces, and the former film audience was now gathering in a coffee house or taverna, watching television. Technicians and performers saw the writing on the wall and hast-
ily found their way into television. The essence of commercial cinema was thus transferred to television, encouraging
the audience to further desert the cinema; the prevailing attitude was that it was foolish to pay at the cinema to see the
same thing that could be seen free on television.

By the time the 1960s were history, so was the commercial cinema. Production statistics would have us believe
Greek cinema was still a thriving entity:

> 1970-71 - 87 films
>
> 1971-72 - 86 films
>
> 1972-73 - 63 films
>
> 1973-74 - 38 films
>
> 1974-75 - 29 films
>
> 1975-76 - 36 films[5]

but approximately two-thirds of those productions were pornos
intended for external use only, and the few remaining were
independents. The big studios were defunct. There simply
was no longer a film industry in the country of Greece.

THE "NEW WAVE":

Independent Filmmaking, 1970-1974

The first half of the 1970s saw the death throes of a 60-year old cinema industry in Greece, and the birth of a new cinematic expression and atmosphere which gave promise of reaching beyond the national confines. With some exception this exciting movement has not fulfilled its promise. The positive rewards of dwelling on what might have been are limited; what might yet come from the Greek filmmakers is only speculative. It is left, then, to attend the dynamic films that were made, glorify the makers only insofar as their herculean undertakings and end results deserve, and wait to see if these artists have the vision and endurance to finish a job so thrustingly started.

It is merely pedantic amusement to theorize how the 1970s Greek filmmaker would have fit into the commercial industry had it not met with such a sudden demise. It is true that many of these filmmakers were working in minor capacities in the commercial industry, but the short films they made at the time make it obvious they were not quietly conforming to the formula methods and concepts of the time. In short, it is clear that the seeds of the 70s film movement were planted long before the filmmakers knew how barren was the soil that would nurture their harvest.

Given the large Greek film audience of the 1960s, it might appear that an "unusual" filmmaker would find his way merely because he worked within an active medium. On the other hand, profits were essential to sustain the spiraling superstructure which, toward the end of the industry, was out of control, having separated from its base of sound business which might have embraced innovative artistic penetration. Furthermore, the forward-reaching filmmaker, assuming the financing problems were solved, might have found the distribution channels competitive rather than cooperative. Actually he may have confronted the same set of problems which were later to plague him, and still do.

The Independent Movement

Technically, Dimosthenes Theos' KIERION was the first film to be made within the "new wave" movement as defined herein. Theos had just completed his film when the junta takeover occurred. Theos' film was made prior to the defined period of the new wave (1970-1974), but the film clearly anticipates it in mood and execution. He took the film and fled to Germany, where he remained throughout the junta. When his film was finally shown in Greece in 1974, he won top honors at the festival. It is enticing to speculate what the film's impact might have been had it been shown in 1968. Would it have been so well received? If so, would it have fostered new ideas about filmmaking within the commercial framework? Might the big studios have responded more actively to non-formula films? How would the audience have responded to the film at the time? Might KIERION, indeed, have been a spark of salvation for the Greek film industry?

As this bit of cinema history will have it, KIERION did not set the stage for a new wave. Two years later Thodoros Angelopoulos made his first film, RECONSTRUC-TION, and had the foresight to stage a private screening for the Athens cinema press prior to its entry into the Thessaloniki Festival. He was motivated by the fear that the modestly subversive quality of the film would result in its suppression from the festival. It was met with triumphant critical enthusiasm.

RECONSTRUCTION is a stark, even grim film, which, coming at the time it did, must have been rather like seeing Satyajit Ray's PATHER PANCHALI suddenly inserted into the middle of a Betty Grable film festival. The junta government was in the middle of its oppressive reign, and the film dared say that all was not glorious in the status quo, a distinctly bold statement for its time. The film world's positive reaction, honoring the film with awards and highly positive critical reviews, was equally bold.

In attempting to define the new wave, it is important to keep in mind the political atmosphere in which these young filmmakers were creating, and under which they had spent a large part of their adult, productive lives. It was one of tight censorship; of threat to one's person and property; of a distinct lack of vocal and creative freedom. Despite this weighty anchor on creativity, the junta served a curiously positive function for the emerging filmmakers. It established boundaries, giving the filmmakers a point of focus. To test and expand these imposed boundaries, to outsmart or manipulate them became a challenge, even a necessity. To destroy the junta's boundaries was the goal; to function with subversive cleverness within them was a mechanism to sustain personal integrity.

Greek history (and the Greek present) is littered with boundary problems: national, cultural, political, familial, sexual, etc. The junta provided a temporary boundary within which the young filmmakers could sense and know their individual positions, both by an awareness of self in relation to the boundary, and in relation to others around them reacting to the same limitation. This only became clear when the junta collapsed, at which time the filmmakers were free to establish (or not establish) their own boundaries, or select from the more commonplace boundaries a point of reference or attack. Unfortunately, many of them floundered--much as the proverbial fish who gets out of water--without the imposed boundaries. To fight and destroy an oppressive limitation is often psychologically easier than the self-responsibility required in knowing one's own personal boundaries and how, if one so chooses, to expand them rewardingly.

Financing

The absence of financing played an important role in the new wave movement. Apparently there was more money available at the time than there is now. But there wasn't all that much, as a look at the films will quickly confirm. What was important, as it always is no matter how much money is available, was the creative imagination called upon to compensate for lack of money. Repeatedly the filmmakers apologize for the lack of technical polish, the dearth of production values, the financial barriers to their fulfillment of an artistic conception. The inspirations or clever touches that remain are viewed by the filmmakers as necessary red herrings--a disguise to divert the viewer from being reminded of what is not there. The disguise, however, becomes a creative reality and it is impossible to compare it with what might have been.

Since these films are earlier statements, and are being discussed by the filmmakers in retrospect, it might also be true that their chagrin at technical execution is a current cover for their unwillingness to admit that their former film statements seem undeveloped and immature to them now. In truth, the modest budgets no doubt spawned a heightening of imagination, a sharpening of talent and skill. Their "smallness" having been effectively realized, became "bigness." Too frequently as these filmmakers went on to "bigger" ideas, their films became "smaller."

Lack of money remains a crucial problem, within which are all the inherent manifestations confronted and conquered by the new wave movement. An additional ogre is faced now: it takes so long to locate and obtain financing that the original product comes to be viewed differently by the creator; enthusiasm has waned; changes of various kinds may actually obviate the desire and will to effect the project.

The "Tone" of the New Wave

The general tone of the new wave was one of starkness, much like that of its earlier counterparts in France, England, Czechoslovakia and Poland. A passionate seriousness pervaded the movement. By 1975 this seriousness was skewing toward ponderousness, but after years of frivolous, tinsel movies, the seriousness of the new wave was water in a wasteland.

Of the ten films herein representing the new wave, six were in color, four in black and white--a seeming anachronism. The point is made in a later interview that the Greek filmmakers are too eager to produce a slickly finished product, without taking time to learn how to effect that goal. Whether this factor comes into play in the selection of the much more expensive color for a first film outing is idle interest. More important is the fact that the mood of the new wave was black and white, and one is inclined to forget that more than half of the films were done in color. Nicos Panayotopoulos' THE COLORS OF IRIS, the most lyrical of the ten, is the single film that is completely suited to color. True, color aids the faded velvet mood of THE ENGAGEMENT OF ANNA, and adds a proper garishness to Costa Sfikas' MODEL, and certainly color adds visual variety to the other films. But the assured definition of emotional and cerebral input from the filmmakers imposes a kind of "black and white" conclusiveness upon the films which overpowers the relative circumstances represented by the variety and shadings of colors. The Rentzis-Zervos film, BLACK & WHITE, even takes this consideration as a content to be consciously explored.

It is definitely not a cheery collection of films! Hopelessness, entrapment, defeat and despair are the joyless messages of these films. Even the surface light-heartedness of THE COLORS OF IRIS ends with a desperate negative intended to motivate the possibility of a positive. [6] This mood was surely an outgrowth and reflection of the imprisonment the filmmakers felt under the junta; it was a prison from which they could foresee no immediate escape. As they could not talk about this openly, they talked about imprisonment in more human terms, thus speaking in a language the entire world could understand. With the downfall of the junta, they disgorged their wrath with such personal passion and intimate knowledge that they temporarily lost touch with the world. They vomited exclusively for a Greek audience who knew and understood why it was being done.

But the new wave--affected, perhaps even created, by insulation--was not insulated in its statements. Since they could not be specific and therefore small-based, as they later were, they made their specific statements in a vague way, which broadened the base of the content. Instead of saying "My government is my enemy, " they said "Authority is our enemy. "

This general, more encompassing statement issues its invitation to be embraced by everyone, for everyone has an oppressive authority in his or her life, even though the forms and manifestations may differ. The later, specific, anti-junta statements were less universal in execution and of much less identifiable interest to the outsider, who was not only untutored in the facts, but also might be in varying degrees disinterested, even if compassionate. This becomes an important point in terms of the business end of filmmaking; Greek films must find a foreign audience if they are to have a future.

The bleak tone of the new wave is not presented as an admired feature that was obliged to continue. Had the new wave survived (and perhaps it has), it would have continued to reflect the position of the creative participants who indeed have discovered better days. Since 1975 the new wave has either been in hibernation, or it is deceased; thus the direction it might take, or could have taken, is merely a speculation.

The anti-authoritarianism which permeated the new wave films was varied in its points of reference and in content execution. RECONSTRUCTION, THE REASON WHY, and GET ON YOUR MARK all examined the hopelessness of the villager, heretofore a backbone feature of the country. With the massive rural-to-urban shift in the population and the ensuing problems, it was a logical choice of subject content. RECONSTRUCTION talks about the joylessness in the village; GET ON YOUR MARK refers to the absence of improvement opportunities; THE REASON WHY, about the organization of a labor union, holds out group power as a counter-action to the death of rural living. BLACK & WHITE picks up the story as the migrant confronts the city in his search for individual rights. KIERION and VARTHOLOMEOS more directly attack the political manipulations whose exploitive and self-serving activities defeat the individual.

MODEL and THE COLORS OF IRIS are more socially (as opposed to politically) concerned; MODEL is an impassioned attack on the personal defeat inherent in meaningless work; THE COLORS OF IRIS is a lightly executed study of the individual's confrontation with an all-embracing system supported by individuals afraid to act outside it. THE ENGAGEMENT OF ANNA and CRANIUM LANDSCAPE may be criticized by the socially conscious as being somewhat ostrich-like, in that they don't meet the then-current situation head-on. Still, their subjects--of understanding and love--were perhaps intended as reflections of a less immediately active, but more positive, long-range way to deal with life. Both films involve themselves with the idea that no "bad" is all bad, and no "good" is all good, a theme somewhat anomalous to the new wave movement.

These ten films, [7] then, epitomize the new wave. There were other films during the period which technically joined in the movement. But these films have been selected because they were made by filmmakers who have in common a first film made under an oppressive political structure, who delivered somewhat similar messages, and who carved new roads through a cinema wilderness created by the collapse of the film industry.

The Nucleus of the New Wave

As most of these films are investigated in greater detail elsewhere in this study, these brief summaries are intended as merely a "get-acquainted" point of reference.

KIERION (Director: Dimosthenes Theos. Made in 1968 but not shown in Greece until 1974. Based on a true story). A thriller about a mysterious political murder.

RECONSTRUCTION (Director: Thodoros Angelopoulos, 1970. Based on a true story). Investigation of a murder case reveals a life of loneliness and desperation in a joyless environment.

THE ENGAGEMENT OF ANNA (Director: Pandelis Voulgaris, 1972. Based on a true story). A study of a live-in maid who hasn't the courage, know-how, or opportunity to find her own life, or to protect herself from the exploitation of those around her.

THE REASON WHY (Director: Tasos Psarras, 1974. Based on a true story). Tobacco workers forming a union are defeated by the defection of one man who is subsequently murdered.

GET ON YOUR MARK (Director: Thodoros Maranghos, 1973. Based on a true story). A village athlete dreams of athletic success as a means of escaping a hopeless life.

BLACK & WHITE (Directors: Thanassis Rentzis & Nicos Zervos, 1973). A young man struggles to find a balance between his personal values and those of others.

VARTHOLOMEOS (Director: Manoussos Manoussakis, 1973). A surrealistic attack on power, authority, force and external controls.

THE COLORS OF IRIS (Director: Nicos Panayotopoulos, 1974). Investigation of an apparent drowning exposes authority corruption, personal evasion, self-centered lethargy. The exploration of real vs. unreal is told in light facade, but under the froth is plenty of body.

CRANIUM LANDSCAPE (Director: Costas Aristopoulos, 1973). The Jesus story again, but with villagers in the roles it has a charming play-acting quality, emphasized by wonderful glimpses of the people talking about their lives and their reactions to being "film actors."

Emphasis on Character Rather than Subject

Aside from the ingredients already discussed as defining the new wave, an additional factor is present during the new wave but changes severely with the demise of the movement. In practically every case, the Greek filmmakers' second films take on a much broader scope of investigation. But the first films have an intimacy and a personal quality which is manifested in character exploration. We care about the people in these films; we care about their problems and their fates; we can take them as they are or see them as the symbols they were often intended to be--which adds a multi-level quality to the films.

--The melancholy Anna Vagena in the title role of THE ENGAGEMENT OF ANNA is a haunting example. Leading a leaden life, having no visible choice to do otherwise, never having known another way, she suddenly has a mercurial opportunity for possible happiness.

--The young man played by George Tsemberopoulos in BLACK & WHITE faces a universal dilemma, that of struggling to find an avenue of personal values and expressions within a system which demands conformity.

--The athlete (Vangelis Kazan) in GET ON YOUR MARK speaks for all our dreams: to run away from our pain, and in so doing convert the dream to a reality.

--The horrific repression and loneliness of the woman (Toula Stathopoulou) in RECONSTRUCTION is a probability in each of our lives, despite the unique setting of her story. Actually the setting has less to do with the essence of the story than was made of it. The film would have us believe that the oppressive environment plays the major role, but loneliness and desperation can occur as easily in Los Angeles or Bangkok as in a dying village in Greece.

--The multi-faceted musician (Nikitas Tsakiroglou) in THE COLORS OF IRIS is, in a way, the most real to us because we see him as a total person (having seen only time- or incident-related aspects of the other characters being discussed). Although an incident draws our attention to the character, we are allowed to see his work, his home, his fantasies, his humor, his seriousness, his sex life, his art, his values, his commitments.

Audience involvement with individuals is equally important in KIERION and THE REASON WHY. In these two films a balance of emphasis is attained between the incidents which inspire the films and the characters caught in the webs spinning out from the incidents. In their second films, both filmmakers made the characters so robot-like that the films suggest that incidents create people, rather than the reverse.

MODEL, of course, is the major exception: there are no people, which is its horrific point. VARTHOLOMEOS is also somewhat an exception. Although there are discernible characters, we don't really like them. And some others are used mostly as prototypes and we are not responsive to their fates on a personal level. And, of course, the Jesus story of CRANIUM LANDSCAPE really needs no further character development, having been molded by centuries of legend and lore.

It is important to note that despite the emphasis on people in the new wave films, there was also a nearly universal view of them as victims of some greater force. It isn't until after the new wave movement (and the collapse of the junta) that there appears a flutter of the idea that individuals may have some modest means by which to direct their own destinies.

Having examined the ingredients of the new wave films, it is essential to view the filmmakers from whom the films emerged. Since each is later examined in some detail, what follows here is a brief attempt to synopsize their motives and reasons for making film, as they melded into the whole of the new wave.

1. Great Desire to Make a Film: Most of the film-makers had made shorts which had attracted enough attention to encourage them, or at least to whet their egos. Making the first film effected an intense involvement which got built into the film. This involvement could take the form of commitment to subject, as in the cases of KIERION, VARTHOLOMEOS and MODEL; commitment to film as a career, as in RECONSTRUCTION, THE COLORS OF IRIS, THE REASON WHY; or an exploration of self through film, as in CRANIUM LANDSCAPE, GET ON YOUR MARK, THE ENGAGEMENT OF ANNA, BLACK & WHITE. This is not to say there were no overlappings in creative motivations and input. THE REASON WHY, for instance, is a film immersed in its subject, but there is little doubt that director Psarras would make films, even with less commitment to subject. GET ON YOUR MARK is certainly an early statement of its director's later-developed political views, but the film is a self-involved examination of his own position in relation to group participation.

Although some of the directors started working in the commercial cinema and could thus see the possibility of a career in film, others were plunging in at a time when film must surely have been, as it is now, a career almost totally resistant to possibilities. There was little hope of making a profit from the film. Financial and physical assistance were sought from friends, family and each other. (It is not uncommon to see other directors appearing as actors. KIERION, for instance, has Angelopoulos, Sfikas and Voulgaris in the cast.)

2. The Smooth Meshing of the Current Totality of the Filmmaker, His Motivations for Making Film, and His Ultimate Product: It can't actually be said that subsequent films were made without commitment, but there is some special ingredient in the first films that rarely lives beyond them. Pandelis Voulgaris hits on it most succinctly when he says, "... everything has to go into the first film because there is the fear and very real possibility there will not be another. So each filmmaker puts whatever he is and has been into the film." This takes a variety of forms: MODEL is a great disgorging of a lifetime of deadening monotony; VARTHOLOMEOS, a lashing-out against the political oppressions in which the filmmaker had spent most of his adult life; a current intensity of involvement with subject is present in KIERION and THE REASON WHY; a summation of personal viewpoint in GET ON YOUR MARK and, to a lesser degree, BLACK & WHITE;[8] and finally, a commitment to film as art or personal success through film can be seen in THE COLORS OF IRIS, RECONSTRUCTION, CRANIUM LANDSCAPE, THE ENGAGEMENT OF ANNA. Again it is necessary to note the dovetailing of categories. One cannot doubt the involvement with subject in RECONSTRUCTION, but Angelopoulos' primary motivation was and is to be a filmmaker. Psarras found the subject for THE REASON WHY long after he had decided to be a filmmaker, but the involvement with subject is so intense as to very nearly obliterate his individuality.

3. Personal Statement: The single most important ingredient of these films is their personal quality. Each film, in its own way, may be viewed as a summing-up of the filmmaker's current position, either from an immediate involvement, or as an expression of conclusions drawn from a lifetime.

* * * * *

If it is true that the new wave is currently dormant

rather than dead, it is also somewhat uncomfortably true that it achieved that status simultaneously with the overthrow of the junta. This in some way suggests that the junta played a supportive role in this burst of art, which is definitely not the case. They are intertwined, however, in that the films are clearly results of the junta, reactions to it, and represent individual stands against it. These filmmakers would probably have emerged in due course, but their statements would have been different.

With the collapse of the junta came an explosion of political films, an understandable occurrence. No longer having the junta as a focus of attention, the filmmakers were released to select their statements. Formerly bound together by a common cause, they scattered now that the cause was in the past. Some have reached far outside themselves, failing to ingest what they have found before taking a stand. Others have turned inward to reveal what is there, taking the risk of defying popular movements. Still others viewed the cinema field more calculatedly and modeled their films within the successful trends.

The turnover in Greek filmmakers is so swift that last year's proclaimed savior is this year's unemployed and forgotten filmmakers. The filmmakers in this study are the "old masters" in Greek films, despite an output of two or three films and a cheerful promise of obscurity. But the streets of Athens seem to be crawling with film masochists, ready to replace these filmmakers in their small and transient glory.

Some of the filmmakers here described, indeed, will fall by the wayside, but others will remain, and not only as national film artists; there is the promise that a few will make contact with international recognition.

The interviews with filmmakers that follow were gathered on tape from June through November 1976, with updating visits in September 1977. Interviews were also preceded by seeing the films. How the material was handled was dictated by the experience: sometimes the emphasis fell on the person, sometimes on the films, sometimes on the experience itself, sometimes on a personal reaction to the experience. The interviews are arranged alphabetically, but in truth the book simply grew like the haphazard happening that is Greek film itself!

Notes

1. Historical information in the first four paragraphs has
    been distilled from "Early Greek Cinema: Karagiozis
    Unchained," by Andrew Horton, The Athenian, June
    21, 1974.

2. Production statistics obtained from O Ellinikos Kinimato-
    grafos (The Greek Cinema) 1906-1960, by Frixos
    Iliadis. Athens: Fantasia, 1960. (In Greek)

3. This and following quotations are from Mirella Georgi-
    adou's contributions to A Concise History of the Cine-
    ma, Vols. 1 and 2, edited by Peter Cowie. London:
    The Tantivy Press, 1968, 1971.

4. Personal interview with film critic/historian Mirella
    Georgiadou.

5. Statistics derived from various issues of International
    Film Guide, The Tantivy Press (London) and A. S.
    Barnes & Co. (South Brunswick, New Jersey & New
    York).

6. This film is constantly enigmatic; this statement is based
    on the author's arguable interpretation.

7. There are other films that should probably be included.
    Tonia Marketaki is a filmmaker who fits into the
    structured niche of the new wave, but her film, VIO-
    LENT JOHN, was unavailable for viewing during the
    research time. Costas Ferris is an award-winning
    filmmaker from the period, but his first film, THE
    MURDERESS, was an adaptation from a famous liter-
    ary source and proves abrasive when trying to fit into
    the "new wave" definition. Pavlos Tassios is repre-
    sentative of the filmmaker who managed the transition
    from commercial cinema through the new wave period,
    finally winning kudos for a post-wave film, THE
    HEAVY MELON.

8. This film was hampered--and possibly aided--by tight,
    constant censorship, making it not a full-fledged
    representation of what it might have been. A more
    detailed discussion may be found in the chapter de-
    voted to Thanassis Rentzis and Nicos Zervos.

Chapter 2

The Importance of Being Mr. Angelopoulos

- THODOROS ANGELOPOULOS -

The Greeks are such handsome people that they don't seem to mind that most of their public places are atrociously lit. It's worth noting, however, that the roof garden of the Makedonia Hotel in Thessaloniki is dimly lit, has a well-stocked bar, and the soft, offensive sounds of inoffensive music contribute to what I suppose may be described as an atmosphere of class. There are other places to rendezvous in Thessaloniki: the fantastically noisy press room at the film festival offices; by the statue of the man on the horse, assuming you are downwind of the harbor; or there are wonderful sidewalk cafes where one can be seen, but not heard; and the rotating tower is O. K. if you are not allergic to heights or tourists. But if you are going to meet Thodoros

Angelopoulos for the first time, I recommend the intimate
formality of the roof garden at the Makedonia.

You don't have to come to Greece to discover Mr.
Angelopoulos. I could have seen THE TRAVELLING PLAY-
ERS in New York, and, in fact, did. A lifetime at the
movies came up the elevator with me; it is not with casual-
ness that a film addict meets a known film director. Thodoros Angelopoulos was there, in person, having a drink
with Eva Kotamanidou, his leading lady. For me, there also
was Mauritz Stiller and Greta Garbo, Josef von Sternberg
and Marlene Dietrich, and even William Wyler and Bette
Davis. I want the Makedonia to know I was impressed!

I doubt Mr. Angelopoulos will grant interviews much
longer if THE TRAVELLING PLAYERS keep travelling. Already there is a sigh before each answer, which has the un-
nerving effect of convincing the interviewer that the question
had all the originality of John Wayne's 19th western. It also
creates a mood of calculation, as though the answer was
chosen from Column B because Column B is the one to which
the interviewer responds most positively.

Mr. Angelopoulos studied law. Perry Mason and
Judge Hardy notwithstanding, my image of lawyers has all
the zip of a documentary on new math. Perhaps weighing
justice, or finding the best way to avoid it, takes its toll of
spontaneity. Nevertheless, Mr. Angelopoulos answered questions with cooperation, intelligence, and dignified charm.
And, in all fairness, I must say we even exchanged a little
bitchy gossip which has been discreetly (and now provocative-
ly) edited into my private memory.

Angelopoulos was never a potential director. From
his first feature he was a full-fledged, developed director.
His was the kind of first film that inspires film students
either to upgrade their concepts or change their majors to
auto mechanics. His second feature confirmed the first feature as no accident. THE TRAVELLING PLAYERS travels
First Class, stopping off occasionally to enjoy the V.I.P.
establishments of international cinema. There is no reason
to assume that Angelopoulos will not continue to provide
Greek cinema with a major voice to the rest of the world,
a by-product of his personal quest.

As an interviewer, I hardly got in on the ground floor
of his ascendency, but I did make the roof garden of the

Makedonia. Fair warning to those who follow: Mr. Angelopoulos has an unexpected little-boy smile which can indeed
sway the jury. It may be his prime witness for the defense.

* * * * *

What has been your reaction to serving on the festival jury?
How do you feel about being a jury member?*

I don't like it at all because this year the filmmakers
are filmmakers of my own generation and I am being asked
to judge, to criticize, members of my own generation. On
the other hand, it is quite interesting to see from the inside
how this selection mechanism works.

Do you think that your growing international reputation gives
you some right or authority to make these judgments of your
peers?

Yes. But on the other hand I know how all these people have made sacrifices to make these films, and what it
means to them, and what is involved. I feel the weight of
this responsibility. I know that the filmmakers know that
all of the other members of the jury are going to ask me,
and in a certain way I am the strongest part of the jury.
So the filmmakers know the decision of the jury really comes
from me, and it makes it very awkward for me.

Could you evaluate the position of the current Greek cinema,
and do you think this festival is really representative of its
current development?

The problem of the festival is always the problem of
the Greek cinema, because it is assumed that every year, the
best films of the year come to the festival. This year, and
perhaps last year, we didn't have the best films. We had
the only films existing. There were no other films. This
means that the industry of cinema is dead in Greece. Even
if the financing comes from someone else, the filmmaker is

---

*Mr. Angelopoulos served as jury member at the 1976 Thes-
saloniki Domestic Film Festival, a competitive festival for
which Greek features and shorts are eligible. He is the first
of the 1970s independent filmmakers to be so honored. Serving as jury member is an acknowledgment of professional
prestige and authority.

now obliged to be the executive producer of the film. The filmmaker has a double job, and he needs more energy and more time, double the time he needed when the industry was an organized industry. Frequently the person who finances the film chooses the filmmaker, but we don't know how he chooses. Why this filmmaker is chosen, we don't know, for we don't know his criterion. He does it in a very anarchistic way. Nobody knows how he chooses, and frequently it is not because the chosen one is a good filmmaker. Therefore, the low quality of films we saw this year at the festival does not signify that the Greek industry is down; it simply means that these people were chosen to do films instead of some other people who might be much better but have not had the opportunity or possibility to do films. We don't know, but perhaps if these other people had the opportunity to do films, the face of the Greek cinema would be quite different. Actually, the possibilities for the Greek cinema are much stronger than what we have just seen.

You and Mr. Voulgaris have proven worthy of international recognition. Do you feel you are now obliged to work outside Greece in pursuit of your own development?

Already my next film is a co-production of the French and German television.* It will be filmed in Greece, however. They called me when they saw THE TRAVELLING PLAYERS and told me they were interested in my next project. We had an appointment in Paris one day at 1:00 o'clock, at which time I told them about the project without showing them anything. The next day we went to Germany and did the same thing, and without seeing anything, they said all right. As to the possibility of someday working outside of Greece, I can't really make any predictions. For the time being, I need Greece and what I have to say is very much connected with Greece.

How did you become interested in film originally?

Until around 1960, when I made my first contact with cinema, I wrote poetry, essays and short stories. I thought of myself as being a lawyer with an avocation of writing. But then I saw Godard's BREATHLESS. It was played in the kind of theater that shows double features, and was pre-

---

*THE HUNTERS completed filming in February 1977. It will play theaters for 18 months prior to its television debut.

sented as a thriller. But I was so impressed that I thought, "That's it! I can't do anything else. I have to work in this part of the art." It was a major discovery. I served my term in the Army and then went to Paris to study.

Your films are nothing like Godard's.

That is not important. He remains my first cinematic love. He is still a very important filmmaker, but I think he has lost himself by going to an extreme. He has been crushed by the results of his own action.

Try not to be modest. I would like to know how you feel about your growing recognition.

It is very interesting and important to know that my films are being shown at the same time in Paris and London and that the reactions are almost the same everywhere. Without false modesty, I knew the film was an important film and would have to play out its history. That is why the public and the critics reacted more favorable outside of Greece than in.

May I assume you had confidence in this film even from the beginning?

I began making the film during the last period of the junta, which was the worst period. My major concern at the time was to make the film without any repercussions to my work. Perhaps another filmmaker would have been more concerned about the content of the film and try to say things in whatever language, without being bothered by the junta. But what I think is important is the language of film, and if my work has some importance it is the language, and I am very faithful to it.

There are various reports as to how long the film was originally. Can we set the record straight?

Originally it was five hours. The current playing time is three hours and 50 minutes.

I have just seen RECONSTRUCTION [his first film] and was quite impressed. Can we talk about it?

Pandelis Voulgaris, Costas Sfikas, Costas Ferris, Athanasios Katakounzinos, and I were approached with a plan

that each of us should do a short story which would be combined into a feature. When the time came to show the producer our products, I was the only one ready. The producer
was a technician in the cinema--an electrician. My script
was not fully worked out, but the ideas were formulated, and
the producer was interested. He actually worked as the electrician on the filming. I was the producer and the director.
The script girl was the assistant director--the everything.
The woman in the film was not an actress. She was a seamstress. We lived in the village during shooting, ate with the
people, lived in their houses. Before it was over we began
to forget who were the villagers and who were the film crew,
we began to feel so much at home. I love this film very
much. It was a film that generated much love.

The producer would have to leave the film site peri-
odically, go get a job in the commercial cinema, then bring
his earnings back to pay for what we were doing. The director of photography would have to handle the lights while
our producer-electrician was out making enough money to
keep us going. When he finally saw the finished product, he
said, "Oh! I've lost everything. Nobody will see this film."
Because it was the time of the junta and I was very much
afraid the film would be censored, I made a private screening in Athens and invited all the critics. I took it to Thessaloniki where it won all the prizes. It then played Paris.
It played the Toulon Festival where it won best foreign film;
then on to Berlin, where it took a special mention shared
with Dusan Makavejev's WR: THE MYSTERIES OF THE
ORGANISM. Then it went to the London and New York Festivals, and Chicago, and more.

Frequently I feel the individuals in your films are strongly
manipulated by their environments, sometimes lost in their
environments, and there are times when the environment
takes over completely.

In the first film, of course, the environment was important, it was the most important thing. There was this
woman whose husband had been working in Germany for seven
years. The village is almost dead and she can find no way
to escape. The conditions of life for women in villages had
also to be examined. The conditions of environment were
very important in this film.
In THE TRAVELLING PLAYERS it is the political
events which influence the behavior of the characters, change
them, mold them, make them behave differently. If these
events had not happened, they would have behaved quite differently.

May we expect this same emphasis in your future work?

  The new film is about a group of people who take part in history. They mold the events, but at the same time are molded by the events. So there is an interconnection between these persons who change the events, and the events which change the persons. They are directly in the events, not just victims of the environment.

Do you feel you are exerting any influence on the Greek film-makers now, even though unintentionally?

  For some years I was a film critic and a teacher at the Stavrakou Film School, so I have had some influence. Also the international recognition has played a role. This year there are many films that are close and less-close imitations. What is sad is that they imitate without knowing. If I use Jancso as a model, I know what I am doing and how I do it, but they don't know. They do it in a way which is not at all clever.

What is your reaction to criticism? How do other people's opinions affect you?

  I can't say. Always the critics have had good things to say of my work. There have been some cases here in Greece. The critics belong to small groups, and each group has its own position. There have been attacks, but I knew in these cases it really had nothing to do with my work. The ingredients of the attacks had to do with other aspects. Because I have been a critic, I know how to analyze my own work. Since DAYS OF '36 there has been a small group which says it prefers the work of Voulgaris because he is a good guy. They don't say his films are better, because it is very difficult to say anything about that. But the essence of their criticism is that Voulgaris is a better guy. Voulgaris and I are very close friends and we both find it quite amusing.

Why are you the heavy of this situation?

  I am very aggressive.

What do you have to say that is particularly unique? That is, what makes you the artist you are?

  I don't think I have anything particularly unique, but it

is a deep necessity for me to express myself through cinema. I want to express my fears, feelings, what I think of myself, my fantasies--through the language of the cinema.

Do you feel that within this expression you touch on any universals? Can other people find personal parallels in your work?

When I do a film, I don't know that. Always the film is a projection of myself, and there is the hope it will be a means to communicate with other people. THE TRAVELLING PLAYERS gave the opportunity to see that I was saying something to other people, that the things I wanted to say were felt and understood by other people. Oshima, Herzog, Truffaut and many other filmmakers liked the film very much and felt very close to his own projection. Bertolucci has seen the film many times, and he finds his own film NOVECENTO has many relations to THE TRAVELLING PLAYERS. They are very similar. In watching NOVECENTO, I saw many things I said in THE TRAVELLING PLAYERS, and many things I would have liked to have said.

I like your film better than Bertolucci's.

So does Bertolucci.

* * * * *

In hindsight it is comfortable to view Angelopoulos' first film, RECONSTRUCTION, as a gong heralding the beginning of a new generation of filmmakers in Greece. Though the film reaped its just due in awards and critical acclaim, it is doubtful that there was an awareness of a new movement; rather there was an awareness of a new film artist. There simply is no question that Angelopoulos was the first of the 70s filmmakers to make his presence known through a major feature film, and he has remained in the vanguard of leadership ever since. His films are the first of the 70s to achieve recognition throughout the world; the first to win prizes at important international festivals. He is the first of the directors to serve on a festival film jury in artistic judgment; the first to be imitated by his peers; and the first to receive a hostile backlash that usually follows success in Greece (this is not to suggest that Greece has a monopoly on such behavior).

Returning from his studies in France (where, inci-

dentally, he shared a room and the learning experience with
fellow Greek filmmaker, Nicos Panayotopoulos), he had an
opportunity to direct a film during the commercial cinema
days. Cinematographer George Panousopoulos recounts this
incident: "In 1965, he and I worked together doing a film
which was a kind of Greek-music version of Richard Lester's
HELP. But he was fired after the first two weeks because
he was too slow. There came another director who does
now a series on television, a director who does very fast but
empty-headed work. The film was finished but was very bad.
So when Angelopoulos was ready to do RECONSTRUCTION, he
came to me. But I was in the process of forming a company
to make television commercials, and I couldn't get away for
the length of time necessary. I suggested Arvanitis, who had
been my assistant on the 'Help' film."

It was a particularly fortunate suggestion; cinematographer George Arvanitis has become a major contributor to
Angelopoulos' overall intent and accomplishment throughout
his four-film output. A major factor in Angelopoulos' success is his understanding that the director is limited or enhanced by the talent gathered around him. Slowly he has
built a repertory cast and crew of accomplished, contributing
talent who attend his leadership with obvious respect. Mr.
Angelopoulos does a large percentage of his creative work in
his head prior to filming. It is only logical to assume that
he approaches the development of his career in much the
same way.

One can admire his awareness of intent and his deliberate movement toward the goal, but it sometimes filters
through as calculation. His goal does indeed appear to be
success, and he is clever enough to analyze its ingredients
and concoct the proper mixture. The international film scene
of the 1970s has been one of cool detachment, and it's one
in which Angelopoulos finds a comfortable niche. Should that
emphasis change, one suspects that Angelopoulos' films would
change also, which is not to say that he would abandon his
quest for a personal point of reference. His commitment to
the content of his work is certainly not in question; nor is
the knowledgeable skill with which he brings it to fruition.
Still, with some presumption, it seems suspiciously accurate
to conclude that Mr. Angelopoulos is less committed to his
message than he is to his medium. Quite frankly, within
the context of the 70s Greek cinema, this self-centered base
is refreshingly honest and accurate, even if it is not openly
admitted. He is simply less confused about what he is doing

and why he is doing it. Within the intimacy of the Greek
social-cinema world, Mr. Angelopoulos asks for and gets respect rather than love. To the world he presents his work
fashioned to evoke success. It is a road on which he will
likely continue to be a travelling player.

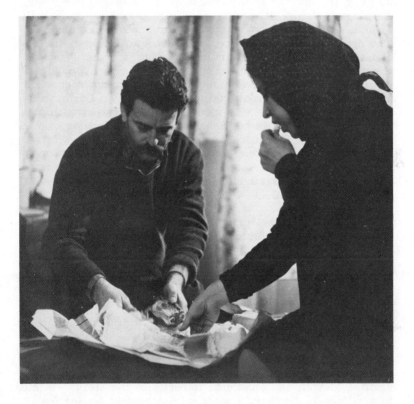

Yannis Totsikas and Toula Stathopoulou in RECONSTRUCTION

RECONSTRUCTION

RECONSTRUCTION is such a satisfyingly complete
film that it is tempting to agree with a widespread Greek
opinion that it is still Mr. Angelopoulos' best film. Its
parts dovetail flawlessly into a whole; to find fault with the
film is to be reduced to minor quibbling. Angelopoulos' subsequent films, for all their artistry and deserved appreciation,

are nonetheless vulnerable to negative reaction to their partisan content, imitative execution, indulgent pacing and deliberate structural confusions.

RECONSTRUCTION was inspired by a newspaper account of the murder of a husband by his wife and her lover. Angelopoulos' film, however, is intrigued with the story only insofar as it served as foreground for his real interests. The dying villages of Greece, the economic bondage, the social entrapment are the stars of the film, and the event of the murder is seen as an integral part or even a product of the milieu in which it was committed. Economic necessity has motivated the murder victim to emigrate to Germany to find work, leaving his wife alone in a village wherein life is harsh and joyless. In her loneliness and desperation, she takes a lover. The husband eventually returns; the wife and lover commit the murder, bury the body in the garden and abortively attempt to escape. The husband's disappearance has provoked an investigation. The lovers are discovered and taken into penal custody.

The film is not primarily concerned with the immediate plot. It is structured as an investigation into the crime by a journalist (played by Angelopoulos) whose retrospective interests give a "once removed" quality to the film, further enhanced by flashbacks which add a "second removed" dimension. The audience is therefore invited to be alienated from the immediacy of the characters themselves, and instead, to view them as typical victims of a social framework which enslaves many.

RECONSTRUCTION has a distant, metallic quality (in no small way a contribution of cinematographer George Arvanitis), despite the emotional intensity of the story. Filmed in a village in Northern Greece with a cast of non-professionals, to the outsider the setting seems quite foreign, unfamiliar, even exotic. Allowing for that difference, its investigation of loneliness and external suppression has a universal quality which transcends its memorable setting. Angelopoulos' work accents the role played by external manipulations, a theme solidly established in his first film. The villain in RECONSTRUCTION, in contrast to his following films, is less animate, less human, less definable, and therefore all the more threatening in that an avenue of combat is vague--the enemy has no identity. "[The film] ... stresses the terrible enclosure of existence in a depopulated countryside, the overpowering landscape, the old men huddled together at the melancholy cafe ... the harsh aspects of rural life, the solitude, the poverty, the ferocious temper of the climate. "1 Angelopoulos' committed attention to the environmental factor as oppressor is summed up in an exhaustingly long and somewhat exasperating shot of the house in which the murder occurred--a kind of visual swallowing of the people and events.

Despite the specifics of the setting, the film reaches beyond itself. Suppression, loneliness, poverty (both material and spiritual) know no boundaries and one woman alone in a remote village in a remote country can evoke a parallel in the steel mountains of New York City or the lost identity of a Tokyo rush hour. Thus the specifics of the setting of RE-CONSTRUCTION actually have less to do with the essence of the content than their depiction would have us believe. Though the cause-and-effect conclusions reached by the film may be expanded, expounded upon, modified, or even disagreed with, even the most confirmed of the "great individuals" would have to soften to an unquestionable recognition of victimizing circumstances, including those that are self-imposed. Thus the film's visual boundaries become merely a question of semantics; its message is perceived by all.

Mr. Angelopoulos' cool detachment works particularly well in RECONSTRUCTION. A story of adultery and murder is charged with emotionalism, and could be treated in a spectrum of ways. By reconstructing the event rather than living it he creates a distance which allows the film room to breathe within its smothering framework. Happily he creates the distance by a kind of icy visual rather than literal camera distance. This opening up--or backing off--makes it possible to encompass the mitigating factors within the event; the end result is to actually accent the emotional aspect of the story without it ever becoming melodramatic.

DAYS OF '36

Within a career marked by boldness, confidence, and success, DAYS OF '36 represents the only hesitation, days of uncertainty. Mr. Angelopoulos is obviously groping for a personal style, a framework suited to his personal structure. Again he looks back on an event which allows for the detachment that served him so well in RECONSTRUCTION. Again he chooses a subject of claustrophobic confinement for which his treatment can push out the boundaries. Again his pacing

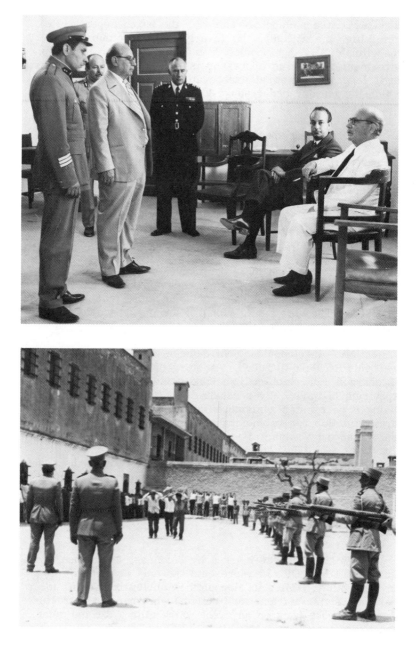

DAYS OF '36

is leisurely, which, in itself, can psychologically add dimension to the intent. But these factors, which served him so well in his first outing, take on a character of calculation when pressed too hard. The distance is too distant. The pace is too leisurely. The "how" turns on Mr. Angelopoulos.

DAYS OF '36 is based on a montage of true stories, similar in content, different in detail. A trade-unionist is murdered. A suspect is taken prisoner. The suspect has previously served as informer for the police. He is visited by a Member of Parliament with whom it is suggested he has had a homosexual relation. The prisoner pulls a gun and holds the politician hostage, demanding his own release and protesting his innocence.

The resolution of this established dilemma inspires the remainder of the film. But again, as in RECONSTRUC-TION, the factors that surround the event become important pieces of the whole. The authoritative machinations set into action in an effort to free the hostage expose "... a sordid sequence of intrigue, betrayal, and political violence. "2

Throughout the entirety of his work, Angelopoulos has demonstrated that he is knowledgeable, thorough and cerebrally far-reaching. He is concerned not only with the cause and effect of an event, but the various aspects of the environment (narrow and broad) in which the event occurs. The prison confinement of the event in DAYS OF '36 opens to allow for the aura of the event: "... guards on horseback trotting through bleached grasses or chalky dust, prisoners tearing through a wheatfield ... galloping horsemen rushing nowhere, men diminished against the sand-brown walls of the prison, the geometry of troops in file.... "3

Not intended exclusively to expand the confines of the setting, these scenes nevertheless serve the purpose. Pieces of the Angelopoulos mosaic are not always met with friendly receptiveness: "... But more frequently the method simply yields to picturesque ways of filling up the screen ... the whole repertory of flashy, long-take cinematics that is virtually a trademark of Jancso that assumes (as I don't) that the pan, the crane, the tracking shot are, like virtue, their own reward. "4

Thus begins the comparison to Miklos Jancso that has plagued Angelopoulos since DAYS OF '36; a comparison which critics found irresistible in discussing the film. The comparison has continued, despite the obvious fact that any modeling after Jancso of which Mr. Angelopoulos indeed may have been guilty, has been so ingested that it is now a consequence only as it regards his formative development. He has clearly assimilated whatever he elected to learn from Jancso and uses it for his own purposes; it may now be viewed as an integrated part of his own artistry. Mr. Angelopoulos, himself, guardedly acknowledges the presence of Mr. Jancso, even if his granting of credit due is not overwhelming. Still, a man whose films clearly state his belief in the importance of external stimulation and manipulation must allow that he, too, might not be wholly his own man.

THE TRAVELLING PLAYERS

THE TRAVELLING PLAYERS is a film that invites a dual point of view: it obviously fits into the pattern of Mr.

Thodoros Angelopoulos during filming of THE TRAVELLING PLAYERS, with Eva Koramanidou and unidentified actor.

Angelopoulos' growth as man and artist, but it is also such a complete unit that it can be adjudged on its own terms, almost as if it were self-born, self-contained. Of course, this is not the case, and furthermore, any film can be so viewed. But it is difficult to discuss RECONSTRUCTION without mention of its primary position in the career of its creator; DAYS OF '36 must be acknowledged as a link between a beginning and a maturity. THE TRAVELLING PLAYERS asks for nothing more than recognition of itself--almost a denial of Mr. Angelopoulos' repeated philosophy that nothing can be seen in isolation. And surely he is right, except that those moments that set standards take on a solitary image, even though they too have their boundaries.

THE TRAVELLING PLAYERS is the first film of the Greek cinema in the 1970s to achieve major international recognition. It alerted the cinematic world not only that Thodoros Angelopoulos existed, but also that there was a Greek cinema bubbling for attention. Greece's seemingly mesmeric devotion to politics nearly thwarted the future of THE TRAVELLING PLAYERS when it refused official sanction as an entry into competition at Cannes in 1976. It nonetheless found its way to the Directors' Fortnightly Section and achieved a major triumph, walking off with the FIPRESCI Prize, which it shared with Werner Herzog's THE ENIGMA OF KASPAR HAUSER. It has since gathered accolades with a nearly boring consistency.

THE TRAVELLING PLAYERS continues the involvement with Greece's history that has thus far served Mr. Angelopoulos well. It covers a period of historical turmoil from 1939 to 1952, during which Greece survived the death of a dictator, a World War II invasion by Italy and Germany, a civil war between the political left and right, the aid of the English--which convoluted into interference into internal politics; and it finishes with the coming of the Americans, who subsequently will likewise be manipulative. The film is ungrounded; not even an event establishes home base. The group of traveling players serve as the thread by which the film is held together, but even they are unbased, on the move. They play out their lives against a historical kaleidoscope which shapes and moves them as though life itself were a role written for them and they are merely the physical embodiments.

Angelopoulos stretches his boundaries beyond immediacy with this film. Time is of greater scope, events affect-

THE TRAVELLING PLAYERS

ing characters are of enlarged proportions, even the length
of the film (it runs 3 hours and 50 minutes) adds to the
grandeur being encompassed. The scraggly players who, in
their real lives, act out the Electra legend, further expand
the time in that they serve as link to ancient Greece. Mr.
Angelopoulos seems to want to take on the entire history of
Greece; and, given his pacing, such a film would run longer
than the actuality!

Pacing serves not only the rhythmical needs of THE
TRAVELLING PLAYERS, but its dramatic crescendos and
diminuendos as well. There are few traditional dramatic
climaxes--not even as ending. The pacing, therefore, gives
the film its urgencies, its rests, its divertissements. Shots
which at first seem simply indulgently long, replace and
serve as climax. The film moves laterally, requiring devoted attention from an audience which may be accustomed
to a more emotionally ingratiating structure. The most
ready parallel that comes to mind is the more episodically-
structured works of Bertolt Brecht or even Jean-Luc Godard
(This comparison to Godard was obviously and declaredly
elusive at the time of the interview.) Whereas Brecht is
theatrical, and Godard is engagingly choppy, Angelopoulos
is languid. Perhaps a more accurate comparison can be
drawn with some of the music of Hector Berlioz which toys
with a theme, drops it, starts a new one, returns to a former theme, develops a favored theme--in general, turns inat-
tentively away from formal, accepted structure.

Pieces of the mosaic seep together seamlessly until
the whole circular pattern is assembled, to be finally effected by the repeat of the opening scene by the closing. It
is as if the audience is at a great height, looking down on a
massive puzzle which can be seen in its entirety only from
such an overview. From this vantage point, the pieces have
melded, are no longer visible.

The pieces are worth remembering, however. George
Arvanitis' camera work is soul-mate and major contributor
to Angelopoulos' intent. The discovery of Eva Kotaminidou
(Electra) is major. She is asked to deliver long monologues
directly to the camera, and received no editing, camera
movement, or other aid from the medium in helping her make
the scenes play. She is on her own, and she responds with
great force. Angelopoulos' original conception of the film is
a piece of the whole, deserving of awe long after the bedaz-
zlement of its execution has upstaged it. The selection of

music incisively captures mood and period, using popular and folk songs of the time to which they were pertinent.

The political distinctly usurps the sociological for the first time in Angelopoulos' films with THE TRAVELLING PLAYERS. Angelopoulos' pro-communist position in the film may partly explain its limited worldwide distribution. (It has never received a theater release in the United States, for instance.) The British (who have released it) get the brunt of the disfavor--in contrast to the 1975 Greek film output, which was vociferously anti-American. Needless to say, there is a strong anti-communist faction in the U.S., and this perhaps inspires some business reluctance to distribute the film. Or perhaps the foolish idea that audiences will not attend a film of such length has militated against it.

Angelopoulos' next film, THE HUNTERS, won the top prize at the Chicago Film Festival in 1977, and it seems probable now that the United States will soon have the opportunity to see Mr. Angelopoulos' work. (DAYS OF '36 has played at least once on American television.) Any retrospective of his work, or of Greek films in general, cannot help but include what is thus far the 1970s' unquestionably most important Greek film, THE TRAVELLING PLAYERS.

THE HUNTERS

Although it was clearly established that Angelopoulos was single-handedly making the Greek cinema movement of the '70s known to the world, he was unable to find financial backing in Greece for his fourth film. THE HUNTERS was financed by French and German television and found its way into competition at Cannes--no small accomplishment. A quirk that may not be peculiarly Greek, but which certainly finds an expression there, is the withdrawal of support for those who have proved successful. Greek critics attending Cannes assured the interested cinema world at home that THE HUNTERS was a failure. When it played noncompetitively (Angelopoulos was the first of the '70s directors to be thus removed from his peer group) at Thessaloniki, again it was affirmed that Angelopoulos had produced less than a success. Undaunted, Mr. Angelopoulos entered the film in competition at the Chicago International Festival and walked off with First Prize.

The Greek critics were not alone in their disdain for

THE HUNTERS. Richard Roud, in the Summer 1977 issue of Sight & Sound, said: "... I have never been an admirer of his. But even those who thought so highly of THE TRAV-ELLING PLAYERS found this new film something of a trial. Although much shorter, it seemed twice as long because the pace was insufferably and dictatorially slow.... The French critics remain loyal to Angelopoulos, but the Anglo-Saxons mostly had to admit they had been bored to distraction. " Rex Reed, with self-conscious cleverness, was less kind: "... a Greek monstrosity that runs three hours and 15 min-utes.... I left in a rage when a prostitute huffed and puffed atop a senile octogenarian who finally looked up and told the camers: 'I can't stand any more of this. ' It was a senti-ment with which I heartily agreed. More than 400 weary festivalgoers had cleared the way ahead of me. "5

THE HUNTERS, historically, overlaps the time cov-ered in THE TRAVELLING PLAYERS, but, generally speak-ing, it picks up where that film left off and continues Ange-lopoulos' study of Greek history to the present time. A group of hunters, marching across a frozen landscape, comes upon the body of a resistance fighter from the Civil War (1949?). The body is removed to their hunting lodge where an investi-gation is conducted, and this inspires flashbacks, memories, and fantasies which comprise the remainder of the film. When no answers to the investigation are found, the body is taken back to the snow and reburied.

Within the focus of Angelopoulos' work, THE HUNT-ERS suggests a possibility of a shift in emphasis. His first three films interweave the lives and fates of the characters so integrally with the environment that they very nearly be-come indistinguishable from such variables as time, place, social-historical environment, etc. And though THE HUNT-ERS is at first glance equally concerned with similar exam-ination, there is some slight difference which may be impor-tant as an aspect of future development. We now see events through the eyes, actions, memories and fantasies of the characters. We are on the inside looking out.

Angelopoulos is not completely at ease with the new-ness of this position. His characters are grouped anony-mously throughout most of the film; they even have no names. But each emerges from the group during the course of the film to reveal a dream, a fantasy, a remembrance of a per-sonal action, a decision or a change of direction in his or her life. This internal emphasis has not appeared before in

THE HUNTERS

the director's work and it hints at a new, personal position, or possibly that his historical study is moving closer to him in time and he therefore sees it within the framework of a more personal viewpoint.

As if to balance this shift, time and events are treated less distinctively than ever before. If the parts of THE TRAVELLING PLAYERS seeped together, they literally flow together in THE HUNTERS, making it sometimes impossible to tell if a scene is a flashback, a thought, a dream, a moment of madness, a present reality. There is an almost eerie quality, as though the film were shot under water. The mosaic of THE TRAVELLING PLAYERS is muted now; a pastel, Debussy-esk haze, brought into focus through the realities and madnesses of the individuals who temporarily capture the attention of the relentlessly staring camera. The lack of definition of time and place--in contrast to their former overpowering dominance--allows the people and their immediate, selected environment (the hunting lodge) to stand in bold relief. It is not surprising that former Angelopoulos devotees have some question about THE HUNTERS; nor that former disinterested viewers may see in it a promise of an Angelopoulos more to their liking in the future.

Again cinematographer George Arvanitis makes his magic for Angelopoulos (and, one hopes, for himself) with memorable scenes of the figures of the hunters emerging from the snowy landscape or dancing somewhat forcedly under strung lanterns. A quite remarkable scene occurs when a parade of boats bearing red flags sails by the hunting lodge, framed by mountain tops in the background, the flags reflecting in the water like blood. Though it is a visual treat, the scene also has a terribly naive connotation: with communism all would be beautiful, lyrical, smooth sailing. Such analysis is unworthy of Mr. Angelopoulos' facile intelligence; giving him the benefit of the doubt, we may assume this interpretation was not what was intended.

Eva Kotamanidou is again on hand, but with far less to do. Nevertheless, when the camera does find her, she responds with a tour de force. The scene is a New Year's Eve party, and she fantasizes seeing the king enter, dances with him, and is seduced by him on the dance floor. The entire scene is done without editing, leaving her on her own to triumph over a fantastically difficult acting assignment.

Mr. Angelopoulos allows himself his moment in the

sun. As a man and woman copulate in the back seat of a moving car, great turmoil erupts and continues around them. Shooting, fighting, smoke are seen and heard through the car windows, but their methodical and emotionless chore continues, accompanied by the woman's monologue and her glazed stare over her hunching partner's shoulder. Mr. Angelopoulos proves that his abilities are not just conceptual; that he has a few pyrotechnic tricks up his sleeve also.

One other scene worth isolating seems to be a confirmation of Angelopoulos' toying with the idea of people as perpetrators rather than victims: there is an empty hall lined with doors at which the camera is aimed, maintaining its silent vigil (it seems) long after the cast and crew have gone home. The characters do emerge from the closed doors, knock on other doors and play scenes off-screen. Hallways, passageways, bridges, doors, arches--all are symbolically interesting structures as connections from one point to another. Even if they become meaningful environments on their own, it is transition. Mr. Angelopoulos' lengthy emphasis on the hall suggests a stage for transition; instead it serves merely as link to the importance of the action off-screen. There is a calculation to this scene; it smacks of deliberate cleverness, and its very impact proves to be its downfall. It is pleasant and provocative to view the failure of this scene as a death rattle of the overemphasis on manipulatory forces which excuse the responsibility of choice.

Andrew Horton, in his otherwise thoroughly agreeable review, 6 defends this scene as eagerly as it is rejected above: "This empty-room technique has been used by others ... but never to my mind as effectively ... to suggest how a room becomes a stage and how architecture assumes personality and influences the individuals involved...."

If Mr. Angelopoulos continues his juxtaposition of time to any greater degree, he will indeed be producing the unfathomable. If he abandons his camera for any greater periods of time, he will be producing still photographs. THE HUNTERS suggests an end to the cinematic and historical exploration in which he has so successfully engaged. If the exploration has led him to people, as THE HUNTERS implies, his next film will indeed be different. It may lose him some of his former admirers, but there is another world, another audience, for him yet to conquer.

Notes

1. Dilys Powell in the London Sunday Times, September 11, 1975.

2. Peter Cowie in International Film Guide, 1974.

3. Nora Sayre in New York Times, April 3, 1974.

4. Film Comment, September 1974.

5. New York Daily News, May 27, 1977. Mr. Reed fails to explain how he arrived at the number of festival-goers who preceded his departure. We do get the point, however.

6. The Athenian, October 1977.

BIOGRAPHICAL BRIEF

Born Athens, April 1935. Studied law, switched to film in 1960. Studied in Paris at Sorbonne Institut de Filmologie. Film critic and teacher in late 1960s. Single. Lives in Athens. Articles and Interviews: (In French) Avant-Scène du Cinéma, Dec. '75; Ecran, Nov. '75; Image et Son, Sept/Oct. '75, Nov. '75; Jeune Cinéma, July/Aug '75; Montreal La Presse, Aug. 15, '77; Montreal Le Devoir, Aug. 16, '77; Positif, Oct. '75; Film a Doba (Czech.) Dec. '75; Filmrutan (Swedish), #3, '75; Cineforum (Italian), Sept. '75. See also: BFI Award 1975, Sight and Sound, Spring '76.

FILMS

THE BROADCAST (28 minutes) (1968).

RECONSTRUCTION (1970). (Director, Screenplay, Actor). Prizes: 1970 Thessaloniki Festival, Best Film, Best First Film Director; Prix Georges Sadoul 1971; FIPRESCI Special Mention, Berlin Festival, 1971; Prix du Bureau Catholique, Mannheim Festival, 1971; Best Film, Greek Critics, 1971; Best Foreign Film, Heyeres Festival, 1971.

DAYS OF '36 (1972). (Producer, Director, Screenplay).

Prizes: Best Director, 1972 Thessaloniki Festival; FIPRESCI Prize, Berlin Festival, 1972.

THE TRAVELLING PLAYERS (1975). (Director, Screenplay). Prizes: 1973 Thessaloniki Festival, Best Film, Best Direction, Best Screenplay; FIPRESCI Prize, Cannes Festival, 1975; Special Prize, Taormina (Italy), 1975; Interfilm Prize, Berlin Festival, 1975; British Film Institute Award for Best Film, 1976; Prix l'age d'or, Brussels; Grand Prize, Figueira da Foz (Portugal), 1976.

THE HUNTERS (1977). (Director, Screenplay, Co-Producer). First Prize, Chicago International Festival, 1977.

(Angelopoulos also appeared as actor in KIERION, 1968, directed by D. Theos.)

Chapter 3

Beloved Enemy

- COSTAS ARISTOPOULOS -

CRANIUM LANDSCAPE, Costas Aristopoulos' primary
film, exerts a resistance to convenient categorization as related to this study. A retelling of the Jesus story at this
particular time of Greek cinema history was a most unexpected choice of film-content. It ignored the deliberate
search for Greekness, at least from the view of surface content. It turned its back on the then current social problems.
From an economic viewpoint, it was impossible to compete
with the similar subject films of Cecil B. DeMille, George
Stevens and Nicholas Ray, and Pier Paolo Pasolini's THE
PASSION ACCORDING TO ST. MATTHEW remains an extremely satisfying version of the story.

Inevitably CRANIUM LANDSCAPE invites comparison
with the Pasolini film. It employs non-professional actors,
is devoid of the slick glamor and technicolor mysticism of
the Hollywood versions, and has a simple crudity about it
that involves the audience in the job of filling in missing artistic ingredients. (One mentally irons wrinkles out of costumes, combs an actor's hair, and, in general, adds grace
notes here and there to make the role of observer less demanding.)

CRANIUM LANDSCAPE has all the charm (and some
of the camp) of those old Sunday School films one shudders
to remember from childhood. It hardly makes a definitive
statement about Aristopoulos' abilities as filmmaker; yet it
has a winning effect on memory. Although not originally
planned as part of the film, there are interviews with the
non-professional actors interspersed during the course of the
film which add much interest to the whole. Aristopoulos became so interested in the villagers playing the roles that he
subsequently filmed these interviews with them and edited the
results into the film. The naturalness of the people, the

COSTAS ARISTOPOULOS

delight one takes in their humor, the respect they command
for expressing their love for life despite its harshness--in
essence, getting to know them--cushions any embarrassment
at the amateurishness of their performances and opens receptive doors to the film itself.

LETTER TO NAZIM HIKMET

Aristopoulos' second film, LETTER TO NAZIM HIK-
MET, fits more comfortably into the general tone of the '70s
Greek cinema. He was moved by an incident of brutality involving a Turkish student, about which he read in a newspaper. The existing antipathy between Greece and Turkey
no doubt inspired the news release, aimed at negative emotionalism against the "enemy." Aristopoulos, instead, focused on the horror of brutality, and saw the Turkish student, not primarily as a Turk but as a victim of a greater
and mutual enemy--authoritarian injustice and cruelty. To
show any sympathy toward a Turk, despite the elevated vision,

was a bold statement--hardly likely to garner popularity.
The incident serving as immediate inspiration became the
springboard to strike out against oppression wherever it existed (e. g. , Chile, Rhodesia, Spain and, of course, Greece).

Despite the obvious satisfaction Aristopoulos registered
with the voice-over commentary of the film (which the Variety
reviewer found "pretentious due to its excessive and forced
poetics"), the film has a hurried look, as though Aristopoulos
felt it time to produce another film but circumstances didn't
lend themselves to a more committed effort. It is not that
his sincerity is in doubt, but rather that it was simply time
to remind the cinema world of his presence. The style of
the film is collage, and attracted little attention at its pre-
mier screening at the Thessaloniki Festival in 1976.

Costas Aristopoulos, like his films, refuses to fit
conveniently into the categories which emerged during this
study. He didn't talk politics, he didn't talk "Greekness, "
he even talked film in a curiously methodical way which suggested dispassion. He made declaratory statements about
himself as though his speech had been prepared in advance,
as though this were a presentation behind which he intended
to remain undetected. His braggadocio was unconvincing;
his emphasis on "being good" (not necessarily successful)
had an element of compulsion in it rather than a simple appreciation of quality. Aristopoulos has spent a great deal of
time in the presence of "being good" at what one does: his
father, known professionally as Arias, is a successful poet,
entertainer, and restauranteur in Athens. Aristopoulos himself attended the Karolos Koun school of acting, admission
to which is highly competitive. Only a handful of actors
scale the heights of the Koun school, which means that
Aristopoulos had success as an actor within likely reach.
Instead, he chose to desert acting, study film in England,
and tackle the near-impossible task of being a filmmaker in
Greece. To confront either of these resistant "establishments" is very nearly foolhardy; to take on both inevitably
invites suspicion that such testing of self is indeed compul-
sory.

His stated reasons for studying acting are far more
practical than these suspicions suggest: "Film had been my
secret love, and I really studied acting to learn what problems the actor had to face. I never planned to be an actor.
But from the beginning I got a license as an exceptional student to play while I studied. So I got the full experience.

Two scenes from CRANIUM LANDSCAPE. Top, Takis Kilakos as Judas.

Some friends of mine, some very important men in Greece, advised me to stay in acting as I could become a very important actor in Greece. But I wanted to be an important film director. When I was younger I was told I could be a very important* basketball player. But I preferred to be a player in filmmaking. "

CRANIUM LANDSCAPE has autobiographical roots: "When I was a child I used to go to see a little man who moved around with a metallic box. You put your eyes to it and it showed some pictures. What fascinated me about it was a picture of the crucifixion with a voice explaining who the people were. This went back to the beginnings of the Greek Orthodox Church and made on me a great impression. So this film has been hidden in me for a very long period of time. It finally came out.

"I decided to make the film despite Pasolini's film, which I had seen but don't believe was influential. My film is one made from the Orthodox point of view, and Pasolini's is one made by a Catholic. The story might be the same, but the details of religion are very opposite. It surprised me when some of the Greek filmmakers tried to say I was imitating Pasolini's film. This happened only in Greece. I showed the film in Italy, where no one made this accusation. I got very good reviews in Italy where they said it was a film which would cause endless discussion, that it was a powerful construction of image. It was also very successful in Holland. If you keep in mind that this film was done on a very low budget, let's say a budget of $12-15,000 and under the dictatorship where it was so difficult to move, it results in something that even nowadays I do respect.

"It was fascinating working with the villagers in the film, but on the other hand, it was like a Greek tragedy. The man who plays God went to America in his early youth and was struck by a car. The accident caused brain damage and he can't think very well. Two weeks before I met him his first son hung himself. The woman who read poetry lost her two brothers during the civil war and she has tried des-

---

*The word "important" is used frequently in Greece by the English-speaking population. Its multi-meanings embrace expressions of quality, success, prestige, historical reverence, innovation, authoritativeness, power, fame, etc. It is a very "important" word.

perately to make something of her life. Every one of them
was more great than myself, so the film didn't come out as
I expected. Their lives meant so much to me that it seemed
to me that I was a ridiculous intellectual who studied in London and came back to make great art. Comparing my art to
their everyday lives, my art was very artificial, out of fash-
ion. In the middle of the film I wanted to abandon it. I
became very depressed. Since there were people involved
in the film who were making their living, it had to be finished. But as time went on I felt more and more desperate.
Finally, following the screening of the film in London, I
spoke to the audience and admitted that I felt guilty about the
film. Through this film I came into a position of being in-
terviewed, starting to establish myself as a director, but the
people in the film remain in the same position. I don't know
if the film improved their lives, while mine was changed for
the better.

"The decision to include those interviews was inspired
by the people themselves. I believe that their biographies,
their speaking about themselves, was like a text written by
saints. I very much respect human beings. It doesn't matter if they are rich or poor. I look to other human beings
to find an originality in them. Even when they are in despair, or very sad, or contemplating suicide. I do respect
the anguish in their lives. "

Early in my communication with Aristopoulos, he
seemed intent on making calculated pronouncements about
himself as related to "being good. " But as we talked about
his films, his enthusiasm for the conversation seemed to
lower his guard, and we eased into a moralistic concept of
the word "good" as opposed to its qualitative meaning. He
began to admit his fascination with the "failures" and the
"bad. " "What does that mean, 'badness'? Why have people
invented this meaningless word? Afterall, something that
may be good for you is bad for me, and vice versa.

"I am planning to do a film about Judas. I have done
the script outline, and I believe it will be most astonishing.
Judas is an example of people involved in other ways of life.
Sometimes these people are rejected by social structures,
but I believe that from them there has been much influence
to many human beings. I want to show that badness is not
so terrible when badness can be exposed very carefully.
Judas represents a person who is suffocated by the greatness
of Christ. I do believe I have seen rare qualities in people

who have been ousted by the social structure. This seems
to be a question of the moral structure. That is, there is
a morality for everyone. By doing this film on Judas I want
to respect Judas, even his betrayal, because it seems to me
a human being is a combination of badness and goodness.

"I am interested in Judas because to some extent I
resemble him. In the last interview I gave to television,
they asked me, 'why don't you communicate with the masses?'
And I told them that I do respect the masses. I don't see
them as masses, but as a mass composed of individuals.
Each individual has his own value, so it seems very artificial
to appeal to them as a superior mind which says, 'Look,
you are going to see this film and after seeing this film your
education is going to be better.' How can I say that to these
people when I don't know my own life? I might love somebody and suddenly, within a very few moments, I hate him.
One moment I may want to murder him and the next minute
embrace him. I have so many contradictions. I have been
so far mistaken, I have been weak and strong. This is what
makes me in love with things, this contradiction. It makes
me interested in Judas. If Christ represents strength and
willingness to sacrifice self, this kind of behavior seems a
little bit artificial. I hate heroes who show off so much.
If heroes react to panic in a way which surprises even them,
that is of interest. So Judas, to me, is a person who tries
little by little to overcome his problems. "

"I hope to start my third film in 1977. It will be
somewhat surrealistic, having to do with modern-day Greece,
wherein many institutions in modern Greek society are at-
tacked in a very poetic, personal way. I do not hate the
older generations, because I do believe I come through those
older generations. There is always a gap, this is something
that is very natural. But even the way I am talking to you,
the language I use, I learned from them. All this culture
I obtained from the older generations. And so I believe that
humankind is a generation that transforms itself as the time
flies, and all these generations together make up 1976 in the
human race.

"What pleases me about me is that I feel very sure
that someday I'll do a good film. Every time I do a film I
stabilize some knowledge. Little by little I'm building a conception as to how it has to be. There are some Greek filmmakers who are a little bit annoyed with me because I choose

a language of honesty. Most of these filmmakers believe
that they are something special. To me this seems a bit ridiculous. I mean, what is so special about them? Why do they feel
so superior? It makes me sometimes hesitate, and wonder if
I am right to do films which cost quite a bit of money. "

"I want to continue directing. There are offers from
television which, till now, I have not gotten involved with because television is too commercial. Greek television is
newly born. But I've finally decided to do what I can, because television is a fact now, and is a common language.
And I do not want to be left behind. But I want to find a
way to do it wherein I can operate on a level that is reflective of me. But I do believe that for the first time in
Greek cinema history, it is starting to establish its true
face. The new generation of Greek filmmakers are quite
well educated, compared to the previous generation. Most
of us have been educated abroad, we've got some technical
knowledge, plus we are interested in many things such as
painting, literature and music. We truly want our cinema
to be a new movement in Europe. "

Aristopoulos is a man who has apparently been driven
to be "good"--in both senses of the word discussed here--
and who now questions the value of that position. His fascination with the "enemy"--the failures, the older generations,
the villains, the actual enemies--seems less an exploration
of the literal focuses of his interest than a psychological
examination of his own capacity to fail, to grow old, to behave on the outside of social acceptance. In short, he is
confronting his own divided self, and his in-depth attempts
to understand the "bad" side--the possibility that he, himself, might be the enemy--is indeed exhilarating subject
matter for future films. Whether films will evolve from his
current involvements is impossible to predict, but the involvements themselves are important attempts to reach a
personal definition of tolerance and understanding. Should
he achieve his goal of being a "good" director, it is currently obvious that as with Mae West, goodness will have
nothing to do with it.

BIOGRAPHICAL BRIEF

Born Athens, 1940. Studied acting, Art Theatre of Karolos

Koun. Graduate of London School of Film Technique. Worked
as editor, cameraman, etc. while in school. Returned to
Greece in 1970. Father is a poet, music hall entertainer
and restauranteur. Married to Anastasias Arsini, painter,
set decorator and costume designer. Lives with wife and
son in Athens. Award: Special Award for Direction, CRAN-
IUM LANDSCAPE, 1973 Thessaloniki Festival.

FILMS

Two shorts (one unidentified).

DRAGONS (Short), 1972.

CRANIUM LANDSCAPE (1973).   (Producer, Director, Screenplay).

LETTER TO NAZIM HIKMET (1976).   (Screenplay, Director).

In Preparation: SLEEP AND DEATH (IPNOS KE THANATOS).
(Producer, Screenplay, Director).   Photography:
George Arvanitis.   Art Direction: Anastasia Arseni.

Chapter 4

The View Is Shangri-La; The Mood Is Mahagonny

- MANOUSSOS MANOUSSAKIS -

In July 1976, Manoussos Manoussakis invited me to
come to the village of Hiliomodi on the Peloponnese to watch
shooting of his second film, POWER. In its present condition, Hiliomodi is not threatened with tourist invasion. It's
a rather glum little village, a large part of which seems to
be owned by the Manoussakis family. The film crew had
taken over at least four buildings, but even then there were
not enough beds to go around. Filled sleeping bags sprouted
haphazardly in sheltered areas at the end of the long work
days, while I, with considerable guilt, accepted the comfort
of a couch.

When not working, the cast and crew seemed in aim-
less pursuit of personal diversions. Only George Tsemberopoulos, the assistant director, seemed to maintain constant
vigilance; with a clip-board of official-looking papers he ef-
ficiently served as link between those who knew what was
happening and those who didn't. (I constantly belonged to the
second group!) Transportation, meals, refreshments appeared magically when needed. Toilet facilities were plenti-
ful--behind the nearest tree! (Though one sound assistant
chose the top of a mountain, arching a modest waterfall tri-
umphantly across the parched landscape.)

Transported to a nearby, smaller, even glummer village, the crew set up headquarters at what appeared to be
the only public establishment in town--a sort of coffeehouse,
post-office, general store combination. Actresses began
making up their faces like Toulouse-Lautrec posters, actors
donned authoritative military uniforms, and the villagers,
with feigned disinterest, continued stringing tobacco leaves.
The surrealistic result was in itself a scene from a Manoussakis film.

Director Manoussos Manoussakis and cinematographer George Panousopoulos during filming of POWER.

The village water supply was located in what might euphemistically be called the town square. Housewives, children and donkeys appeared as though on cue, and found themselves participants in the magic world of the silver screen. Rough soldiers herded them (and the by-now over-painted harlots) into the back of a wagon, under the command of Manoussakis himself in an immaculately tailored officer's uniform, complete with braid, riding crop, and ten sandaled toes popping incongruously from under his trousers. When the women were subserviently huddling in their vehicular prison, the driver suddenly stripped off his shirt and, bare-chested, returned calmly to his coffee while a stand-in driver took off with his human cargo, going I know not where until I see the film.

Towering above the village was a mountain which served as protective foundation for the ruin of an old fort where, in the distance, stick figures could be seen in prepa-ration for afternoon shooting. After lunch, everyone mys-teriously picked up the chairs on which they sat and started, single-file, to climb the mountain. Manoussakis, in one of his frequent and (to me) amazing moments of awareness of my presence, advised me to do the same. With chair in hand, camera and equipment lurching from my neck, I joined this strange, silent parade, marching a route through bram-bles, sharp rocks and donkey droppings.

The gutted interior of the fort had been transformed into an open-air theater with a tiny proscenium stage adorned with multi-colored crepe paper streamers blowing maniacally in the wind. The juxtaposition of a vast natural background of neighboring mountains, and the silent observation of the ruined fort itself, gave the proceedings a kind of nightmare quality; the site was Shangri-La, but the mood was Mahagon-ny.

The painted girls became entertainers on the windy stage, the men and chairs became the theater audience, I became a frenzied photographer, and when the sun became unbearable, two donkeys carting water and coffee became re-freshment dispensers to wet down the parched intermissions.

The following night presented rare excitement in this mountain village: under glaring electric lights three drunken men were to rape a nervous actress. The necessary phys-ical transformation of the male anatomy for the accomplish-ment of such foul deed would be heartily challenged by the

Manoussos Manoussakis during filming of POWER.

frigid night air. It is doubtful whether any rape victim ever
had such a vast and curious audience. Families arrived from
the surrounding darkness; crying babies tested the patience
of the sound engineer; a carnival atmosphere engulfed the entire village. I snugged into a long-sleeve farmer's undershirt
and had a lengthy conversation with the electrician on the
merits of veteran director-cinematographer Rudolph Maté.
Manoussakis should have filmed the filming.

Two days were not enough to fathom what Manoussakis'
new film is all about. There is promised corruption and violence. (I was invited to return to become a victim in a big
slaughter scene but, alas, my film debut as a corpse was extinguished by chance.)

Manoussakis' first film, VARTHOLOMEOS, is a surrealistic attack on authority; I have little reason to believe
the second film any less kind to the establishment. I didn't
understand much of VARTHOLOMEOS, and strongly suspect
I am not alone in my confusion. But its anti-authoritarian
message is loud and clear. It is a daring film, and says
much for the boldness of Manoussakis. Once a reputation
has been established, an artist can fairly safely take a chance
on a product that might go broadly misunderstood. But to
make such a major thrust into uncertainty on a first film requires a gambling on self for which few persons have the
courage.

It is inconceivable to talk of surrealistic film without
mentioning Buñuel, but VARTHOLOMEOS struck me as being
more akin to the work of Dusan Makavejev. A girl beats
endlessly on a bucket upended over her head; a bride eagerly
mourns an array of deceased husbands; a hangman thrashes
the ocean in punishment or chops down a staircase on which
an accident has occurred. One scene inspired me to conclude
that Manoussakis was making an anti-victimization statement,
but then I discovered it was an actual historical reference,
and I wondered how many smugly stupid conclusions are based
on ready satisfaction with self-advice, without waiting to make
decisions until other pertinent variables are gathered. Which
is by way of saying that if I did not comprehend all the details of Manoussakis' message in VARTHOLOMEOS, its pro-
vocativeness sparked examination and thought, and perhaps
that is actually what it is really all about anyway.

Manoussakis may be the most unbounded filmmaker
working in Greece today. Tradition, either of the medium

or cultural, go unattended in his work. He is a bit wild;
whatever discipline exists is attuned to his concept of its
reality. The viewer is tempted to soar with his somewhat
chaotic originality, or to step aside and view the whole thing
as a dynamic mistake. In either case, the director's lack
of film inhibition demands an involved reaction.

Manoussos Manoussakis is a man who has discovered
the secret of popularity; the unanswered question is whether
or not he makes calculated use of that knowledge. He is
never too busy to give a fleeting personal acknowledgment to
each individual, allowing the recipient of his attention to interpret it as an intimate exchange. But his films cluster individuals into types and symbols and tools, with little or no
revelation of them as individuals. Is the one-to-one exchange
offered in his real life and the absence of individuality in his
films a legitimate dichotomy, or are we willing victims of
his charm, which dissolves our personal masks and exposes
a category-layer to which he relates? Whatever the answer
(if, in fact, the question is accurate), Manoussakis is extremely well-liked, and I (stated suspicions aside) happily
join the ranks of his admirers.

His presentation is one of ease and casual good-nature,
but his films speak of serious concern for present and future.
In private, the easy-going Manoussakis reveals the discouragement and personal psychological threats inherent in the current Greek cinema--and beyond. "When I went to England,
I had already decided to study film. There my tastes developed because I was interested in the arts generally. But
I had already decided that film was the best way to express
myself, rather than painting or poetry or literature. And I
hope to continue making films, but I don't want to wait another three years to make another film. There are many,
many times I do not know if films are the way to do things
nowadays. There is a question I have if it's the proper way
to say something. I'm not sure making films allows me to
live the way I want. You find yourself running around for
three years just to find the money to make one film, while
all during those three years you have fucked yourself up and
lost contact with the film you were going to make. So you
have fucked up your life. So why make films? It is a big
problem for me. I want to live.

"I don't know if it is the proper way to fight, especially now when it costs so much money. When I think of the
amount of money I am going to spend on the new film, it
makes me crazy.

Two scenes from VARTHOLOMEOS.

"I can't just withdraw to a village and live out my
life in peace and quiet until I die.   What I mean when I say
that film may not be the way to create development is that
I am really in chaos as concerning the rhythm of our times.
I am in chaos when I think that we could very easily die any-
time, as a species, that is.   If films are active in preventing
such a thing ... but you look around and you see life absolutely overrun with threats and yet you stay and make films.
Sometimes I think it would be nice to withdraw to an island,
or maybe have a theater group and travel around to the villages and make personal contact with the everyday rhythm of
everyday life.   Of course, I'd like to continue making films,
but the way you have to make them is completely discourag-
ing--the way the system is set up, not the medium, or whether or not you can pass ideas through the medium.

"As to some future recognition, it depends on what
might be asked of me in return.   How would I have to change?
If they like me as I am, I would say yes, because I have an
ambitious character.   But there would be limits as to what
I would do in exchange for that.   I could be very easily
thrilled with money, and international acknowledgment.   But
these things can very easily eat up somebody.   I do not say
that I could stand against them, or fight against them, or
that I am some kind of hero who can't be touched by them.
Of course I could be touched by them.   But then, I haven't
been confronted with the problem yet!"

* * * * *

Manoussakis is calm and controlled when working.
He is infinitely patient and even-keeled.   Disruptive problems,
no matter how petty, were dealt with rationally and efficient-
ly.   Nervous actors were soothed; forgotten lines were
prompted without evidence of concern for the dwindling budget; village women (surreptitiously smoothing their aprons or
recovering a wisp of wandering hair) suddenly found themselves charmed into a film debut.   He seemed to be the
focal point at which the chaotic maze of filmmaking converged
into a clearly marked road, straight and almost carelessly
undemanding.

A magnet is needed to collect the scattered pieces of
filmmaking in Greece because a day's pay for a day's work
is simply not applicable.   Manoussakis is just such a magnet.
He jokes his way through the village with the ease of never
having lived elsewhere.   He winks paternally at me (consid-

erably his senior in age) and reassures me that I am not as
unbased as I feel. He puts a comforting arm around a dis-
traught actress and she delivers what he wants. He dis-
cusses technical problems with the photographer with time-
saving efficiency. Effortlessly, he turns a lot of discomfort
and hard work into a party; with a smile a host of volunteer
workers feel they are guests.

* * * * *

1977 UPDATE: The excitement that accompanies the first
screenings of a finished film had swept all doubts of a future
in filmmaking from Manoussakis. POWER was ready to be
shown, but it was in severe trouble. It had failed to obtain
an O. K. from the censors, who objected to the excessive use
of the adjudged vulgar street language, despite its realistic
correctness within the context of the film. They also were
displeased with some of the sex scenes, with which the film
abounds. These scenes, too, seem inevitable outcomes of
the film's intent, and are handled with an inspiredly correct
balance between sensuality and an animalistic lack of emotion, as befits the characters depicted. The film is so accurate in fulfilling its intent that one cannot help but be suspicious of the motives of the censors. In truth, the film is
boldly, intentionally, and emphatically anarchistic, and it is
difficult not to suspect that the censorship problems have
more to do with this permeating element rather than the ones
stated. Without censorship approval, the film cannot hope to
be released to theatres, though it can play festivals.

Trouble was compounded when the selection committee of the 1977 festival rejected the film, the rumored reason being that the committee could not understand the film.
Subsequently the film played out of competition, and attracted
the second biggest audience of the festival (following Angelopoulos' THE HUNTERS).

POWER, in my opinion, is the most passionate, imaginative, and involving film made in Greece in 1977. The
chaotic fever of Manoussakis' first film has been harnessed
into disciplined fervor. Still working in a bigger-than-life
framework, Manoussakis depicts the corruption of the government, the church, the military, big business, diplomatic
relationships with the outside, and even the "little man" workers, who normally are treated as sympathetic victims of the
aforementioned powers. Manoussakis lets no one off his
scathing hook. While the powerful classes negotiate and

During filming of POWER.

juggle for more power, the little men dig for archaeological treasures, the sales of which will make them rich and powerful.

A carousel of sexual scenes occurs throughout the film, each of them devoid of partner-involvement. They are merely acts, with no love, tenderness, or even healthy passion. No class or group escapes the biting camera which snoops into the world's bedroom, there to discover it rutting gracelessly, even with minimal physical involvement. "Little man" gets a bit of a break here, though not much. At least the soldiers, in their drunkenness, register a full-bodied lust, though it is manifested sadistically and is definitely power-based rather than love-based.

POWER shares some of the philosophy of Pier Paolo Pasolini's film SALO, without resorting to any of SALO's visually repulsive sensationalism. Both films declare the "have" classes to be cruel, selfish, imprisoning users, driven to seek satisfaction in extremes because of a deadened ability to experience their own humanity. The "have not" classes are willing to be used out of fear or ignorance. Even worse, they cooperate--their acceptance being an affirmation of their belief in and emotional sameness with the behavior of the user classes. In short, the used class hopes someday to be the user class.

Whereas Pasolini sees the users continuing in their struggle against impotence by reaching toward grotesque extremism, Manoussakis is more definitive in his conclusions-- it is hopeless and its only justice is total destruction. In the end, he simply sets the entire world on fire. *

This all sounds terribly grim and nihilistic. Yet there is a certain belief in life registered in Manoussakis' film--not through literal content, but through execution. All scenes involving the soldiers are particularly dynamic; they are climaxed by an all-male, drunken party wherein Dimitri Meletis does an unusually erotic striptease, part imitative of a female stripper, but dominantly male nevertheless. The drunken soldiers hoot and cat-call, and even caress his but-

---

*Watching scenes from the movie being filmed, the "feel" had been that of the Kurt Weill/Bert Brecht opera, "The Rise and Fall of the City of Mahagonny." They, too, set the world on fire at the end of the opera.

tocks during the dance. But he ends this homosexual-erotic scene by licking a pinup from a girlie magazine, and then reaching a sexual climax by stuffing the picture down the front of his undershorts.

There is also a memorable rape scene, made distinctive not by its brutality but through the repressed desire of the victim to be so used. Sexual repression, and lack of joy in the sex that is not repressed, adds to the message that at the core of human behavior is power-seeking. The film does not make clear which it believes comes first: power attainment and its subsequent deadening jadedness, or the absence of healthy sexual fulfillment which converts to power-seeking. Furthermore, the obvious pleasure Manoussakis had in making the film keeps the totality of the film from being completely oppressive, and even erodes the message a bit.

There are no outstanding roles in the film, but the cast is universally good. Some incongruous and outlandish costumes add an exaggerated quality to the film. The tendency toward exaggeration in Manoussakis' films results in caricature, which again weakens the whole. By distilling the essence of his characters, and then lifting that sediment to the surface, he creates distortion. The essential horror being expressed is thus rendered somewhat foolish. There is a certain arrogance in this treatment--a looking down on the users--which minimizes their villainy. Although the users are depicted as individuals, the audience understands that they are representations, and therefore less identifiable. *

In POWER, the "used" class receives a more realistic treatment; the film thus might garner some adverse attention by those who are irrationally "pro" the working class. More importantly, Manoussakis has invited this criticism by making the used class more identifiable to the audience; the depicted negatives of the class are therefore felt with greater penetration. From a structural point of view, this is a subjective imbalance in favor of the workers, but it really

---

*This approach is one shared by many of the Greek films in the 1970s, the outstanding exception being Theos' KIERION, wherein the horror is dispensed by individuals for whom the audience can feel real fear, rather than some disassociated, cerebral understanding.

has the opposite effect. That is, the users are allowed to escape because they are rendered unreal; the used, for whom more sympathy is felt, are strongly called to task through the more realistic treatment.

These conceptual flaws do not seriously thwart the overall impact of the film. Manoussakis obviously did not get all his disgust out with VARTHOLOMEOS. He has now honed his message, refined it, digested it, and spews it out with mature force in POWER. There is no love, no lyricism, no surface hope in his message. But it is a very potent film about the impotency of power!

BIOGRAPHICAL BRIEF

Born Athens, 1950. Studied film in London. Lives with wife and son in Athens.

FILMS

VARTHOLOMEOS (1973). (Producer, Director, Screenplay).

POWER (1977). (Producer, Director, Screenplay).

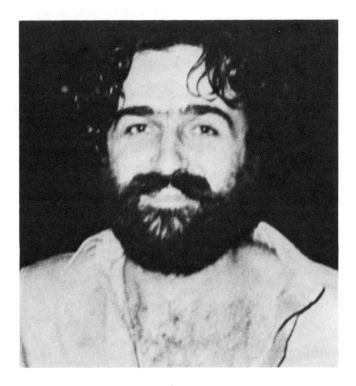

Chapter 5

The Party's Over ...

- THODOROS MARANGHOS -

I first met Thodoros Maranghos in 1975. He struck me as reclusive and a bit hostile, or, at the very least, distrustful. He had enviably voluptuous hair threatening to engulf his shoulders, and the kind of massive beard which tends to trap the lower eye-lashes. He seemed literally to have disappeared, leaving nothing behind but a pair of eyes. Even they refused a direct contact, adding to the illusion of buried identity. This man with no face had produced two quite remarkable films: GET ON YOUR MARK and STRUGGLE.

Photo of Thodoros Maranghos, above, courtesy of The Athenian magazine.

At the 1976 Thessaloniki Festival I saw a smashingly handsome man who seemed vaguely familiar--especially the eyes. It turned out to be a naked-faced Maranghos with trimly clipped ear-lobe-length hair, and an easy outgoing quality which cast doubt on my memory of him. The face-less Maranghos had refused to pose for photographs, so he too has now disappeared.

The 1975 festival was a celluloid eruption of political statements. Having lived the bulk of their adult lives under a repressive government where such open opinions were not permitted, this outpouring was not only understandable, but probably necessary. Unfortunately it made for a rather dreary and one-dimensional collection of films--the art of filmmaking had been subverted by passion for subject.

STRUGGLE boded ill; ho-hum, another interview film exploiting the filmmaker's current favorite social injustice. But from its crude opening shots, executed with mobile subjectivity, it plummeted on its biased but believed course which took it through glittering on-the-spot footage of the triumphant overthrow of the junta, and on into the more calculated and cool investigation of the existing social strife, and, of course, a dogmatic proposal of the panacea for those ills. Propaganda crystalizes ills and offers cures with such pious assuredness that its message frequently is declared cure-all for all ills at all times at all places. STRUGGLE shares a bit of this naiveté, but it is so earnest and so passionately created that it is easy to overlook the very thing it hopes to convey.

There are six accredited directors of STRUGGLE, and despite their refusal to reveal who did what, it is reasonable to assume that Maranghos was the directorial apex around which STRUGGLE revolved. As an individual filmmaker he had produced three shorts and GET ON YOUR MARK, an exceptional first feature which put him high on the list of promising Greek filmmakers.

Maranghos is much more extroverted and communicative now than when I first met him, but good-natured teasing, intended to urge him to get on the mark for another solo film, met with serious mouthings of slogans sounding vaguely like television commercials prepared by some Moscow version of a Madison Avenue junior executive. Any hopes that the reappearance of the physical Maranghos might symbolize renewed contact with the individual Maranghos behind the attractive exterior were quickly put to rest for another year.

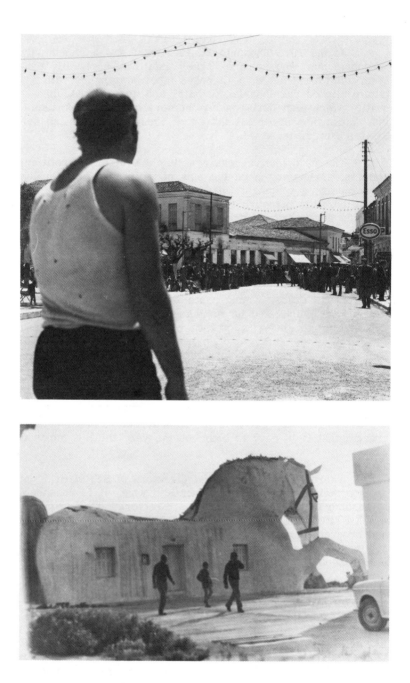

Scenes from GET ON YOUR MARK.

Maranghos created a scene in the festival theatre during the screening of MINUS-PORTRAIT, a short film by Leonidas Papadakis. Two large Greek flags were erected as backdrop, and items were thrown into camera range that both actually and symbolically turn Greece into a trash dump. Political references were made, as well as the expected commercial products that litter our lives; an American flag and symbols of the dictatorships found their places in the growing heap. Maranghos raised a furor when he adjudged a photograph as being of Lenin and could only be pacified when he was assured it was not Lenin, but the Greek dictator Metaxas. Those political authorities all look pretty much alike to me, too!

Maranghos, or at least the part of him under control, had been unhappy with Tasos Psarras' film MAY, because it depicted the people behaving as a disorganized animalistic mob, much as we actually have behaved repeatedly throughout history. Presumably the power of positive thinking is now the more dynamic statement, and the workers are to be shown smiling and whistling while they work--even if that cartoon has already been done by Walt Disney.

Of Maranghos' two major children, STRUGGLE unquestionably enjoys daddy's favoritism. There is little argument that STRUGGLE is an engrossing and superior documentary, but his other offspring, the currently neglected GET ON YOUR MARK springs from a creator with original imagination not yet molded by the dictatorship of group alignment. It is a tragi-comic story of a village tailor who dreams of escaping his deadly life by becoming a famous athlete. When he finally gets his chance to enter a race, time and ignorance of productive training are his real opponents, and he is beaten easily by the younger runners. His dream destroyed, he moves to Athens to take up a dismal life as a factory worker.

Maranghos had attracted attention as early as 1969 with his first animated short. His background was advertising, and he lacked formal film education or experience. GET ON YOUR MARK has an unfinished look which actually adds to the emotional punch of the film. It parallels and enhances the ignorance of the village athlete whose dreams must remain dreams because he doesn't know (or can't even realistically consider) how to effectively act out the dream. He trains as best he knows, but with no opportunities to move closer to the goal his incentive dwindles. When finally an opportunity does occur, it is simply too late.

Actor Vangeles Kazan and real-life counterpart in GET ON YOUR MARK.

      Although hopelessness because of the absence of opportunities was the focal point of Maranghos' interest in doing the film (a retrospective conclusion), the individual in the story is of such interest that the emphasis ultimately falls on him, rather than on the victimizing forces which inspired the film. Furthermore, Maranghos was from a village and now found himself emerging successfully through the maze of confrontations we all face in our efforts to find a balance between ourselves as individuals and our position within the group. The Greek film world is hardly economically permissive, and GET ON YOUR MARK was made during a period of heavy censorship. Despite the hostility of the system, Maran-

ghos had succeeded in being recognized as a talented individual. His own experience had to influence his ultimate decision to spotlight the individual in GET ON YOUR MARK,
despite a conscious inclination to zero in on social oppres-
siveness.

Maranghos is disinclined to show GET ON YOUR MARK
and has little patience with others' interest in it. The star
of the film, Vangeles Kazan, was not reticent about discussing
it (or nearly anything else!), so he was sought for observa-
tions of the film.

"I was with Maranghos just yesterday and we rem-
inisced about the old days. After two or three years, since
we made GET ON YOUR MARK, Maranghos said to me,
'You were right when you said don't go far away from the
characters with your camera. ' I think watching MAY was
what convinced him. 'Now I understand what you meant by
that, and I believe you are right. '

"Even after three years I feel very happy about this
film. I took the courage at the time to speak up, because I
had 20 years of experience behind me and Maranghos had
only one. The film actually began with me because I am a
sports fan, and I had always thought I would like to do a film
about a runner attempting to reach the goal. When I mentioned this to Maranghos, he said, 'Oh, I know just such a
story, and we can do this film. '

"During the shooting I felt hungry; that is, I felt a
lack of satisfaction with the development of the character.
Maranghos was inclined to treat the story more objectively;
that is, more symbolic of the dreams and struggles of the
villagers to obtain meaning to their lives. He kept at too
great a distance from the character. I didn't say to him,
'You know I am the leading player and I want some close-ups, '
nothing like that, although in truth I was an important col-
laborator in the film and had some right to say that. But
I felt a closeness to the character was essential, and by in-
sisting, the other roles subsequently were developed because
the concept has to be constant throughout the film. But
Maranghos said, 'I'm doing the film for the director, not to
show the actor. ' After this confrontation, I simply agreed
to do what he wanted.

"Maranghos and I are currently discussing the possibility of doing a sequel to the film. The person on whom the

film is based tried to commit suicide. The village in which
he lived had at one time been very prosperous. It was good
land and there were many farmers. But now it is dead. He
came to Athens, as shown in the film, but he has returned
to the village. He is a farmer now. The day he attempted
suicide was a holiday, and suddenly the bells started to ring
and the sound of the bells actually prevented the act. It is
really a very tragic character, even though in the film there
are some comic sequences. Despite the fact he fails to
realize his dreams, he is a hero.

"Maranghos' ego would not allow him to recognize anything wrong with the film, even now. But I believe that even
Maranghos recognizes that were we to do it now, we would
be more correct to focus in on the problems of the character
and through those problems the problems of the provinces
would be shown."

* * * * *

I have not a whisper of interest in organized politics,
but it is impossible to view Maranghos without acknowledgment that his politics now seem to have permeated his life
and art. Of course he has every right to find meaning and
comfort in his chosen way, and I take no stand against his
way except to selfishly bemoan the loss of a new Maranghos
film on my visits to Greece. It simply boils down to not
wanting to go to the party with Maranghos even if he has
proven in the past to be an interesting companion. He himself denies personal authorship of STRUGGLE, which reduces
his feature-film output to GET ON YOUR MARK, and his
party-line thinking results in his semi-denial of the worth of
that film; in the final analysis this means that Maranghos
has traded his personal art for group shelter. If he scorns
GET ON YOUR MARK, and claims to have been only one
equal participant in the creation of STRUGGLE, in essence
he denies that he is or ever was a filmmaker. By that admission he therefore denies his position in this book. But
GET ON YOUR MARK is an example of the small, personal,
unusual film which might possibly be an answer to Greece's
problems of entry into the international market.

Without money, Greek filmmakers must rely on recognition of unique stories and, in particular, maintenance of
personal creative viewpoints. By adopting an organized philosophy, creative output is necessarily flattened to suit the
philosophy, putting the creator in the position of being in

STRUGGLE.

competition with others who make the same philosophical (and/or political) statement. In filmmaking, it then boils down to who has the most money or imagination and can say the same thing in the most eye-catching way. In financial competitiveness the Greek filmmaker is not only at a disadvantage--he is not even in the race. His only salvation, and future, lies in personal creativity. He, like the French New Wave, the Czech filmmakers of the 1960s, the English "angry young men," must simply go his own way, having the courage to be different, believing in himself and his vision. GET ON YOUR MARK is just such a statement.

It is difficult to anticipate Maranghos' next move. After all, a reassumed visual identity is a move toward individuality. It is doubtful that Maranghos as independent

Artwork courtesy of Jim Berenson.

artist is in the near future, but talk of a sequel to GET ON
YOUR MARK may mean that Thodoros Maranghos, submerged
these years in an anonymous group, will bob up again and
take a rightful place in Greek cinema. As to international
cinema, slogans and platitudes have to struggle mightily for
an audience. Even Bertolucci's NOVECENTO seems to know
that a few hours of flag-waving needs two minutes of Robert
Di Nero nude.

Meanwhile, Maranghos seems to be somewhat non-
productive, which is sad because he possessed a goodly share
of talent. The absence of that talent on the Greek scene only
furthers my doubts about the value of group therapy. I never
did like parties anyway!

1977 UPDATE: Maranghos was prominently on the scene during the festival upheaval (see Thessaloniki Festival coverage
for 1977). He adds EVIA-MANTOUDI 76 to his credits and
collection of awards, but not as director.

BIOGRAPHICAL BRIEF

Born Filiatra, Messinia, 1946. A skilled designer and ani-
mator prior to entry into "main-stream" filmmaking. Worked
at an advertising company before making first short. He and
wife live in Athens. Awards: At respective Thessaloniki
Festivals: 1969, Best Fiction Short, TSOUF; 1971, Best
Fiction Short, SSST; 1973, Best Film, Best First Feature
Director, GET ON YOUR MARK; 1975, Second Prize, STRUG-
GLE; 1977, Best Photography, EVIA-MANTOUDI 76. See
also: "A STRUGGLE Well Worth It," by Mel Schuster, interview with five of the six directors of STRUGGLE, including Maranghos, Journal of the Hellenic Diaspora, April
1976.

FILMS

TSOUF (1969). (5-1/5 minutes).

SSST (1971). (8 minutes).

TO IKOPEDON. (Short, repressed by the junta).

GET ON YOUR MARK (1973). (Producer, Director, Screen-
    play, Editor).

STRUGGLE (1975). (Produced, written, photographed and directed by six filmmakers).

EVIA-MANTOUDI 76 (1977). (Photography, Sound).

Chapter 6

The Man That Got Away

- NICOS PANAYOTOPOULOS -

Nicos Panayotopoulos is Greece's secret weapon. He is so secret, even Greece doesn't know about him! Both he and his film are enigmatic, certainly, but there is nothing secret about puzzles except the solutions, and the Panayotopoulos puzzle is more rewarding than most solutions.

The prime clue to Panayotopoulos the artist thus far is THE COLORS OF IRIS, itself, a bit of a mystery. It jolted me into an unabated enthusiasm, not only for the film but for the new Greek cinema--an irony in that though it made me aware of "Greek" films, it ill-prepared me for the discovery of the struggle to define "Greekness" which is so eagerly debated by films and filmmakers.

There is nothing uncertain about Panayotopoulos' rebuttal to the criticism that his film is not Greek: "Some of the directors show the customs and pictures which present the idea of Greece which outsiders have come to expect as being Greek. It is a very misunderstood notion of Greek art. They give the answers in Greek folklore as if that were the important thing. It's true even in paintings and books. But everything that is produced by Greeks is Greek. Our national poet Dionisios Solomos was thinking in Italian because that was his language. We have thousands of stimuli from all over the world now. When you make a film, you make a proposition for a dialogue--a conversation on a certain subject. I don't see any reason why I can't make a conversation with Europe too. I was accused of showing things that don't exist in Greece. Of course they don't exist. The film comes out of the mythology of American movies. The whole film is a reference to movies."

In a strange way Panayotopoulos is possibly the most Greek of those filmmakers with whom I have had contact.

79

NICOS PANAYOTOPOULOS.

Examples of the split personality of Greece and the Greeks are so numerous as to be redundant. The answer to this enigma is that the answer is an enigma. Panayotopoulos identifies with that enigma and in his efforts to solve riddles, finds additional questions. Perhaps it is the and/or quality of Greece which compels many of the filmmakers to find a ledge and declare it foundation. Panayotopoulos seems to continue peeling away layers which expose additional layers which, he suspects and probably knows, cover new layers. How truly Greek!

THE COLORS OF IRIS is all about those layers, fortunately presented in far less somber terms. In defense of this sobriety, Panayotopoulos quickly established his seriousness by requesting questions in writing, allowing him time and thought to present himself most accurately. He then proceeded to a detailed account of his new film, described as a "grotesque fable with social connotations" but which provoked a tape-full of laughter. Mr. Panayotopoulos' humor is delivered behind a Buster Keaton mask, and it is only by a quickening in his eyes are you able to discern real from reel.

The opening sequence of THE COLORS OF IRIS lets you know instantly that the film was made by someone who knows what he is doing and cares that he is doing it.

A television commercial is being filmed on the beach, and while waiting for sunrise, the electrician tests his limelight, illuminating each of the characters both literally and figuratively. Without verbal aids, the light is the informer of the role each person has in the filming and in the film. With the exchange of night for day, they start to film a female on-the-beach high-fashion ad. Suddenly, a fella with an umbrella wanders into camera range. When he becomes aware he has blundered into this imitation of life, he turns and walks deliberately into the sea, * leaving only the bobbling umbrella as clue for the search that follows later. The investigation that results from this strange interlude

---

*I would have liked the Liebestod here (HUMORESQUE), or, at the very least, Judy Garland singing "It's a New World for Me" (A STAR IS BORN).

provokes a moment of truth for the composer*
working with the film crew. The detective(s) and
police officials eventually advise and consent to let
the matter drop, and occupants of the executive
suite at the agency agree not to be indiscreet by
pursuing the matter further. The music man, however, develops an odd obsession with this mysterious man who never was, and manages to obtain a
blow-up of his rather funny face. Is it a portrait
of a mobster? Is it a man who knew too much?
The detective story that follows is a breathless
gambit as the hero goes on the town to track down
the mystery man's identity. If ..., but no, there
is no exit. The closing sequence is a repeat of
the opener, only now the crowd gathers to watch.
The band plays on while drum majorettes strut.
But before the parade passes by, the musician,
carrying an umbrella, wanders into camera range,
excuses himself, turns and walks into the sea.**

It would have been an easy solution to make a multi-
leveled comedy and though Panayotopoulos does have a lot of
fun with the film, *** his concern that the film be correctly
explained leaves it unquestionably clear that having fun is
serious business. 'THE COLORS OF IRIS is an auto-sar-
castic film. It wants to be an avant-garde film, but the
drama is that it must reject itself. Everything is phony.
The actors play all the time. The decorations are false.
The story too is false because it is not something that can
really happen. I did this to show that artistic creation is
something autonomous. I believe that film has its own truth.
It's not important that a film show a realistic story or a
non-realistic story, but through the film to be able to get in
touch with life. I used this story not because of the content

---

*Marvelously played by Nikitas Tsakiroglou, who occasionally
looks like a mature Jean-Pierre Leaud.
**Panayotopoulos says there are 100 movie references in
THE COLORS OF IRIS. All of them are considerably more
subtle than the 32 I've managed. But then I omitted the
scenes from a marriage, the girl in black, and the aging
chanteuse with a song in her heart.
***In itself practically a phenomenon since the "new wave"
Greek cinema seems to frown on fun. In fact, it is rumored
a film was rejected from the 1976 festival on the grounds
that it was a comedy!

THE COLORS OF IRIS.

of reality, but to go further than the simple experience of my own life. The hero in this film is false. He is an actor. Because he doesn't know what to do, he plays. When he wants to become a real person, he will get out of the show. "

In a piece he wrote for the March 1974 issue of Film, Panayotopoulos offers further explanation of THE COLORS OF IRIS: "Because I don't believe in the effectiveness of films on a directly political level, I made a film in color above any objectives and aspirations. It is not that the objectives of the film are vague. Simply there are no ideological components in the film. Those who look for keys to decode the film would better search to find these keys in themselves. It was Renoir, I think, who said that films which tell everybody the same things are bad films.

"If the surface frivolity of the film disturbs the middle class 'seriousness' of the Greek intellectuals, let it disturb them. Everyone can gain something from that.

"It is not a film of the absurd. The illogical fact of the disappearance comes to remind one that the reality of the cinema is not the objective reality but a product of creative imagination. It is a film which attempts to understand what a film is, in an effort to define life. It is a study on the rights of a progressive cinema not to register reality. That's why the film is full of references to life and at other times to cinema--identifying the uncertainty inherent in the film to the uncertainty existing in human relationships. "

Nicos Panayotopoulos has not been very successful playing the game of director in Greece, a game which requires diplomatic skill, social malleability, and plain old salesmanship. He simply is an independent functioning on the outskirts of a system that demands juggling for position within a power scheme. The end result of his reluctance or inability to play the game is that he has been somewhat ignored. A further complication is that the rules of this game are either nonexistent, in flux, or not defined. In creating a facade of frivolity in THE COLORS OF IRIS, Panayotopoulos has surely encouraged the view of him as a bit of an outlaw in that, generally speaking, the new films in Greece thus far have disallowed any pleasure for its own sake; their inability to laugh at themselves finally becomes comedy, created by their own cumulative gross seriousness.

Panayotopoulos commits sins which further alienate him. He has not made the obligatory overt political film. He has not taken a position on the plight of the disintegrating rural life. He has not aligned himself with a group, or even a clique. He made a film frequently described as "European" --meaning "non-Greek, " even though various maps assure one that Greece is still in Europe. He has wasted precious film by including two delightful musical sequences when he could have been instructing us, or at the very least imitating some other director, preferably one who is politically left. He has difficulty delivering in a framework of immediacy, pre- ferring instead to select his own method of accurate presenta- tion--an anomalous timing factor in that the norm is to hit the climax as quickly as possible after arousal. And not a sin, just simple bad luck, is the fact that the producer of THE COLORS OF IRIS also produced THE TRAVELLING PLAYERS, and the former has become somewhat lost in the resulting ballyhoo over the latter.

Bad luck plagued a prospective second film. The script involved a Greek working family in Germany, detail- ing the isolated life of people unable to assimilate into their new environment, with the result that they are exaggeratedly dependent and involved with each other. The tyrannical fath- er eventually makes life unbearable, and on the celebration of his birthday the other family members murder him with the knife used to cut the birthday cake.

The Greek Film Center agreed to finance the film; contracts were signed, actors selected. The script was sub- mitted to the censorship committee, normally a formality. When they rejected the script, an appeal was made to an overriding committee which accepted the script by the major- ity of one vote. Two days before the planned departure for Germany, the Minister of Information personally called Panayotopoulos and cancelled the project. "In effect they feared for the external image of Greece and the encourage- ment of the erosion of internal status quo. The killing of the father was seen as a symbol of revolt. " The fact that the script happened to be based on a true story seems not to have been a factor. An illusion can often be created by suppressing a reality.

Obviously Panayotopoulos has not been idle since THE COLORS OF IRIS, but not one frame of film will prove it. This may be corrected in the near future. A script, with a role tailored for Harriet Andersson, the Swedish actress, was

sent to her. A trip to Sweden and Paris has secured not
only the services of the actress and French actor Pierre
Clementi, but also the bulk of the necessary funds.

Director Panayotopoulos with actor Nikitas Tsakiroglou on
set of THE INDOLENCE OF THE FERTILE VALLEY.

"It is a parable, an allegory, a grotesque fable with
social connotations. " (That should up his standing in the
serious world of Greek cinema!) 'It is about a family, a
father and three sons who inherit a large sum of money and
a house in the country. " (Perhaps it will get rejected on the
grounds of its revolutionary threat to the value of the mother's role in the family.) "They live an idyllic life in the
country. " (You see, he is involved with the villages after
all.) "But eventually they get bored, and begin to withdraw
from all activity. " (Lack of social consciousness?) "Eventually they do nothing but sleep. The maid ... " (The working
class) "... has to do everything for them. The youngest
son ... " (Youth) "... imagines work to be something very

romantic. " (Should get approval from the political left.)
"He wants to get a job in a factory, to which the maid starts
to carry him on her back, but he is so exhausted he curls
up in her arms and goes to sleep. " (Enigmatic end.)

"For me, the family represents the different expressions of the bourgeois class. The father is the fascist, the
oldest brother is the traditional right, the second brother is
the right, the youngest is the liberated right, but his roots
are still there. The maid is the working class who in actuality supports the bourgeois class. Their dreams are her
dreams. She admires them. They can't exist without her
support. She feeds the whole system by her support. It intends to be very absurd and grotesque and unreal. " I had
hoped his next film would be a musical! Oh well, I can wait.

His involvement with the class structure, be it ever
so unusual a treatment, sounds suspiciously compromising.
His preoccupation with weeding out the real from the unreal
seems far more inspirational to him. Obviously it can be
applied to any framework and will surely be present in his
proposed new film, but it sounds frustratingly lost in the facade of the snoozing bourgeois.

"When you make a film you try to include reality, and
while making it you realize that it is very difficult or impossible to make a reality because there are always things of
reality that escape you. You must choose certain things to
put in your film, and then you realize that this is not enough.
With this logic you see that the film is nothing. So when
you make a film you must include its own denial.

"I don't know what is truth. When I talk about the
show, life too is a show. I do this because I want to be honest with myself, but I am very confused in myself. * I can't
propose only one thing, so I take the different elements of
life and play. Pasolini said that a man can only be judged
when he is dead, because as long as he lives he is an open
case. At any minute he may change or reverse his course.
This creates a confusion. We don't know what he really is.

"The problem in my first film is, what is cinema?

---

*Andrew Horton, in the April 1975 issue of The Athenian,
quotes this pertinent moment from Panayotopoulos' script:
"I can never tell when you are serious or not. "

I don't know, and I made the film to ask that question. Maybe after four or five films I will have the answer. For the first few films that a director makes, apart from the story, there must be the question, 'What is this that I am doing?' When the Americans first started making films, they didn't question what they did. They made films as natural as though they were breathing. I would like very much to make a film that naturally. But when I do a film I want to believe that I am really doing something. But when I make a film I think that ... it's a Greek expression ... that I make a hole in the water.

"Perhaps I don't love film enough. I have two things inside of me. One is my great love for films, my great admiration for films. The other is a desire to destroy that admiration. But the joy I feel in making film is greater than any the audience could obtain. That's why I want to use the game in my films, because I believe that the game is an element of freedom. That is why I have all the characters playing games. But the minute they want to be serious, they have to get out of the film. They have to return to real life. "

The difficulties Panayotopoulos has in functioning in the Greek cinema scene may necessitate his leaving it. He will not leave film, and if to make films he has to go elsewhere, he will go. It is not enough for him to be a director in Kolanaki Square, i. e. , to talk about it. His options are to learn to function within the no-rules Greek game, or face the game on new grounds. Characteristically, with his new film (Swedish-French-Greek co-production) he finds his own way by trying both. Or is it neither?

It does seem likely that Greece will eventually lose Panayotopoulos, but it will no doubt wish to reclaim him in the future. He is high on the small list of Greek filmmakers with potential to break through to international scope. He has a clear, grounded view of the distance between now and his quest, and states no illusions in mapping a course to that goal. He has personal style, wit, intelligence, vision, ego, humility, curiosity, taste, and a passion for his art. One important ingredient he lacks is salesmanship. But if he can find a way to prove his worth, buyers will come to him.

There is a kind of fury in him which he tries to soften with flippancy. It could bring him greatness, but it also presents the danger of destruction. Panayotopoulos'

ambivalence about film is a flirting with exorcism; a desire
to gain a sense of control over his own life. But, if you'll
pardon the excess, the only way for Panayotopoulos to gain
his life is to give it up, for film and life are inextricably
melded. As he far less melodramatically put it, "I have no
choice. "

"Well, if you have no choice, " I ask, "why don't you
just give up all that conflict?"

And either the real or the game-playing Panayotopoulos
answered: "It's not so bad to have all this confusion. I can
always put it on film. "

1977 UPDATE: The new film was in shooting in October.
Complications necessitating rescheduling resulted in the un-
availability of both international stars, Harriet Andersson
and Pierre Clementi. They have been replaced by Greek
performers. There was negotiation in progress with the respected actress Elli Lambetti to do a guest bit in the film.
She has not made a film for several years and was reluctant
to endanger a highly regarded image. Fellow director Costas
Sfikas (who played the man with the umbrella in Panayotopoulos' first film) had joined the cast. A deserted house in
Kafissia, a once (and still) fashionable suburb of Athens, had
been renovated and furnished for the film. Filming was
going on with a minimum of problems and the picture should
be ready for 1978 festival consideration.

BIOGRAPHICAL BRIEF

Born Lesvos, 1941. Moved to Athens, 1948. Finished film
school along with high school. Went to Paris at 18. Graduated Sorbonne Institut de Filmologie. Worked many films as
assistant director in Paris and Athens. Made industrial
films in Paris. Lives with wife in Athens. Has daughter
from previous marriage. See: "The Colors of a Fertile
Filmmaker" by Mel Schuster, The Hellenic Journal, Nov. 30,
1978.

FILMS

SUNDAY (1966). (25 minutes)

ANDREOU (1969). (30 minutes)

THE COLORS OF IRIS (1974). (Direction, Screenplay).

DANKESCHON-BITTESCHON (1976). (Unrealized script).

THE INDOLENCE OF THE FERTILE VALLEY. (1978). Reviewed in Variety as "The Slothful Ones of the Fertile Valley" (Aug. 23, 1978); won top prize at Locarno International Film Festival in August 1978 as "The Lazy Ones of the Fertile Valley"; took Best First Film award at 1978 Chicago International Festival as "The Idlers of the Fertile Valley." Took four prizes at the 1978 Thessaloniki Festival, including Best Film. Greek Film Critics added Best Film and Best Director citations.

BELOW: Yorgos Dialegmenos and Olga Karlatos in THE INDOLENCE OF THE FERTILE VALLEY.

Chapter 7

It's a Long, Long Time from May to December

- TASOS PSARRAS -

There was an excited air of expectancy at the premiere screening of MAY.   Loud arguments over seating arrangements erupted, and a human sea began to overflow
into aisles and doorways.   Far left political films at the
Thessaloniki festivals seem to breed chaos.   MAY offered a
match for emotional fuses which, when lit, sputtered and then
fizzled to a quiet, subdued anti-climax.   The film displeased
those who had anticipated verification of their political positions; it amused those who were politically opposed; it bored
the non-affiliated.   The boos and bravos which greeted the
end seemed more a release of frustration than a comment on
the film.

Photo above shows Tasos Psarras during filming of MAY.

Not having liked MAY at all, I was somewhat reluctant to meet its director, Tasos Psarras, for fear that objectivity would be totally elusive--it being an improbable state
under the most hopeful conditions. My fears were fulfilled,
though not in the expected way. The reception to MAY obviously had been bitterly disappointing to him. One review
had been so venomously destructive that it actually swayed
sympathy toward the film. Psarras was clearly under great
strain, and granting an interview to an American (and all
that that image implied) added suspicion and an "on-guard"
atmosphere to the meeting.

Psarras was confronting the total experience with such
dignity that I did indeed lose sight of objectivity--but the subjectivity reached out to him. He seemed like a bewildered,
hurt, gentle animal who had mistakenly wandered onto a fir-
ing range. He became the most severe test I encountered
in my attempts to be fair, open-minded, and judgmentally
clear-sighted. MAY was a bold, aggressive, smug film. I
could not find Psarras in the film; I could not see the film
in Psarras.

He has been involved with film for eleven years and
one senses that of all the filmmakers in Greece, Psarras is
the survivalist of the lot. He will anxiously pull a lock of
hair, grasp at a bit of face-saving rationalization, then continue on. Should the overwhelming disappointment that constantly confronts the Greek filmmakers drive them all to
opening advertising agencies or start driving taxi cabs, Psarras will still be making films.

"I always liked the cinema and went often. When I
was 16 I was given a camera. I made a lot of home movies,
but then I entered an amateur filmmaking contest and won
first prize with a film about a morning in the life of a young
man who is bored and doesn't know what to do with his life.
The prize was a three-year course in filmmaking in Thessaloniki. I had not finished high school, which I did before
going to the film school. When I finished that, I went to the
Stavradu School in Athens. The family was not totally supportive. They said, 'O. K. , you can study film, but you have
to finish the university. Then if you want film for a hobby,
O. K. ' To please them I studied to become a veterinarian. "

Even his willingness to go along with his family's
wishes on the surface, but persist in his own personal reality seems to add weight to the feeling that Psarras lives in

From Psarras' short film, MELELE.

an insulated world. His first film is a case history of a tobacco workers' strike and is intricately detailed as though
this were the world's first labor-management disagreement.
He talks respectfully of the world of Bertolt Brecht with a
kind of wonderment. (Brecht is enjoying a vogue in Greece
comparable to that in the United States in the late 1950s.)
Psarras' discoveries are very personal, as though he is un-
aware that a large number of people also possess the same
information. Through his films he seems to be assuming the
role of a teacher (both his parents are teachers) who is giving first-year lessons to fifth-year students. Perhaps that
is a bit unfair, for when THE REASON WHY was played in
villages, "the women would come because it was free, and
then they would beg us to play it again so their husbands
could see it." There obviously are students for his lessons.

This isolated individualism does not extend itself into
his conscious philosophies, although there is some conflict
in his description of his work: "I am interested in the way
to approach a subject. I like to reconstruct a real event
through my own personality.... In the first film it was the
groups that interested me. The second film is about classes.
It is not the persons who constitute society, but the groups
that give meaning to society." The individuals who comprise
the groups that comprise the society seem to have gotten lost
somewhere along the way; so, necessarily, must his own personality.

MAY is a mishmash of ideas, techniques and concepts.
The working class "is out on the streets fighting for their
rights. The other class is not in the streets. The classes
were used as symbols and nothing was intended realistically.
To be realistic you have to go inside and deal with individuals." The result is that the working class, constantly filmed
at an impersonal distance, appears a disorganized mob whose
sole purpose is to wave flags, shout slogans, and clash with
the equally impersonal police. In short, they are as boring
as some of Brecht's more "informative" plays.

The class in power is depicted as exaggerated fools,
a curious way to bring glory to the working class since they
must be a foolish lot indeed to have fallen under the power
of these effete buffoons. But at least we see them as individuals, and by treating the working class merely as a dehu-
manized object, Psarras, in a way, aligns himself with the
aristocracy, which has historically viewed the working class
as a usable object.

Poster from Psarras' MAY.

MAY was based on an important and true incident from Greek history (a strike by tobacco workers) which inspired the poet Yannis Ritsos to write his famous "Epitaphios," which in turn inspired composer Mikis Theodorakis to some of his best-known music. Over-influenced by his interest in the theories of Bertolt Brecht, Psarras elected to film the story in short scenes meant to involve the audience informatively rather than cinematically. The bulk of the action is filmed at a deliberate, unengaging distance and even climaxes are avoided by the discreet panning away of the camera. Exaggeration and repetitiveness add to the unreality, a quality intended, but certainly misjudged. Despite Brecht's intentions, he was a man of the theatre and the sheer theatricality of much of his output worked as counterpoint to his intentions, each adding new dimensions to the other. MAY is devoid of theatricality.

MAY was filmed in Thessaloniki under most trying conditions. Not only did the winter light shorten the work day, but much filming could be done only at the end of the business day because facades of store fronts had to be period-dressed after the stores closed each day. Psarras has a particularly alert eye for detail, and decor and settings have made major contributions to both of his films.

His first film, THE REASON WHY, is also about the plight of the tobacco workers. Based on a true incident involving the murder of a tobacco worker who sells his tobacco and destroys the power of a fledgling union, Psarras has made a film rich in detailing village life. In the course of telling his story, the camera pokes and probes into houses, the mechanics of working tobacco, and the life of the village itself. There is nothing glossy or commercial about the folk setting of the film--it is engrossingly real and informative. Of all the films under consideration in this study, THE REASON WHY is the most revealing of the physiognomy of a Greek village. Thodoros Angelopoulos' RECONSTRUCTION chillingly captures the repressive psychological atmosphere, but is not so concerned with the kind of day-to-day existence vividly shown in THE REASON WHY.

Most of the Greek filmmakers have grown up in cities, but repeatedly show an avid interest in the problems of village life. Psarras explains: "There is another conception of cities here than elsewhere. We have one eye on the city and another on the village. With the movement to cities, we now have to buy food productions from outside rather than

Scene from MAY.

produce it ourselves. It is important to explain to the people that they should stay in their villages and work there, and they will be more happy in the villages. If they can work within a system, they can earn more money. The city is not paradise."

Psarras is not alone in his belief that the villagers should stay in the village. The movement from rural to urban areas has indeed created a severe shortage of agricultural produce in Greece, as well as overcrowded city populations. Concern over this problem is a real one. Still, it appears repressively judgmental to "... explain to the people that they should stay in their villages...." It's a bit like explaining to Psarras that he should forget making films and go vaccinate a few sheep.

"Making films about the village is also a reaction to the commercial cinema, which was always in the city, about the good boy who was going to marry the good girl, or the poor girl who was going to marry the rich boy. The subject

of the commercial cinema was not interesting to the people
who lived in the village because they saw films about people
who had nothing to do with them. "

  This may be a bit of hopeful thinking, since popular
TV fare seems only an extension of commercial cinema. Investigating Psarras' theory, it is clear that the "Cinderella"
quality of commercial cinema would have collapsed sooner
but for the support of the villages. TV transmission was
slow to work its way to the villages and thus the tail-end of
commercial cinema was supported nearly exclusively by villages. Furthermore, the atmosphere is somewhat akin to
the U. S. depression of the 1930s, when most of the major
film successes were the most blatant escapist fare, e. g.,
Busby Berkeley musicals, runaway-heiress comedies, etc.
And it appears no accident to be reminded of the 1930s in
the United States in relation to Psarras. He would have made
films with John Garfield or Burgess Meredith urging us to
unite our way through our mutual depression.

  Psarras' social consciousness "came instinctively. I
didn't seek it out. I have never declared myself communist
or leftist or anything, but that's what the public sees in my
films. " His healthy belief in self, combined with his interest in group behavior, inspired the most memorable scene of
THE REASON WHY. In a coffee house, the tobacco workers
meet to organize a union, elect officers, decide their course
of action. The mobile camera, moving in cramped quarters,
examines the whole spectrum of individual versus group:
the individual views the group; the group views the individual;
the group segmented into a collection of individuals; the coming together of individuals to mold smaller groups within the
whole; the banding together of small groups into a whole; the
absorption of the individual into the group; the loss of identity within the group; the retention of identity within the group;
the discovery of identity within the group. The "how" of
what is being said very nearly makes redundant the verbalizing of "what" is being said. It is a masterly bit of filmmaking. Psarras planned the entire scene in advance,
though whether his intentions match this interpretation is a
moot point. Calculated or not, this detailed examination of
a situation was a Psarras creation. His visual ability is
far more effective than his verbal.

  THE REASON WHY evolved quite accidentally. "I
was visiting a village and out of curiosity I began asking
about the tobacco workers, their problems, their lives.

Psarras during filming of THE REASON WHY.

They began talking about their lives, and while so doing they talked about this particular event which you see in the film. When I returned home I began writing the script.

"The film had commercial distribution in the three big cities (Athens, Thessaloniki, Patras), but the producer gave two other prints to be shown in schools, unions, colleges. He didn't care any more about the Greek distribution. It went to Cannes and was shown in the Director's Fortnightly and was bought by Holland, Belgium, Australia, Sweden, Germany, Mexico and Italy. Many countries asked for the film, but they offered only about $1,500, and the producer was not interested, saying that for less than $5,000 it wasn't worth the bother.

"The public liked it and the journalists liked it. At the Thessaloniki Festival, the day of the awards, I waited for something, but it got only an acting award. The public was angry and some of the other directors and producers refused their prizes in protest, although they took them later. This was the first year of our liberation. As an excuse, they said that I showed the leading man as a communist and also a murderer. They said this would be an offense to the communists, despite the fact that both communist parties accepted the film. The jury was mostly middle-class people and they kept themselves safe by not supporting any partisan ideas. "

Perhaps the overly epic scale of MAY persuaded him toward the intimacy of the ideas for his next hoped-for project: "It is about a musician who plays an instrument similar to a Scottish bagpipe. He comes from a village to the big city, and it is about his experiences and development. He is a shepherd, goes to the small town, and then the city. It is a fictional story. He ends up being a doorman at a big apartment house. He can't breath and one day he goes up on the Acropolis and begins to play his instrument. "

Even though his products thus far have been heavy on the message side, he asserts that the art of film comes first with him. "I didn't have a message first and then go out and find a medium by which to express it. First was the film. Of course I want what I believe to be expressed on film, and what I believe, what I hope for myself, is that we grow as we go. I always see things that I want to know, develop, learn. "

At our second meeting, three weeks after the unhappy reception of MAY, Psarras had recovered. He had assimilated the disappointment, survived the negative reactions-- even the cruel ones. It would be understandable if he were expressing dreams or hopes for his future, in the face of an unpleasant present; but there was only determination and a kind of blind confidence. I felt guilty for not having liked MAY, while he, wasting no emotion on the past, went off to re-edit the film. After all, June is just around the corner.

* * * * *

1977 UPDATE: MAY was never shown commercially. Psarras was off on a trip around the world making a television documentary about the merchant marine union.

BIOGRAPHICAL BRIEF

Born 1950, in a village near Thessaloniki. Grew up in Thessaloniki where family moved when he was two. Parents are teachers. Won three-year film course in amateur filmmaking contest. Also studied film in Athens. Is accredited veterinarian. Single. Residence in Thessaloniki.

FILMS

PRESENCE (9-minute short).

40-38-22-87 (30-minute short).

SUPER SHOW 71 (13-minute short).

MELELE (25-minute short).

THE MIRACLE (18-minute short).

THE REASON WHY (1974).   (Screenplay, Direction).

MAY (1976).   (Screenplay, Direction).

Top, Thanassis Rentzis.   Bottom, Nicos Zervas.

Chapter 8

Double Exposure

- THANASSIS RENTZIS & NICOS ZERVOS -

Visiting Thanassis Rentzis is to be projected into a
world of film memorabilia. Posters from his own films as
well as others' find featured positions on the walls, or get
special mention in less glorified corners. Photographs and
audio tapes scatter the room, which looks like a child's play-
pen, attesting to the on-going work on a film Rentzis' wife,
Gay, is preparing.* Copies of Rentzis' own magazine Film
are in evidence, and a large, well-rounded library of film
books adds a scholarly dimension to their live-in movie museum.

Rentzis himself is thin and quiet, with cool, choco-
late eyes that evoke the uneasy feeling that they see more
than they reveal. His infrequent, incisive comments are
punctuated with a gesture from an otherwise disconcertingly
motionless body.

Nicos Zervos, on the other hand, is as comfortably
messy as Rentzis is precisely neat; moves, articulates and
opinionates with gusto. He has a restless outgoingness that
suggests a great deal of energy which has not yet found a
proper depository.

They are an unlikely duo, and the qualitative success
of their first film, BLACK & WHITE, indicates that their
personal differences were complementary, or at least melded
into a new whole which produced a film of easy charm (Zervos) and quiet dignity (Rentzis). BLACK & WHITE is a
small statement about the rights of an individual to find his
own answers rather than accepting those ready-mades offered

*MONASTIRAKI, produced and directed by Gay Ageli. 20
minutes. Won an award given by the Mayor of Thessaloniki
in 1976.

Gay Ageli filming MONASTIRAKI.

by groups. The directors regret its lack of development in certain content areas and what they view as technical inadequacies. Yet, curiously, these very "failures" make major contributions to the simple and honest success of the film. The very boundaries imposed on it have prevented any of the over-indulgence that frequently comes when young artists, with the vitality of new eyes, think they have the answers.

BLACK & WHITE is the story of a young artist who moves to Athens in search of stimulation and a more meaningful life. From this simple opening it is evident that we are dealing with an unusual individual, for leaving home is often a major undertaking in Greece, where family ties can be oppressively binding. He is able to support himself financially by selling paintings, and this allows him time to explore the possible rewards of group involvement, sex, materialism and finally artistic expression. These extensions into the world around him are efforts to find yes or no (black & white) answers which might add definition to a questioning life. But he finds only other people's answers, which, to him, are grey. He is confronted with the needs and be-

liefs of others, and is sometimes able to compromise, sometimes not. His art agent's eventual refusal to buy the kind
of paintings he wishes to create symbolizes the defeat he
feels from external manipulations, and in the end he accepts
a dull but secure job and sinks again into an only slightly
more developed expression of the greyness he had sought to
escape.

It should be no surprise that the film is in black and
white--a fact imposed by financial considerations. Black and
white seems completely appropriate, however, and the directors have made the most of their medium. Scenes are
frequently connected by an all-black or all-white screen--a
technically effective addition to the content.

The film got some good notices, but on the whole was
not really well received by anyone. Its investigation into the
possible supremacy of the individual was an unwelcomed idea;
in fact, such an idea is likely to find disfavor whenever or
wherever it surfaces. Authoritarian organizations realize
that their power rests on their ability to suppress individualism. Prejudice, custom and tradition, as tools toward that
end, are far more effective than force or violence. But the
greatest enemy of individualism is individuals, who find it
far less difficult to simply think and do what they are told or
what is expected. It is much easier to delegate responsibility than to assume it.

BLACK & WHITE does not develop this theme in depth.
Censorship would not have allowed it. But just to be exploring the individual at a time when strength seemed to be found
only in groups, was to make a bold and long-ranged statement. Even the youthful intelligentsia of Athens rejected the
film--and perhaps have not yet caught up with its message.

The boundaries imposed on its creation may have inspired BLACK & WHITE to reach out beyond the boundaries
of time and nationality. It is a modest film, but when the
more lavishly produced, loudly applauded "now" films become yesterday's curiosities, BLACK & WHITE will still be
pertinent.

Perhaps the directors, too, feel a sense of greyness
about the film, in that a first-film enthusiasm was constantly
dulled by censorship; compromise and deviousness were utilized to complete the film. It was made in 1973, a time
when censorship was strict. "We were constantly having to

Scenes from BLACK AND WHITE. Top, Vicky Potamianou and George Tsemberopoulos.

deal with censorship. Every step of the way we were having to ask 'Can I say this? Will they let this stand as is?' Sometimes the form of the film was molded not because we wanted it to be like that, but because it was a way of saying something that could not be dealt with more openly. " These restrictions had the end result, though, of inhibiting excess-- which is not in any way to condone censorship. Nevertheless, one feels strongly the simple effectiveness of BLACK & WHITE could easily be imbalanced by the slightest excess. There is a general impression that the directors regret that their stronger statements were not expressed, and George Tsemberopoulos (the film's star) openly states that he does not like the film. This is regrettable because since the advent of less strict censorship, many of the products of the young Greek filmmakers have been ultimately lost in their own relatives. The ingredients of BLACK & WHITE have been leveled, resulting in a whole which is not eroded by over-emphasis on any of its parts.

Devoid of the relatives that surround the making of BLACK & WHITE, it appears a youthful comment on a mature theme. However, for the film to be made at the peak of a repressive government, a time when the immediacy of that fact left little energy for thinking beyond the oppressive present, is a quite remarkable feat. The film transcends its own time and deals instead with timeless and placeless problems. Stepping back in order to get closer is rare indeed in Greek cinema in the 1970s. Most of the filmmakers have been distortedly close to their subjects, the resulting illusion being entire films in close-up, disallowing time and physical perspectives. It is hardly surprising that BLACK & WHITE was not well received; it did not address itself to an audience which was literally possessed by an immediate experience. Even now Rentzis and Zervos discuss the film as product, downgrading its timely uniqueness. If they refused to be swept on a tide when it was devastatingly demanding, they confirm their position in retrospect even though it would be easy to reap some slight glory by touting an exclusiveness.

"The major difference in making film now from that of during the junta is freedom. There is always the money problem, of course, but during the junta, once you passed the censors, it was not so difficult to find financial backing. But now the primary concern is financing, and then comes the censors.

"During the junta it was very specific what you could

and could not say. Now it is supposed to be free, and in truth there is more freedom now. But we are not allowed to make statements against religion, or strong statements against the family. The army cannot be insulted, and things Greek-sacred, such as ancient history, must be treated with respect. The sexual act is not permitted. * We produce some pornos, but it is not supposed to be permitted. The pornos are done in two ways--one way for local distribution and a more explicit way for exporting.

"There is also a financial difference, which is more a function of history rather than political structure. Films were simply less expensive to make at that time. Greek cinema can no longer support itself exclusively from domestic distribution, and we haven't yet found a way to distribute internationally. A film like ELECTRA might do well internationally, but this is more thanks to Cacoyannis, who is well-organized. That is, he knows people all over the world. "

Their initial interest in film, as Zervos says, "... was not very original. I went to the movies a lot. I had an 8mm camera and my interest in filming grew. " Rentzis "... spent a lot of time at the movies, too. " Neither finished formal education; Zervos quit and took a job as an assistant director, Rentzis switched to a cinema school when he was 16. "There was a school in Athens with a good teacher, Costas Fotinos, who is now director of the Audio-Visual Department of the Montreal University in Canada. For a while I worked as a photographer doing stills and montage. "

Zervos: "BLACK & WHITE was really Thanassis' idea. It was the first film for both of us. Most people start out by doing a short film first. I knew Thanassis and at that time I had a little money and I wanted to make a film. We talked and talked for some time and in the beginning he preferred to publish his magazine rather than make the film. But finally we decided on the film. "

---

*Either this means a sexual act may not be explicitly depicted, or else the restriction has been softened. Angelopoulos' THE HUNTERS has two rather defined copulation scenes; Manoussakis' POWER is liberally laced with sexual scenes; Panayotopoulos was filming sexual scenes for his new film which were not anticipated to end on the cutting room floor.

Rentzis managed also to start the magazine <u>Film</u>, which is one of two serious film publications in Greece. It resembles Jonas Mekas' <u>Film Culture</u>, published in the United States; in fact, Rentzis' second film, BIO-GRAPHY, is dedicated to Mekas. Of <u>Film</u> he says, "It is a specialized magazine, mostly theoretic, which means it also has a specialized audience. It takes certain subjects and analyzes them carefully, but is aimed at people who already have some background. The magazine is not really concerned with the problem of the number of people who might understand it." <u>Film</u> is a quarterly and is into its third year of publication.

The partnership of Rentzis and Zervos has not been unbroken. Since BLACK & WHITE Zervos had made a short documentary about women working in factories. He is particularly interested in counteracting what he views as severe sexual inhibitions within Greece, and ascribes to the concepts of psychologist R. D. Laing. "I am trying to do a film on drop-outs or outsiders. I don't know in English what those terms mean, but I am not just talking about drug addicts. We don't have many hippies. But we do have a number of people who really don't want to work. They have no social consciousness or culture. The family system here, as everywhere, is disintegrating. What I see most is young people who want to fight, for lack of a better word, the system. The biggest number go into the communist party. But lately, most of the students have begun to think of themselves as anarchists. I don't know if they fit theoretically, but it is a kind of general reaction against things. Of course, the junta time played a big part in it. And young people, in order to act organized, they find the ... well, I don't want to say the 'easy' way, but they don't really examine what Marxism is all about, they just get into a group so they can fight the establishment. That is why it is such a big thing now. I don't believe it is out of a consciousness of Marxism. It is fashionable. Don't get me wrong, I'm not anti-communist. I just don't believe it is our solution."

Rentzis is General Secretary of the Directors' Union and is much in evidence during times when the union's needs and desires surface. Watching him in action somewhat contradicts the impression that he is a quiet, internal man. Still, it seems no accident that he became interested in experimental filmmaking because there the artist is left alone with his medium without the interference of the non-technical/non-artistic aspect of a director's job. This interest was in evidence even in BLACK & WHITE, via a verbal homage to the American experimental filmmaker, Stan Brakhage.

Poster for BIO-GRAPHY.

BIO-GRAPHY played the 1975 Thessaloniki Festival and won third prize. It is a "collage" film which traces the middle-class rise to power during the 19th century via a series of gravures. Collage films enjoy a certain popularity in Greece, at least among the filmmakers themselves. A comparatively low production cost is no doubt one reason for the decision to work in this form. Admitting that sitting through a collage film is very low on my list of favorite things to do elicited some black and white proof that others don't share that opinion. BIO-GRAPHY played the Rotterdam Festival, and though there are no prizes given there, polls are conducted to gauge opinions. A rating system of 0.00 (low) to a high of 5.00 is utilized. BIO-GRAPHY garnered a 4.05 from the critics and 4.17 from the audience, placing it third in over-all festival ratings by critics and audience alike. It is noteworthy that the much-heralded

THE TRAVELLING PLAYERS placed fifth and seventh with
critics and audience respectively. Further support for BIO-
GRAPHY can be found in the many favorable critical notices:
".. one of the most impressive and noteworthy films of the
festival ... " (Variety); "... one of the delights of the festival ... " (The Athenian). So much for my minority distaste
for collage films!

"There are three kinds of films being made in Greece
now, " explained Rentzis. "There are documentaries, sometimes made by teams of filmmakers, like Maranghos-and-
company's STRUGGLE. They find an outlet through meetings,
factories and universities. Then there is the more conventional story-line film which can hope to find a way through
the traditional commercial cinema network. The third is experimental film, such as my film BIO-GRAPHY and Sfikas'
MODEL. These films express the research we make on the
cinema, and are not exactly Greek films, but are simply
films made by Greeks, but on the international level of cinema. These films are the most interesting to me. I am not
a nationalist.

"The problem of distribution for the experimental film
is a problem of organization. For instance, BIO-GRAPHY
was sold in France, Holland and England. From these three
countries I clear the cost of the film. The film can be sold
cheaply, anywhere from one to ten thousand dollars. Therefore, if there is a multi-sale, we end up with a profit. I
see this as the hope--to sell cheaply to many. BIO-GRAPHY
will be shown in Paris next month. If it has any success,
there is the possibility of it selling to many countries. "

His "sell cheaply to many" solution may have a built-
in discouraging psychological factor: low cost equals low
quality. Not an absolute, of course, but frequently an unfortunate fact.

Rentzis currently works on a fiction film "which
starts with Karaghiozis* getting stoned on hash, and the
whole thing will be his trip. " It seemed a perfectly natural
question to ask if it was autobiographical, but it remained
an unanswered question. He seems to be moving into a more

---

*Karaghiozis is a famous puppet character in shadow theater,
an import from Turkey which the Greeks have made their
own through adaptation and development.

cerebral position as regards his work, a kind of exploration of medium for medium's sake. It would be a loss if the element in him which produced BLACK & WHITE were extinguished. There seems little doubt his future will be film-oriented in some capacity or other. Selling cheaply notwithstanding, he may be confronted with the very problem of his character in BLACK & WHITE, who wants to paint pictures for which there is no economically sustaining outlet. Meanwhile his characteristically succinct wish for his own future is, "I just want to do the films I want to do."

Zervos may conceivably become one of those dropouts in which he is currently interested. But his "drop out" has a hopeful "drop in" sound to it. "I would like to do films that I can produce myself. But also I would like to have the money to produce films. I don't want to be Finos Films, but I would like to be able to give the money to young filmmakers to make films. I don't mean in a kind of Christian way. But I would like to help create a kind of New Wave in Greek cinema."

* * * * *

1977 UPDATE: Thanassis Rentzis moves more into the role of resident "filmologist," a particularly useful position in the Greek film world, given its lack of organization. Rentzis thus serves as a kind of dependable one-man clearinghouse for the many problems or needs which emerge. He was in the forefront of activity during the 1977 Festival problems (see section on 1977 Thessaloniki Festival); his magazine thrives; the Karaghiozis film has been shelved in favor of a collage film tracing the evolution of the human body (CORPUS--see filmography). His wife, Gay Ageli, is active in various women organizations, and hopes there is another film in her future. Nicos Zervos, like many other Greek filmmakers, has been working in television. Within the various aspects of his TV involvement, he made a short film on the making of THE HEAVY MELON (Director: Pavlos Tassios), the top prize-winner at the '77 Festival. Zervos has also worked on a documentary about rembetika. He remains committed to filmmaking; hopes to make a feature which examines the various authorities which contribute to, or detract from, the development of individual character.

Scene from Zervos' short ATTEMPT FOR A SOCIOLOGICAL
RESEARCH IN GREECE 1974.

BIOGRAPHICAL BRIEF

THANASSIS RENTZIS was born in Aegion, 1947. Moved to
Athens, 1960. Switched from formal education to cinema
school at 16. Edits quarterly film magazine Film. General
Secretary of Directors' Union. Particularly interested in experimental film. He and wife Gay (also a filmmaker) live
in Athens. Award: Third Prize to BIO-GRAPHY, 1975
Thessaloniki Festival.

FILMS

BLACK & WHITE (1973). (Screenplay, Co-Director).

BIO-GRAPHY (1975). (Screenplay, Director).

CORPUS (Being completed in 1977).

BIOGRAPHICAL BRIEF

NICOS ZERVOS abandoned formal education to work in film.
Worked as assistant director before co-directing first film.
He is divorced, lives in Athens. Award: Honorary Mention
for AN ATTEMPT FOR A SOCIOLOGICAL RESEARCH IN
GREECE 1974, Thessaloniki Festival, 1974.

FILMS

BLACK & WHITE (1973). (Co-Director).

ATTEMPT FOR A SOCIOLOGICAL RESEARCH IN GREECE
    1974 (1974). A short concerning the communication
    gap between the working women discussing their prob-
    lems, and the sociologists who are interviewing them
    in a "scientific" way.

CATCH 76 (1976). Short experimental film. Repressed by
    censorship on the grounds it insulted the Greek na-
    tional character and for being insolent (it questioned
    the authorities of church and state).

HAPPENING. Incomplete short.

Chapter 9

An Original Model

- COSTAS SFIKAS -

While you and I sit around watching reruns of Hawaii
Five-O on television, Costas Sfikas, for relaxation, translates Balzac, Dante, and "other light classics" into Greek.
While you and I breezily go off to the movies, he painfully
and slowly creates them. While I, bursting with my own
judgmental facilities, declare his first film dazzling, stu-
pendous, exhilarating, rejuvenating, marvelous!--he folds his
hands in his lap, bows his head as though I were patting it,
and expresses such appreciative modesty that I want to buy
him an ice cream cone as a token of apology for having
somehow tried to corrupt his innocence--a strange reaction
to the oldest member of the new Greek cinema. Yet, there
is something wonderfully child-like about the openness of
Costas Sfikas. If he is complimented, he is proud and grateful. If he disagrees with you, he says as much. If he is
worried or concerned, his face reveals it. If you are warm
and kind toward him, he reciprocates. If you want to exchange an idea or a bit of life with him, he is enthusiastic.
He appears guileless, without negative design. It is no wonder that most people find him strange and somewhat unap-
proachable!

I first met Costas Sfikas in London and, without preconceived opinions, fell into easy commune with him--that
is, as easy as his limited but eager English would allow.
He had purchased a book and was so enraptured by it that
it became essential that he unwrap it, with some effort, for
my perusal. I have forgotten the book, but not the vicari-
ous excitement. He was as enchanted as a child with a fairy
tale and I became equally so. Then and there I asked Mr.
Sfikas to show me his first film, and I looked forward to a
lyrical, joyful experience.

A couple of weeks later I finally settled in for the

115

COSTAS SFIKAS

film. With the opening shot, a rather geometrically stark image (which first appeared animated), I thought, "Oh no! He's pretending to be Zagreb, but he's really Disney at heart!" The surprises were to continue as though on an assembly line.

MODEL is a film so unique in imagination and execution, as well as in its flawless delivery of content, that it is only wariness about authoritative judgments which prevents me from calling it a masterpiece. It is the kind of film likely to cause a scandal at each screening; there are those who would find it a big "put on"; those who would judge it pretentious; those who would be hostile to the responsibility they are asked to assume in relating to the film, for the most consistently important ingredient of the film is a built-in void which the audience is invited and given time to fill. Accepting that invitation is to see a film as exciting as a suspense-thriller, as limitless as science fiction. Yet the film is endlessly repetitive, boldly monotonous, and so unyielding to traditional film form as to provoke spectator alienation.

The surface content of the film is a rather simple anti-automation statement, but the structure of the film encourages viewers to develop this theme to any degree to which they are able or willing. Once you become a participant in the film, you are left free to create as you choose. Having temporarily exhausted my visions as related to the film's content, I began restructuring the film, giving it climaxes, syncopating its rhythm, designing a "socko" ending. I was happily and busily destroying the film and creating one which was far inferior, more structurally polite and familiar, enjoying the delusion that my alterations would make the film more engaging. The verve with which I recreated the film was itself witness to the success of Mr. Sfikas' film. His fear that we are becoming robots asks that you make contact with your personal uniqueness; the fear is eventually so frighteningly visualized that I, for one, fell over myself trying to withdraw from my robot expression of self. The film inspires you literally to embrace yourself, recapture a curiosity about self, look in the mirror and get acquainted again. Mr. Sfikas may declare mechanization the villain, but I suspect that the very uniqueness the film encourages us to contact is mistakenly equated with isolation, which in turn inspires fear, and thus serves as first step to robot-land. He needs now to make an equally potent film to help us confront that fear of isolation, to find joy in our uniqueness. This

Frame from Sfikas' film MODEL.

would be a double bill of catalytic proportions--a real zinger
for the Saturday night crowd at the Bijou!

The "plot": The opening shot is the interior of a deserted factory. This shot was originally five minutes long.
It now lasts a mere 2-1/2 minutes. (I asked Sfikas for a
still of this shot and he gave me a frame from the film. So
now the shot lasts one whisper less than 2-1/2 minutes, and
I wonder how many frames he has given away to so shorten
his film's opening.) F-i-n-a-l-l-y, there appears in the
d-i-s-t-a-n-c-e a moving dot which, as it s-l-o-w-l-y moves
toward the viewer is discerned to be a robot, walking mechan-
ically through the l-o-n-g deserted hall. This is repeated
for a few hours.

Suddenly a bell rings and the factory workers rush to
their machines. Some of them stand at attention by their
machines and some of them actually get inside the machines
and stick their feet out through holes. Another bell rings
and they all start to work furiously, moving in unison. The
noise of the machines is deafening. You hear and feel the
ghastly monotony of the work being done. This goes on for
an hour or so.

Unexpectedly, in the middle of the screen, appears a
bathroom sink. It starts moving toward you, growing larger,
like some monster from a cheap science fiction movie. It
is on a conveyor belt which moves off the screen and into the
theater; then, teeteringly, it turns. The object's profile ob-
literates the screen, consumes the workers, becomes a distorted blob in its overwhelming close-up, all the time reflecting a neon-type colored light from some unknown source. It
has turned into a horror movie!

The objects keep coming across the world like giant
indestructable beasts. A bell rings and the workers disappear briefly for a joyless coffee break. But the home ap-
pliance monsters have become self-procreating; they continue
their relentless march. This goes on for four or five hours.

When you are exhausted from having filled in all the
missing passages of this story, you notice a few visual diversions. The robots are continuing their dirge-like proces-
sion, while in the upper-right corner of the screen, there is
a rather perky parade of pastel-people; they occasionally enter the factory, never to exit, and possibly to go directly to
the dressing room where they change into robot costumes.

Poster for MODEL.

The factory workers return from their break and re-
sume their output, although by now it is clear they are not
needed. Toilet stools, baskets, lamp shades, chairs--all
bathed in sickening greens or purples or pinks--advance
across the landscape like the ants in THE NAKED JUNGLE
which destroy everything in their path.

You know for sure it is a horror movie when pieces
of human anatomy begin showing up on the assembly line.
True, they are limbs and torsos and faceless heads of man-
nequins, but imagination has worked overtime (at time-and-
a-half, let us hope!) and they have become real, bloody,
grisly, dismembered appendages. You hate mechanization!
You hate unions and management and canned peas and plastic
whipped cream and Sears Roebuck & Co. and Detroit, Michi-
gan, and efficiency experts!

While I struggle for something else to hate, one more
kitchen sink is threatening to wipe me out. But the lights in
the auditorium come on and the projectionist says, "That's
all," and, somewhat shell-shocked, I wander out into the
comparatively peaceful shelter of the Athens traffic.

Actually, this isn't the way the movie is at all--
which is just the point. The film is really quite simple,
the very simplicity being its profundity. There are no coffee breaks, no bells, no noisy machine sounds. In fact, the
entire film is played in deafening silence. The pacing is
slow, but my exaggeration is only to indicate that I was given
so much time to add to the film, imagine and feel its content,
that it seemed impossible to cram so much into so short a
time. Time became elongated to accommodate internal activity.

In the March 1974 issue of Film, Thanassis Rentzis
contributed a rather lengthy study of MODEL, explaining the
film's Marxist philosophy. Sfikas gave me a translated copy
of this piece, indicating his approval of Rentzis' analysis.
There is no argument that the film is Marxist, but it is not
that limited. The absence of overt dogma, combined with
the uncommanding pace of the film, opens the subject content
of the film to the capabilities of the viewer. The utter joylessness of the workers, and the time allowed to contemplate
that state of being, invites expansion beyond dogma. MODEL
stimulates many ideas and must accept responsibility (and
reward) for that stimulation, even should it stir up a few
thoughts with which the filmmaker himself might disagree.

Scene from METROPOLIS.

Sfikas has been well-tutored in mechanization. "I have worked for the post office for nearly 30 years. During those years I have seen people become nothing but accessories in the function of something else. They have no sense of personal reward in what they are doing. Big mechanisms exist without consideration of human qualities.

"Originally I wanted to be a violinist. But I finally had to admit that I had no talent for it. I was only 16 at the time of the German occupation and I had to go to work. I have been working ever since, except when I resigned during the junta.

"When I first saw Eisenstein's BATTLESHIP POTEMKIN I decided then and there I wanted to somehow work in film." Since that decision, Sfikas has functioned as writer, actor and director. His opportunity to make a feature film was earned by winning a script contest sponsored by the film magazine Contemporary Cinema. MODEL was the result. It shared first prize with KIERION (co-scripted by Sfikas) at the Thessaloniki Festival, and has since made its way to Rotterdam, Berlin, London, and Toulon--in all of which it created an uproar. One man in the London audience loudly announced that had he paid admission, he too would have

created a scandal. But there has also been support from
fellow directors like Jean-Marie Straub.

"If people do not like my films, there is nothing I
can do. But if they do not understand them, I try to explain that it is a new form and shape of film. People who
understand the film ask why it was done in such an absolute
way. For instance, only a small part of mechanization is
shown, and even it is shown without personal reactions. It
is simply a mathematical expression--an equation of what I
believe."

Sfikas has a reputation for being somewhat unapproach-
able. He has an aristocratic presence, a straight, regal
bearing, and a rather distant, preoccupied look in his eye.
Apparently this is mistaken for aloofness. My enthusiasm
for his film may have inspired him to respond to my over-
tures, for I found him warm, enthusiastic, eager to communicate. A torrential rainstorm hit during our meeting;
wet and cold, we continued to deliberate the robot-creators
of the world. Mr. Sfikas' fears for his own loss of humanity are indeed a mistaken identity; 30 years at the post office
have made no discernible dent in his uniqueness. His re-
sistence has been a victory for the individual, and MODEL
proves it.

His second feature, a collage film entitled METROPO-
LIS, "is like an audio-visual symphony. Music is used to

express how the bourgeois feel about what they think is important in their lives. Frequently the visual image of the film says the opposite of what the music expresses. At other times it is used to extend the images, as during the reading of the Proust passages where the music adds depth and meaning to the words. "

Sfikas had been approached to do a film on the beginnings of the First World War for television. "I began working on it while waiting for them to give the final go-ahead. As I made the choice of pictures for the film, I could see the structure of the film evolving very far from what had been conceived for television. I decided it would have to be a film for the festival. I worked sometimes up to 18 hours a day on the film. The major problem was finding the pictures, because I did not want to use sensational images-- those with shock value. I didn't want the audience simply to react. I wanted them to find the meanings in the film themselves by just going with the experience of the film. The television people had wanted a more straightforward reportage. But I selected pictures with multi-meanings. They could be interpreted in many ways. If it had been shown on television there would have had to have been a running explanation. But the pictures should be self-explanatory.

"When I say I saw it as a visual symphony, it is because different elements are repeated and then repeated again in variation. For instance, the picture of the elephant we see three times: first when it is killed, where it is a symbol of Africa. Then we see it as the dominant figure in a coffee house where prostitutes congregate. Again we see it as a symbol of physical strength relating to the western world's domination of eastern countries.

"Silent newsreels of the time were always informatively reported in favor of the imperialistic viewpoint. This fact is used in the film, as well as some scenes from fiction films of the day. Nuns and priests are intercut with the manufacture of weapons to comment on the role the church played in the war. There is always a relation between the church and the bourgeois mentality. Nuns reappear repeatedly, making various visual comments. "

Repetition has been a predominant factor in both of Sfikas' films, though he claims it is unintentional. "But repetition has played an important role in my life, so it is not surprising it shows up in my work. If a person knows how to use repetition, he can arrive at positive results. "

A third film, in the planning stages, will be a study
of time, as seen from the viewpoint of people doing things
they don't want to do.

Sfikas creates very slowly; it is no wonder that he expresses great admiration for J. S. Bach, who not only composed a new cantata for each Sunday's church services, but
also found time to produce 20 children! If Sfikas continues
at his present rate of production, his films are fated to be
few. Furthermore, his creations are unlikely to attract a
large audience. He must therefore find his own reasons for
continuing. The external will offer him little more than a
respectful place in obscurity, although there is hope for some
recognition within the comparatively limited world of experimental film. Those few who do make contact with his work
cannot help but be enriched, even if they hate it.

Mr. Sfikas has retained his curiosity about life and
maintained his contact with his own creativity, despite his
stated fear of becoming a robot. Instead of celebrating the
very thing that keeps him marvelously alive, he chooses to
dwell on the externals which threaten to dehumanize him.
Fortunately, they have done little except give him food for
thought and occasional melancholia.

On the surface, MODEL is about automated mass production and its effects on humanity, but actually it is a loud
and clear tribute to an individual and his original creativity.
It is too bad Costas Sfikas cannot be mass produced!

* * * * *

1977 UPDATE: Sfikas has been working on documentaries
commissioned by the postal department. He is playing a
small but important role in Nicos Panayotopoulos' new film,
but was eager to impress that he is not an actor, despite
the growing list of performing credits.

BIOGRAPHICAL BRIEF

Born Athens, 1927. Early ambitions toward music. German
occupation necessitated employment at age 16. He worked in
post office nearly 30 years (gave up his job during the junta).
Lives with wife and daughter in Athens. Awards: Critic's
Prize for DAWN OVER THIRA, 1967 Thessaloniki Festival;
Best Film, MODEL, 1974 Thessaloniki Festival.

FILMS

As Director: INAUGURATION (1962). (Short).
EXPECTATIONS (1963). (20 minutes).
DAWN OVER THIRA (1968). (20 minutes).
MODEL (1974). (Screenplay & Direction).
METROPOLIS (1975). (Screenplay & Direction).

As Writer: YOUNG APHRODITES (1963). (Dir: Nikos
Koundouros. Screenplay by Sfikas and Vas-
salis Vassilikos).
KIERION (1968). (Dir: D. Theos. Screenplay by Theos & Sfikas).

As Actor: KIERION (1968). (Dir: D. Theos).
DAYS OF '36 (1972). (Dir: T. Angelopoulos).
THE COLORS OF IRIS (1974). (Dir: N.
Panayotopoulos).
THE MISTAKE (1975). (Dir: Peter Fleisch-
mann).
THE PROCEEDINGS (1976). (Dir: D. Theos).
THE INDOLENCE OF THE FERTILE VALLEY
(1977). (Dir: N. Panayotopoulos).

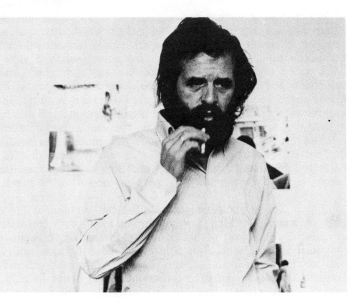

Chapter 10

Bring Me the Head of Citizen Theos

- DIMOSTHENIS THEOS -

Dimosthenis Theos is a man charged with the electric-
ity of his own beliefs, expressing them and himself with the
near fanaticism of a religious zealot. As the ideas get more
lofty, you can almost see him reaching for them, much as a
singer goes after a high note. If there is no humor to al-
leviate the results, his own excitement and sincerity is
pleasurably contagious.

He has made two feature films to date. The second
film, THE PROCEEDINGS, is a visually static expression
of a currently emphasized cerebral involvement with his life
and work. Having seen this film first, I was totally unprepared for the fluid self-assuredness of his primary film,
KIERION, nor the excited animation of the man himself.

Theos' sister is a talented architect (she did the costumes for THE PROCEEDINGS) and I was invited to dinner

at her memorably designed apartment, an evening during which an amazing amount of suspicious profundity was exchanged, counterbalanced by an ultimately amusing lack of comprehension. The bartering of conclusions is a slow process under the most ideal circumstances, requiring patience, tolerance and a good deal of hope. Filtering these and additional ingredients through a language barrier resulted in what is probably a massive, though blissful, amount of misunderstanding. Neither of us, not even for one rational moment, allowed the impossible to influence our mutual sermonizing and we both attended happily to what was voiced; that is, I delighted in what I was saying, and he, in turn, was enraptured by his own words. We both enjoyed it very much!

Theos vociferously extolled the virtues of his current philosophy, which has something to do with the discovery and development of behavioral models, and I began to feel uncomfortably like an IBM card--each opinion offered was another code punched. I, in turn, offered forth my favorite theme on the divine individual, no doubt equally categorizing. All in all, we both were exhilarated by our own philosophies and parted happily, knowing that each was dedicatedly opinionated and willing to express it with Wagnerian duration.

Through the haze of the language barrier and the difficulties of communicating philosophical ideas, it would be presumptuous to try to explain his theories, or even to express agreement or disagreement with them. But he pursues them with serious and devoted intent which evokes great respect for his commitment, his energies and his pursuit.

Apparently Theos reads research reports and academic studies with the zest of the New York subway rider immersed in the latest Harold Robbins novel. Facts and figures were offered as proof of points, and I had visions of Theos heading a network of researchers gathering endless data to guide sales and services to countless Greek housewives; compiling massive reports to be lost in bureaucratic files, or perhaps happily remembered on a tax form as a business expense.

Report on Dimosthenis Theos

I.   BACKGROUND

   A.   Initial Interest in Film

1. "I went to several films a week and began to be interested in the medium as an art form. The Hollywood films in particular were influencing. The quality was so high, I began to question why we made the type of commercial film we did. "

2. "In specific I liked the American thriller. Howard Hawks' SCARFACE, Samuel Fuller's SHOCK CORRIDOR, John Huston's THE AS-PHALT JUNGLE and THE TREASURE OF SIERRA MADRE are particularly memorable. "

B. Participation in Film

1. "I took a job in the commercial cinema as a technician. At the time there were about 80 films a year and it was a very good job. I worked all year long. "

2. "I worked both as an assistant director and as director of production. "

II. THE FILMS OF DIMOSTHENIS THEOS

A. Hundred Hours In May

1. A short which tells factually the story of Costa-Gavras' film, Z. *

2. "It is the story of the murder of Grigorios Labrakis in Thessaloniki. It was made at a time when I was working with a group of technicians and the facilities were available. I started filming the documentary when the murder occurred. I put my own money into the film. "

B. Kierion

1. Interviewee's Comments:

   a. "I began shooting this feature in 1966. It

*HUNDRED HOURS IN MAY played the Tours Festival in 1968.

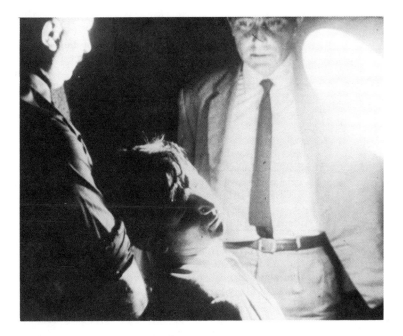

Scenes from KIERION.

was a period of considerable political turmoil, so all the young directors were very
excited to make statements about what they
saw happening in Greece. This was just
before the junta and after the civil war.
It was impossible to make direct political
statements. When artists began to talk
politically in 1966, we were not really sure
we were free to say things openly, so I
made a political film in the guise of science
fiction. We don't see where the events
take place. We don't know the country,
nor the time. I don't want you to think I
was shooting a political creed. I simply
wanted to show the truth, as I believe do
the other directors. For example, the film
shows a policeman beating a person in prison. It was not permitted before this period
to show such a thing. "

b. "As basis for the film we took a real
event, the murder of an American journalist who came to investigate the civil war,
and was found dead on the beach near
Thessaloniki. This actually happened in
1948, and only recently the State Department has published some papers that show
how he was murdered. It was a time when
the Americans and the English were quar-
reling about who owned what, and the English murdered him. The Greek government found it convenient to blame the communists. The Americans were caught in
the McCarthy period, and they too found
this solution acceptable at the time, since
the journalist was a known liberal. "

2. Interviewer's Comments:

a. KIERION is a superior thriller which captures an atmosphere of threatening authori-
tarianism and individual victimization. It
invites comparison to Costa-Gavras' highly
successful Z, which likewise fictionalized
a true incident in modern Greek history.
The minimal production values of KIERION,
as compared to Z, contribute to the ulti-

mate superiority of KIERION. Filmed in
grainy black and white, it has the frightening result of audience involvement. We
are not left comfortably sitting in our lives
watching a movie--we are experiencing a
real piece of recent history that could indeed surface again, engulfing the innocent
and guilty alike in its thrashing. The
threat and fear of such possibility finds
immediate visual expression in the film,
resulting in a thoroughly ominous and un-
forgettable film.

3. A Brief History

"KIERION wasn't yet finished when the junta
came in. I made the copies in France and
showed the film in Venice in 1968. It got very
good reviews in the Italian papers. It was sold
to Canada and Sweden TV. After the junta I
returned and redid the sound of the film, which
had deteriorated, and showed it in Thessaloniki.
With the money gained from the prize it won,
I had a small profit on the film. It played in
Athens for one week and was purchased by
Greek television in 1974. "

C. The Proceedings

1. An Introductory Note on the Film*

"The film borrows the Antigoni's legend from
the myths of the ancient Theban cycle. The
events of the myth have been transferred to
the Aegean.... The action takes place in a
hypothetical island of the Aegean--Lycabettus.
It is a small kingdom, with political dependence
on the sphere of influence of the Minoan Crete.
Asia Minor belongs, at its major part, to the
sphere of influence of the Hettean Empire.
With the presence of the Maeceneans, the balance of powers is destroyed. (The Maeceneans,
in the film, are mentioned as Achaioi or as

_____
*As quoted in a published 8-page "note" explaining the pro-
ceeding of THE PROCEEDINGS.

Costas Haralambidis, Anghelos Sfakianakis, Yannis Totsikas in THE PROCEEDINGS.

Achijawa and are considered as a larger alliance of clans.)" (Author's note: well, you get the idea!)

2. "Considerable research was done on the costumes, and though we learned that the priests dressed as women, the current view would not allow us to handle this authentically. However, in essence the costumes are accurate. Money for the film was found from various sources. The producer is a school friend and he put up some money out of friendship, but also as a business venture. I put up some money of my own, and the rest was found here and there. The film took one year to make. We would get interrupted for various reasons. Once the problems were solved, the cast would have to

reassemble and we would pick up where we left off. "

3. A Note on Reactions to the Film*

a. In all fairness, I cannot hope to have an opinion on the content of this film. Memory projects a great deal of static pageantry, suggesting staging of paintings from archaeological finds. Most dynamic in recall is the decapitation of a goat. I believe that at this point of Theos' cerebral detachment it is no accident that a beheading should occur in his film. That he depicts it as a sacrifice may relate to his stated belief that this film, like Orson Welles' CITIZEN KANE, will find its appreciative audience in ten years. There is something sacrificial in this attitude, considering the statement was made prior to the film's official premiere screening.

b. The film created an uproar at the 1976 Thessaloniki Festival. Catcalls and boos interrupted the projection, and Theos denounced the audience as barbarians. He, in turn, was similarly labeled for having made the film. Following the screening there evolved a spontaneous open forum on the film, with Theos explaining that it was quite experimental. Part of the experimentation was to guide the actors to walk through their roles without emotion, suggesting an objective-as-possible approach to presentation. Why so much money was spent on an experiment remained an unsatisfactorily answered question. Everyone I asked renders a different account of this festival confrontation, so it is assumed that the final, absolute resolution to the event was the hour: 4 a.m.

---

*Loosely based on author's inept deciphering of either the film or the 8-page Introductory Notes on the Film. Also incorporated is some hearsay as to the scandal it created at the 1976 Thessaloniki Domestic Film Festival.

Costas Haralambidis in THE PROCEEDINGS.

III. THE FUTURE OF DIMOSTHENIS THEOS

A. Some Current Thoughts

"I would like to research the way the social structures are assimilated by individuals, and their way
of behavior is nothing more than the assimilations
of these models. That is what I want to investigate, explain and describe in my films. What I
don't like, and want to show in my films, is the
men who want to save the world, in one way or
another. You always discover as you examine
their lives, they are people who can't save themselves, but they want to save the world. From
this point of view I am very much like the ancient
Greeks--they didn't want to save anyone. They just
went on their way. In ancient Greece, and we
don't know whether we have any real relation with

ancient Greece, it's that we never had people who
wanted to impose their way of life, their own way
of doing things. They were speakers who went
about telling their opinions, and people said you
are not well, you are crazy, and they threw stones,
and the speaker went away, and another took his
place. "

B. Film Projects

1. "I want to make a film about a torturer from
the junta. I will show how he assimilated the
anti-communist social structure, the Turkish
element, why he behaved as a Nazi torturer.
I want to show that he became what he became
through the social structures that existed while
he was young. I want to show this in an objective way so that the film does not become a
fascistic film from the point of view of communism. I want it to be very, very objective
and scientific, the explanation of the behavior
of this man. I am collecting the data. I will
use the actual transcripts from the court at the
time he was condemned. He did not appear in
public frequently. He was always the person
behind another person, but he was the real
boss. There is another man I am interested
in as a subject who was the leader of the communist party. I want to do a similar study of
this man. The method can be used within the
framework of any ideology. "

IV. CONCLUSION

A. Interviewee's Concluding Statement

"Film is my first expression, but I would consider
a book. But even should there be a book, I would
want eventually to state my conclusions on film. "

B. Interviewer's Concluding Statement

If our behaviors are modeled on some admired or
influential "hero, " system, or state of being, what
remains unclear to me is on whom or what the first
of a kind was modeled. What is very clear, how-

ever, is that KIERION ranks high in the "new wave"
movement and should have indeed served as model
for those who came after. This doesn't suggest
they should imitate its content or film noir style,
but rather its tone of commitment, personalness,
and inventiveness, all of which overcame economic
modesty. If Theos used his Hollywood heroes as
models, he has integrated and personalized their
messages, rendering their influence a mere ingredient within a new model.

Ten years may indeed reveal the elusive treasures
of THE PROCEEDINGS. Meanwhile, I should like
to see the original and fully integrated filmmaker of
KIERION at work again--a man motivated by a complete point of view; one that embraced emotion,
body, thought, energy, blood (mostly for internal
use only), craft, intuition, and an involvement with
an art form in balance with its selected and executed content.

*   *   *   *   *

1977 UPDATE: Theos has been cinematically inactive since
THE PROCEEDINGS, which was not released to theaters in
Greece.

BIOGRAPHICAL BRIEF

Born 1935, in Karditsa, province of Thessaly. Worked in
commercial cinema in 1960s. Self-exile in Germany during
junta. Worked in a factory until he learned the language,
then became a reporter for television. Currently works in
ceramics when not occupied with film. Lives in Athens with
his wife (a lawyer) and two children. Awards: KIERION,
Special Honor, Venice Festival, 1968; Best Film (shared
with MODEL), Best First Film Director, Thessaloniki Festival, 1974.

FILMS

HUNDRED HOURS OF MAY (1965). (17 minutes).

KIERION (1968). (Producer, Director, Co-Writer). (Was
    not shown in Greece until 1974).

THE MURDERESS (1974). (Screenplay).

THE PROCEEDINGS (1976). (Screenplay, Director).

As Journalist: "Film in Griechenland," <u>Filmkritik</u>, August 1973 (in German).

Chapter 11

Love Makes the World Go 'Round

- PANDELIS VOULGARIS -

Comprehending Pandelis Voulgaris and his films requires foregoing preconceived evaluative tools. He has not
identified himself with groups, causes, dogmas, philosophies
or goals in an effort to find himself. He simply is. He
leads life on his own loving, intuitive terms. He remains
aloof from the Greek fascination for bickering. He avoids
proselytizing. Even his opinions are expressed with empathy
for the next guy's position. If he has enemies, it is through
their hang-ups, not his. He inspires warmth wherever he is.
In fact, he is even half-jokingly referred to as Saint Pandelis.

Above, director Voulgaris (right), with actress Diane Baker
and actor Stathis Yalelis at the 1976 Thessaloniki Film Festival.

Any attempt to define Voulgaris is to impose an image that instantly must self-destruct, leaving only his uniqueness. Any concrete explanation of him is bound to distort his reality. Nevertheless, within the Greek cinema world, where the cerebral enjoys great respect, Voulgaris remains blissfully and healthily unconscious. While the other directors are busy thinking, analyzing, plotting, Voulgaris simply acts and responds from an intuitive level, not asking too many questions or seeking too many answers. Though one might suspect such a position to be one of blandness or of lateral movement, the essence of Voulgaris is ... one wants to say "pure, " and thus his message is easily misunderstood. His creative profundity must be felt or absorbed. To meet it head-on is to find a confusion, an enigma, an imposed solution.

Pandelis Voulgaris transcends language barriers in conveying his humor, his lyricism and his sense of joy. He was imprisoned during the junta, and personal tragedy has intruded in his life, but there is no evidence of bitterness. His personal warmth is unpretentious and contagious. His films are as difficult to "read" as he is, because they too do not fit into neat categories. They are excellent, though unintentional, teachers or reminders that understanding, knowledge, and evaluation are not always cerebrally based. He is vulnerable to the same fate as Federico Fellini, who made beautiful, unconscious films until the world told him how clever he was, at which point he started making conscious but less profound films.

It is very important that the world discover Voulgaris, but equally important that Voulgaris not discover too much of the world.

* * * * *

"I was young and impressionable at the time Cinema-Scope was introduced. This excited me, and it became a game. We wanted to do what we saw, and be what we saw. We would sit on the steps in front of the house and watch people go by and imagine what they could be. This one would be a Count or a Countess or whatever. In school I had no special talent for anything, and one day I saw some people filming for the commercial cinema and I saw a boy I knew. I asked him what he was doing there, and he told me he was the assistant director. I was curious as to how he had managed this, and he told me about a private school where you could go without passing any examination, which interested me because I didn't want to have to pass examinations in ancient Greek and mathematics and things like that. So I said, "That's very nice. I'll go there. ' And I did.

"Fortunately the teachers were very good and professional, and they encouraged me. It was there that I wrote the script of my first short, and there was a director from the commercial cinema who helped me make my first short. Then he took me with him to the commercial cinema, and I worked as an assistant in the commercial cinema from 1961 to 1965. The atmosphere was wonderful, and I liked it so much that it is an atmosphere I want to recreate every time. I learned a lot of things, especially from the negative side. I saw lots of things I didn't want to do. I felt they had lost the real thing--the sensitivity--and that was much to learn during the four years.

"Toward the end of the commercial cinema, which collapsed about 1968, the big producers were making about 110 films a year, but they were so much alike that when you saw the advertisement for next week's movie you thought it was for last week's. People simply stopped going to the cinema. TV was the second cause. People began to be aware that they were seeing the same people on the small screen that they had seen in the 110 films on the large screen, so why go and pay? Independent filmmakers had wanted to have the chance to show the big producers what they could do, in hopes of getting some financial help from them. But there was no time to do that because the producers of the commercial cinema lost all their money before we could show what we could do.

"So financing became a real problem. Many of the directors thought of the solution of making an advertising firm which would make money to be used for film production. Everyone of us thinks that the first film will also be the last, because we don't know if we will ever find financing for a second film. And we want the one film to show that the film is Greek, that the film is experimental, that the film is European ... all that and more in one film. It is a real problem, because you think you will not find money for a second go-round. When you want to paint a painting, or write a song, or make a film, you want to feel free when you have finished, but when you have the financing to worry about, you begin to put on your Sunday clothes to face the political person, or the critics. The result is the probability of losing the real thing you wanted to express.

"I can't minimize the financing problem, but there are other problems--that of essence. That is, how to show in our films the character of Greece, how we operate in relation to other countries. A whole generation of poets, musicians, composers, writers made the character of Greece 20 years ago. And now, even the old houses like you saw in THE ENGAGEMENT OF ANNA are going. We have to build again on the new apartment houses--the new face of Greece --a new character. We have nothing on which to build. This generation which contributed is now something of the past. The music of Hatzidakis, the paintings of Tsarouchis, these old houses that don't exist any more, have a connection. But these things don't exist any more. Expressions of tradition, or expressions that became tradition, have collapsed, and having lost that, we have to find a replacement. Even the tradition of the family visiting the old woman in ANNA each Sunday is a thing of the past. Now the family gets in the car, and the old woman stays alone.

"The replacement of these things is very concrete. The new generation feels very much alone, and because they feel lonely they go to a group. They want to go somewhere to not feel alone, and where they meet is in a building made of concrete. The new filmmakers want to show the good and the bad, with nothing in between. The concrete architecture becomes symbolic of the absence of pliability. Formerly people were not good nor bad. The good had bad, the bad had good inside. The new generation wants this thing to be concrete.

"When the last generation of artists was young, they had groups, but they were individualistic groups. They were together because they were in school together, but they searched for answers because they wanted solutions to their problems as individuals, not as a group. Now it's the group. Even then the political parties were not so well organized, which left some freedom to the individual, but now there is no freedom. You have to do that because you belong to that party. That is the line to follow. And that's what I'm afraid of.

"Reaching out to a group to find self is very limiting in subject matter, content and expression. And even if you are not in a group, you begin to think to what group is this film oriented? What group is going to like this film? What group will offer protection to this film? But when something is real--a song or a film or whatever--when it is real, everyone will like it, regardless of the group.

"I don't think there are any special problems in Greece that don't pertain everywhere, as regards making films. But the difficulties we do face which are not so prominent in many other countries are technical problems. We do not have schools, nor ways to learn. But those are only details. When you have the love, and you want to do something, these things become merely things to be overcome. We do have an advantage here in that we can turn to each other for help. If I need a photographer or an actor, I can turn to them and just simply ask them to help and they do. This doesn't happen in, say, Italy or France. Through this love that surrounds the film we teach ourselves.

"We have unions, and the unions have rules that we must respect. But they are within the reality. That is, they say you are obliged to have seven technicians, and that is something within the Greek reality. That isn't something you do because it is forced on you. Since the collapse of the Greek commercial cinema, which began in 1965 and was totally gone by 1968, we have had no films. We don't know even if we can find seven films to show at the festival in Thessaloniki this year.

"Of course, there is always a censorship problem, but it is minor because you can always fool them. Even during the junta. You give them a false script, as they did with THE TRAVELLING PLAYERS, and then you change things. The problem is really what are we going to show. Are we going to make films which are only for those few who support 'art' films, or 'experimental' films, or are we going to try to find a way to say to those abroad, 'Come, here is the new Greek cinema.' We haven't found the answer to this yet.

"International recognition? Certainly it would help when you're looking to finance the next film. But what is more important than international fame is when four or five people that I like, and accept their criticism as just, don't like what I have done. This makes me very sorry and sad. I have been lucky to be around people who have committed their lives to being true in their art and have tried to show honest relations between people. That is what is important. All the other is important, but only superficially.

"I make films because something inside of me is inspired. The short, JIMMY THE TIGER, was a response to actually having seen a performance by a person on whom

Jimmy is modeled. THE ENGAGEMENT OF ANNA is a
story that was real. In fact, my family didn't speak to me
for some time after making the film because the characters
are based on real family. But after doing ANNA, I began
to feel guilty because everyone started asking me what was
the political side of the film. Now I have made a film about
the concentration camp experience. We are political prisoners, but I have tried very hard to not draw distinctions between the good and the bad. That is, some policemen are
good and some prisoners are bad.

"I don't see my future as other than a director. But
my dream is not to make a film every other year, but to
make a film when I feel like making a film."

* * * * *

It is hard to imagine Pandelis Voulgaris working outside Greece, which is a limiting factor in work opportunities
for him. On the other hand, this gives him relative freedom of expression, for he is greatly respected and loved,
and this opens doors to him that are closed to other filmmakers (such minimal doors as do exist, that is). He is
somewhat unsure of his worth; needs constantly to be reas-
sured of his artistry. At least that is the facade presented.

International recognition surely hinges on his ability
to continue producing. With the success of such films as
ROCKY, DAY FOR NIGHT, THE MAGIC FLUTE, and COUS-
IN COUSINE, there is a hint that the pendulum may be swing-
ing away from the less passionate style of filmmaking that
has reigned for some time. If so, Voulgaris' films should
find their way into the international stream. His cumulative
output is the most original expression in Greece in the 1970s.
His work is uncontaminated by imitation or trend influences.
He has experimented with structural style but the far more
important element of personal essence has been solidly on
display from the first film. Voulgaris' films are not so
much about what you see as they are about Voulgaris and
what he is, or was, at the time of filming. He uses film
to unconsciously analyze and reveal himself, and that has
served as artistic content for many great artists. Perhaps all.

THE ENGAGEMENT OF ANNA

It is pedantic to talk about the direction the New Wave

Scenes from THE ENGAGEMENT OF ANNA.

in Greece might have taken. What might have been completely changed course with the collapse of the junta, which is not
to say that the junta government was in any direct way responsible for, or supportive of, the New Wave cinema. It
simply means that with the comparative freedom of post-junta
Greece, the filmmakers are talking in different terms about
different subjects. In essence, they have started all over
again, and invite a completely new and different evaluative
framework.

In the heyday of the New Wave, THE ENGAGEMENT
OF ANNA was the model for what might have been. It had
the youthful eagerness that characterized the New Wave, but
it also had a professional finish. It was modestly financed,
but rich in imaginative execution, both behind and in front of
the camera. Its content was not distorted by a personal passion. It had drama without melodrama; sentiment without
sentimentality; distance with disengagement; commitment without self-indulgence; tenderness without triteness; compassion
without condonement. It remains a model of unselfconscious
Greekness. It takes for granted its Greekness, opening beyond that restriction while simultaneously embracing it.

THE ENGAGEMENT OF ANNA is a remembered part
of Voulgaris' past. Anna, a live-in employee, is treated
much as a family member while being a domestic servant to
it. The family arranges for her to meet a suitable young
man, with matrimony the objective. Though this is done
with a genuine desire for Anna's future happiness, the realiza-
tion that she might leave elicits an array of selfish, cruel,
ignorant, insensitive reactions from the family members.
Additional pressure is exerted when Anna's mother is con-
sulted; she responds with a plea for Anna's continued sub-
servience because of the financial assistance Anna supplies
her family. Anna can find neither the courage nor the opportunity to act otherwise, and continues her life with the
family as though the event had not occurred. (In real life,
Anna continued on as companion until the family matriarch's
death; then she married.)

THE ENGAGEMENT OF ANNA is a cool movie; the
camera observes with detachment, making no comment, asking for no specified reactions. Its distance is counteracted
by its true story base, which lends an intimacy to the film
that prevents it from being unduly objective.

Whether deliberately or instinctively, the directorial

execution is underplayed, which allows the peaks to emerge as they will. No effort is extended to make an issue of the sexual repression which permeates the entire film; the hot, lazy Sunday afternoons get no enhancement; no subjectivity is applied to the characters. They are simply allowed to speak for themselves. The cast responds to the mood with impeccable individual and ensemble professionalism.

"THE ENGAGEMENT OF ANNA was realized because Dinos Katsouridis* came to me with the suggestion we do a film. I had written ANNA some time before that, but had had no success in getting it financed. I had nothing else to show at the time, so I dragged ANNA out of a drawer, and he liked it. ANNA won five awards at Thessaloniki, but the most interesting reaction was from the middle-class people in small neighborhoods where the film played. People were frequently embarrassed by some scenes, especially the scene where the man goes into Anna's room and makes advances to her. Some of them were moved, and some of them told me that it was right to say that Anna went back because that was the real thing. Some people refused to talk about it. We sat outside the cinema and asked them what they thought of it as they came out.

"ANNA played the Forum Section of the Berlin Festival. I was a prisoner in the concentration camp at the time and the news came over the radio that the film had won a prize. The policemen didn't know how to react. The only person who could move freely through the prison was a doctor who was also a policeman. He heard about the prize and wanted to tell me about it. He was so moved by the situation that I offered him a cup of coffee."

THE ENGAGEMENT OF ANNA also played the New Directors series at the Museum of Modern Art in 1975. Following the screening, Voulgaris was subjected to a question and answer period, during which time the audience labored earnestly to extract their own conceptions of the film from Voulgaris. They wanted Voulgaris to confirm that the film was a statement of the social climate in Greece, or that the film was really about the abuse of one class by another, or that the film was disguisedly political. Voulgaris met each question with a disarming simplicity, claiming that the film

*Dinos Katsouridis is a producer, director, and cinematographer.

was simply a remembered story from his past, and he meant
nothing else by it. His work has continually met this same
kind of audience and critical determination to impose a meaning presumed to be more profound. Film (London) said,
"... it is in the second half of his film that political concerns
come to the fore." The October 1975 Jump Cut concludes
that "... ANNA is concerned with what are undoubtedly the
two most important elements of the Greek social landscape;
the relationship of the lower classes to the middle class ...
and the relationship, in all its ramification and variations,
of the woman to her society."

Voulgaris' art will continue to elicit individual evaluation and assorted conclusions because it springs from the
enigma of a personal view.

THE GREAT LOVE SONGS

THE GREAT LOVE SONGS was a complete turnabout
from THE ENGAGEMENT OF ANNA in style and execution,

Voulgaris between performers during filming of THE GREAT
LOVE SONGS.

as well as in content. ANNA was a reflection of his past,
executed somewhat distantly and straightforwardly. THE
GREAT LOVE SONGS is, to use his description, a product
of dreams and is executed with rich subjectivity. While
ANNA is formally structured into a beginning-middle-end
story, THE GREAT LOVE SONGS ambles episodically. At
first it appears that the film is held together by the Hatzidakis songs which inspired it, but Voulgaris' genuinely positive, lyrical, and sometimes magical view of life combines
the pieces into a flowing whole. As with any revue-type
structuring, there are elements which work better than others, but the film remains constant in its celebration of joy.

Like ANNA, THE GREAT LOVE SONGS finds a balance, though its requirements are different. The romanticism balances the experimentation; comedy rejects invita-
tions to pretentiousness; an acknowledgment of ugliness
grounds a tendency toward excessive lyricism. There is no
effort to interpret the Hatzidakis songs; whatever inspirations
they afford are in mood only, but the execution is delicious-
ly unexpected, constantly imaginative.

"THE GREAT LOVE SONGS was something I had
dreamed of doing back in film school. I had heard some
songs Hatzidakis had adapted from some folk songs and
wanted to do a film about them. Finally the time actually
came when Hatzidakis proposed that we do the film. It was
very badly received at the Thessaloniki Festival because it
was during the junta period and nobody was in a receptive
mood for lyrical things. It was a 16mm and therefore not
likely to be largely distributed. It was really meant for television but it was played in an art cinema three days before
the polytechnic school uprising, and after that I went into the
concentration camp. The film played at a Greek week that
was organized in a New York university. This film is very
valuable to me because I found you can do a film without any
plot, without any restrictions and whatever realistic talents
I have were used in ANNA, and now I feel free to move into
other frameworks, such as the lyricism of this film. There
is no fiction in the film, it is a presentation of the songs.
The film has two parts: the first part shows how the song
is written by Hatzidakis, how a composer writes a song, and
the second part is dreams inspired by the songs. I didn't
try to translate the songs literally, but reached out for the
ambience of my response to the songs. "

Although ANNA is Voulgaris' most complete work,

Scenes from THE GREAT LOVE SONGS.

there are moments of THE GREAT LOVE SONGS which soar
above ANNA: the camera literally swimming through the
multi-faces of the city streets; a young man admiring a new
haircut; a marvelously handsome man playing cards with
childlike concentration.

The expected goes without attention. A beautiful duet
in the musical work is staged in the subway. The boy sings
on the soundtrack and we see the boy on the train. The girl
sings and we see a girl, and one thinks, "Aha! He's finally
selected the obvious." Then the male voice sings the next
line, but the camera stays on the girl, then leaves the train
completely and starts a new visual theme, only to return at
the end of the song for a surprise ending to the little subway
vignette.

THE GREAT LOVE SONGS is even more personal than
his first film. Without plot, it is to be expected that some
sequences are better than others. The more calculatedly
staged scenes are the least effective, and though I'm told Voulgaris has a special brand of humor, the humorous moments of
THE GREAT LOVE SONGS are not really very funny. But
the marvelous inventiveness of the visuals accompanying the
Hatzidakis songs frequently rises to a triumph of creative
ingenuity. Somehow he manages to make art of the ride on
the subway, a crowded city street, the destruction of a building.

If Voulgaris refuses to take a position in ANNA, he
doesn't hold back in THE GREAT LOVE SONGS, and if the
message is read correctly it is, "Love is magic; the ugliness, the absurd, the grotesque, the foolish are made toler-
able by love. Love makes it all go 'round."

That sounds beautiful and it is. But there is a flaw.
Magic, as visualized in the film, is an illusion--a make-be-
lieve. The next to last scene in the film is of a magician
whose magic is clearly established as trickery and illusion.
This scene flows into the concluding and summarizing sequence of the film. A giant ferris wheel turns; the night
and multi-colored lights capture the magic of an amusement
park while disguising its harsh daytime vulgarity. The circular movement is then mirrored by a circle of couples com-
prised of various characters from the film. They change
partners in the circular dance, creating varied combinations
of absurdity, ridiculousness, incongruity, poetry, and beauty.
A couple emerges from this partner-changing ring and they

meet each other in the center. It is executed with nearly
excessive romanticism. Love is magic. Magic is unreal.
Ergo.

Throughout the film we constantly have been allowed
to see faces which somehow assume an immediate identity,
even though on the screen briefly. It is only at the end,
when love is symbolized, that the boy and girl remain ob-
scure. They are lost in the message, and actually become
an opposite to the essence of the rest of the film, which
seems to be Voulgaris' simple and profound ability to clearly
and affectionately attend each person he encounters.

Still, there are truly great moments in THE GREAT
LOVE SONGS. It is the kind of film you'd like to own, to
screen again and again. Voulgaris' vision, the camera, and
the editing are in themselves a great love song.

HAPPY DAY

The magical image of love meets with some confusion
in HAPPY DAY, but the confusion is the audience's, not
Voulgaris'. Even the villains of HAPPY DAY, for whom he
might have felt and shown a hatred, are depicted as a human
admixture of good and bad, as are the prisoners, for whom
we want to feel complete sympathy. Voulgaris has refused
to resort to simplified stereotypes, and by so doing he in-
curred the displeasure and disappointment of a political audience which wanted to see an important film director voice
their understandable thirst for revenge.

Politics permeate Greek consciousness, and though
Voulgaris had indicated little interest in dealing with the subject, his imprisonment during the junta inspired urgings that
he make a political statement. In an interview with Willard
Manus in The Athenian, Voulgaris claims to have been un-
justly accused of making a film during the Polytechnic uprising and smuggling it out of the country. He was incarcerated on the prison island of Makronissos, and this experience, combined with an adaptation of the book THE PLAGUE
by Andreas Franghias, serves as springboard for HAPPY
DAY.

To have yielded completely and made a more defined
political statement would have been uncharacteristic of Voulgaris; thus far he has not given himself to any external align-

Scenes from HAPPY DAY. Below, the "queen" (George Sar-ri) being greeted by the priest (Costas Tzoumas).

ment. HAPPY DAY may really be a compromise, a response to popular urgings, but the balance of the emotional contract is more to his reward than those with whom he negotiated.

It takes a determined imagination and a steady sense of direction to utilize a prison camp setting as a furtherance of his investigation of love. THE ENGAGEMENT OF ANNA expressed a love for tradition, even while acknowledging its repressive negatives. THE GREAT LOVE SONGS continued the nostalgic theme: the old houses being demolished are dramatic losses; the long opening of the drive through ugly modern Athens is finally absorbed by the embracing quality of the film. HAPPY DAY turns a barren island prison camp into an object of beauty, even though it is forced to serve man's ugliness.

Stylistically, HAPPY DAY is the amalgamation of the caressing reality of THE ENGAGEMENT OF ANNA and the episodic structure of THE GREAT LOVE SONGS. The rough edges of the latter film have been smoothed, leaving the framework, to which is then applied the velvet of ANNA. The result is likely the answer to the style questions asked in the first two films, and probably points the direction of Voulgaris' future work.

The tone of the film is one of suspension. We don't know why the prisoners have been incarcerated. We don't know who they are, or where they are. The island itself is geographically disassociated from the rest of the world. We don't know who the authoritarian visitors are who inspire the happy day. We don't know why the prisoner refuses to confess, or even what he is expected to confess. We are given nothing but the mood. Other ingredients add to this sense of timelessness and placelessness. One long tracking shot floats ever so slowly across the camp at night, as though hovering over a microcosmic world. The priest, when choreographing a dance for the theatrical, doesn't so much dance as move haltingly, countering the musical rhythms as he moves. The music itself occasionally utilizes a chant effect, adding a kind of religious mysticism to the atmosphere.

Considering Voulgaris' clearly stated ability to embrace, he would seem to be the logical and likely Greek director to investigate sexuality, a subject to which the new Greek cinema has not seriously addressed itself. Voulgaris, too, seems to avoid the subject. In THE ENGAGEMENT OF ANNA, Anna, in her innocence, is accused of physicality with

the gentleman caller. One of the guardians of her virtue
then tries to seduce her with a kind of leering lewdness that
often is seeded in repression or distorted morality. We do
not know if Anna and her gentleman caller are sexually attracted to each other, but if they are, it remains unrequited
and is dealt with no further.

Sexual leerings again occur in THE GREAT LOVE
SONGS, but are treated humorously. We may presume that
sex will be a tool used for the expression of the romantic
love envisioned in the last scene, but the atmosphere is so
spiritual that it is difficult to extend it into a beautiful but
sweaty sexual reality.

Homosexuality is in casual evidence in HAPPY DAY.
A prisoner sells his body for creature comforts, and the
priest is apparently having an affair with a poetry-reading
companion. Again, sexual references are just that, and do
not get explored.

The last scene of HAPPY DAY is highly erotic, despite its presumed philosophical meaning. A prisoner is
found tied to a post in the water, having been drowned. Another prisoner gets into the water with the corpse, tenderly
washes the salt from the dead man's face, then lengthily
kisses him on the mouth. He is clearly picking up the gaunt-
let of resistance thrown down by the prisoner's death. But
the kiss is so sensual that it is impossible not to consider
sexual love of male for male. Finding a parallel statement
in Voulgaris' earlier films, however, it seems more an extension of his love for the past, and sadness at seeing it die,
i. e., the tradition of the family (despite its internal flaws)
in THE ENGAGEMENT OF ANNA, and especially the beauty
and sadness of the shots of the old buildings being demolished
in THE GREAT LOVE SONGS. This is interpreting out of
context of the story of HAPPY DAY, but then there is no
clear-cut story in the film, and its vagueness strengthens the
theory that Voulgaris continues his preoccupation with love
(be it ever so pure), even in the degradation of a prison
camp.

It is not so much the sexuality in HAPPY DAY that
continues the thread of Voulgaris' love theme as it is the
sensuality. The island itself, the tasteful beauty with which
nudity is handled, the obvious joy the guards find in physical
movement (the volley ball game), the admiration for the commitment to principle expressed by the prisoner who is ulti-

Top, Voulgaris during filming of last scene of HAPPY DAY. Below, Stathis Yalelis and Stavros Kalaroglou in that last scene.

mately killed because of it; the innocent pleasure the prisoners take in preparing and performing their musical theatrical, the relish with which they wear their fanciful costumes on the "happy day"--and more--combine to visualize a love for life which transcends the demandingly dynamic anguish it may present.

I was told a strange story: an official during the junta ordered a raid on a bazouki, during which a customer killed a policeman and was sentenced to life imprisonment. Following the overthrow of the junta, the officer was imprisoned in the same prison as the condemned killer. They have since become lovers.

Voulgaris captures an expression of this "let bygones be bygones" attitude (which may be a reflection of a sense of timelessness) in his handling of the "villains. " When the unidentified "queen" comes to visit the prison camp (the occasion of the happy day) she behaves as a wise and kindly mother, even though officially she is responsible for their imprisonment. They respond accordingly, and happily present to her an entertainment on which they have willingly and pleasurably spent time and energy. The prison official who has the prisoner killed is saddened by his obligation. The priest who obsequiously attends the queen, and hurries to prevent the flag from touching the ground, reads poetry and serves as a warm father figure to the prisoners.

From a career point of view, Voulgaris' timing is dreadful. At a time of social and political chaos, he makes an exquisite valentine. Later, when the audience wants a grim vendetta, he gives them a psalm to life.

Fortunately the medium of film allows for another set of relatives to be applied to it. Thus HAPPY DAY should get another chance when the social climate may be more receptive to it. It is a quite remarkable film which asks not to be cerebrally understood, but simply embraced.

Like an unfulfilled love affair, it lingers in memory, evoking imagined possibilities. It projects a yielding quality, but having accepted its invitation, one finds that it gives only if you meet its terms. Thus, to obtain its rewards, you become the yielder, not it. This inspires a feeling of competition, and it then is a question of whether one is willing to be "taken" by the film. This can produce resistance. Beyond this comes the final mutual intercourse with the film.

Viewers drop out at various shading points of this chain of reactions and realizations, which likely explains the gamut of opinions and conclusions reached about the film.

Based on the variety of critical and audience responses, HAPPY DAY is the least understood film made thus far in the 1970s. Voulgaris' films are so evocative that to attempt to explain them proves irresistible. But his vision and message refute categories, remind one of the ineptitude of words. Here is wonder and delight at life in itself and in self.

* * * * *

1977 UPDATE: HAPPY DAY had a successful run in Greece, despite the variety of receptivity to it, though it failed to pass the curious selection criteria at Cannes. Voulgaris is currently working on a future-film script, but is not actually in planning stages. He has directed a stage revue since HAPPY DAY, and in September was in the northern part of Greece filming for television.

BIOGRAPHICAL BRIEF

Born Athens, 1940. Studied at Stavrakou Film School in Athens. Worked as assistant director in commercial cinema. Political prisoner during junta for having filmed student uprising of November 1973 at Polytechnic. Strong potential for international recognition. Married. Lives in Athens. Awards from the Thessaloniki Festival: 1966, Best Short Film, JIMMY THE TIGER; 1972, Best Film, Best First Feature Director, THE ENGAGEMENT OF ANNA; 1976, Best Film, Best Director, HAPPY DAY; THE ENGAGEMENT OF ANNA, FIPRESCI Award, Otto Dibelius Award, OCIC Award, Berlin Festival, 1974. Interview: "Pandelis Voulgaris and Happy Day" by Willard Manus, The Athenian, November 1976; "Pandelis Voulgaris--Out-of-Synch Filmmaker" by Mel Schuster, Coffeehouse #9, 1979.

FILMS

THE THIEF (1965). (18 minutes).

JIMMY THE TIGER (1966). (15 minutes).

DANCE OF THE GOATS (1971). (22 minutes).

THE ENGAGEMENT OF ANNA (1972). (Co-Script, Director).

THE GREAT LOVE SONGS (1973). (Screenplay, Director).

HAPPY DAY (1976). (Screenplay, Director).

Voulgaris also appeared briefly as actor in KIERION, directed by D. Theos.

JIMMY THE TIGER, Voulgaris' 1966 award-winning short.

Chapter 12

GROWING PAINS FOR THE NEW WAVE:
1975-1977

    The films produced during the life of the new wave
were highly personal films; each, though quite Greek in atmosphere, told a story that could be understood and experienced outside national boundaries; each stayed properly within
modest budgets and intent, giving them a fulfilled, finished
distinction. The primary involvement was political; the movement was essentially a united front of filmmakers using their
medium to speak against the oppressive socio-political conditions. With the collapse of the junta, the reasons for this
cinematic fraternity became less compelling, and the unity
of the movement dissolved. There was no ritualizing of the
disbanding of a group, for there was never a formal group--
only a grouping of individuals who made new contact with their
individuality when the cohesive effects of a commonly felt external force ceased to exist.

    For many of the Greek filmmakers (and for most oth-
ers in Greece, for that matter), the end of the junta was a
time of triumph and a time of trauma. Young adults who had
never known (or had forgotten) the right to choose, had now
to grapple with the responsibility of freedom; they had the
"luxury" of selecting personal relevances. This doesn't mean
there was suddenly a total abandonment of censorship, but the
new government was eager to disalign itself from any taint of
junta and a much greater freedom of speech became the norm,
including a permissive attitude toward voices from the political left. The far-right junta had actually created a moderate
middle road among the conservative population, which still
thought of itself as right but was now only too well aware of
where extremism could lead. This tolerance was evident at
the 1975 festival where a bombardment of rational- to propa-
ganda-left films reeled freely, even capturing the bulk of
awards.

    This new-found freedom and responsibility so severely

altered the direction and informal structure of the new wave that it literally ceased to exist. The "group" disintegrated, the individuals released to travel separate, elected roads. The explosion of political films in 1975 was a potent and necessary post-junta evocation, and created the illusion that the new wave was still a functioning organism. Instead, the dam was bursting, in a somewhat ecstatic death scene for the cinematic group movement.

The collapse of the junta resulted in at least two more important changes in the Greek cinema scene: there was less money available to the filmmakers, as people moved back into a more self-based lifestyle; many directors living out of the country during the junta returned to Greece to vie for what little money there was, and also brought back with them new views and new ideas. The pressures of the junta were so demanding that the subject matter and conclusions drawn in that period were of a highly insulated nature. One of the problems confronting the filmmakers now was a rediscovery of their position as Greeks in relation to the world. Having been cut off from the world for several years, they were faced with ripping off the junta prophylactic which had discouraged self-evaluation, in order to find a broader scope of consciousness.

Perhaps this new and somewhat "unreal" world was responsible for the frequency of stage theatrics in post-junta films. THE TRAVELLING PLAYERS is the most obvious example, in that the characters in the film are actors, performers, role-players, whose "real" identities even are borrowed from a theatrical source. The major occasion in HAPPY DAY is a theatrical presentation; stage entertainment is used in Manoussakis' POWER as an appeasement for the masses, and also as a stimulant for a mass rebellion. THE COLORS OF IRIS overtly investigates a real-versus-unreal spectrum, and ALDEVARAN (Thomopoulos) is heavily laced with theatrical performances (though in nightclubs and coffee shops). Creators obviously are prone to make statements about their own involvements and there have always been backstage movies, but given the atmosphere in which these films were conceived, the "theatricality" takes on the shadings of a new, unreal, play-acting meaning as related to life itself.

Released from the pressure to make political statements, the filmmakers have floundered a bit. The junta lasted seven years, during which time the thought processes of these artists were honed by their experiences within an overtly political framework; their conclusions, no matter how valid, were necessarily narrowly focused. Let free to tackle an unlimited universe of ideas, it was not an easy task to become students again--students of new thoughts and possibilities--after having been producing adults. The practical demands that they do so, however, could not be ignored. Greek cinemagoers no longer supported the costs of filmmaking and the rest of the world was not particularly interested in a narrow-visioned message.

In actuality, some of the new wave filmmakers had begun to cope with this situation even before it was thrust on them. After having garnered prizes and attention for a first film, they found their second films barnacled with new problems. Finding money became an even more consuming undertaking. Lack of technical proficiency was less easily disguised, since the enthusiasm and passion which sustained the first film was not so easily re-created, and the result was sequences (or whole films) which were thought through rather than lived through. The general impression is that films emerged too quickly from time of conception through execution, despite the length of time devoted to obtaining financing. (Perhaps the time and energy required to locate financing detracted from that available for the creative ingredients.) The ideas and concepts they intended to convey were simply not yet ingested; instead of producing health or muscle or growth, the intake had produced flab, sallowness and constipation.

A lifetime of involvement and conclusions was built into the compositions of the first films. Generally speaking, to some degree or other, the second films have been less personal, more oriented to an idea or external situation to which the filmmakers have attached themselves rather than one they have taken into themselves. It is this failure to internalize the subject before speaking on it which has contributed greatly to the retardation of Greek film maturity. There certainly are exceptions: Voulgaris' THE GREAT LOVE SONGS, despite his personal experimentation with form, is a product of integrated thought, feeling and response to the songs which inspired the film. Manoussakis' POWER may be viewed as an extension to his first film; instead of striking out into a new direction he restated his former, somewhat youthful film, with a forceful and developed maturity. If Angelopoulos' DAYS OF '36 seems less successful on its isolated terms, it obviously serves as useful learning tool lead-

ing to his subsequent evolved and successful films. Angelopoulos, having been a film critic and a committed student of
cinema, was not unknowing about developments elsewhere.
He was soundly accused of imitating Miklos Jancso in this
second film. Angelopoulos proved in his third film that he
knew the difference between imitation and absorption.

There are other, more practical reasons for the second film failures. A dearth of film educational facilities ill-
prepared the Greek filmmaker for large and speedy output.
George Panousopoulos points out, with discouragement, that
filmmakers spend what little money there is on big films
which double as finished product and learning tool. He maintains that they could better secure their futures by investing
in 8mm production simply to learn what they want, what they
don't want, and how to get what they want.

Solving the educational problem is only the first step;
the benefits of experience are more difficult to come by.
After a successful first film, and a tasting of a kind of fame
(be it ever so local), they were eager to follow through.
And, of course, there was the very real desire to get on
with their art. The financial problem is probably responsible
for the existence of a film form rarely seen elsewhere.
"Collage"* films are obviously relatively inexpensive, and
they are highly suited to dubbing should they find their way
to another country. They have been a second-film solution
for Thanassis Rentzis, Costas Aristopoulos, and Costas
Sfikas.

Educational and financial problems aside, the real
problem with the second film is an "objective" viewpoint.
The close-knit nature of Athens living, coupled with the
lengthy junta repression, has resulted in limited experience
with objectivity. Having taken a summation stand with a
first film, a more "objective" film was a temptation that has
proven irresistible. The result, too frequently, is sopho-
moric, underdeveloped, or pretentious. It is usually a case
of self-segmentation, as though the subject were viewed with
only one eye. The subject may be explored and studied in a
creative way, but the conclusions reached lack the integrated
commitment which throbs through the first films.

_____
*"Collage" films are a series of still photographs, advertise-
ments, newspaper and magazine clippings, or what have you,
that when assembled, photographed, narrated, and musically
scored if desired, become a motion picture.

Literary Content of the Post-Junta Films

The first major showcase for Greek films made after the junta was the 1975 Thessaloniki Festival, a literal arsenal of political films. Despite the understandable motivations and empathetically pitched passions, in the cool of distance many of these films settle into self-indulgence, immaturity, and an irresponsible cry of victimization. These conclusions may be most aptly applied to the barrage of short films made that year, and the further variable of youth may also be tapped to soften the criticism. The "old masters" were seasoned by this time, and despite their equally intensive positions, most of them were beyond this kind of adolescent bravado.

Angelopoulos unreeled his THE TRAVELLING PLAYERS that year, and with its success in traveling around the world, the concept of going beyond the Greek audience was seeded. Not only was there some competitive envy of the film's success, there was also the very realistic recognition by other filmmakers that they too must travel a similar path if they hoped for development of their own careers, or, more altruistically, for the survival of Greek cinema.

THE TRAVELLING PLAYERS is certainly political, but the historical distance, as well as the filmmaker's less emotional style, removed it from the pitfalls that entrapped many of his colleagues. The junta cannot be solely credited (or blamed) for the obsession with politics. Repeatedly one hears the statement: "Everything is political." Be that as it may, it is equally pertinent to say that everything is sexual, or everything is personal discovery, or everything is economic, etc. That the Greek filmmakers select "political" as their point of reference has much to do with the small size of Greece, where political gyrations, of which there have been a multitude in Greek history--even modern Greek history --have an immediate and intimate effect on the individual. It is probably impossible to take an ostrich position, as one easily can in a larger, non-communist country like the United States. Furthermore, the everything-is-political attitude is an euphemism for finding one's position on a pro- or anti-authority scale. The least political of the filmmakers are less inclined to resist authority, simply because they are privately more anarchistic and therefore less subject to the dictates of authority. They have found a way to make their films in their own ways, about the subjects that are of primary concern to them, without being unduly influenced by current socio-political dynamics. Such filmmakers as Voulgaris, Panayotopoulos, Aristopoulos and Thomopoulos went against the trend to make their very personal films, but even some of them "buckled under" when their heroic efforts met with popular apathy despite the quality of the finished product.

The everything-is-political attitude takes its toll on the filmmakers in other ways which can become crucial to an existing career or a future one. Should an outsider come to Greece to learn, to obtain films for showing (or buying), or even with a desire to hire film personnel, the "authoritarian" contacts, in whatever areas, use their power and prejudices to guide the outsider to his/her personal choices. It thus behooves the filmmakers to genuflect, or at the very least remain amicable with those who are currently useful connections. This is an unhappy game-playing necessity from which very few of the filmmakers find an escape. Voulgaris is universally liked (even loved), so he is somewhat aloof from these incestuous maneuverings. Panayotopoulos is a loner and is often "punished" for it. Theos is pronouncedly independent and reaps enemies who either don't like his independence or dislike being reminded of their own dependency. Even the far-left filmmakers who disclaim personal ambition which might remove them from the power struggle have to accept a more limited audience exposure as well as meet the approval of fellow comrades. This on-going acceptance of "using" and "being used" is heavily responsible for the loss or potential loss of many of the artists (not just filmmakers) from Greece who find the "role" of filmmaker a deterrent to, or even destroyer of, the act of making films.

Discovering "Greekness"

Following the 1975 orgy of political films, and with the junta beginning to ease into history, the subject of "Greekness" has come to replace the junta as an insulating symbol. Off the record, filmmakers frequently criticize other directors for not using their talents to state "Greekness."

Even a casual dip into Greek history since the Roman invasion quickly explains this reaction. Greece became an independent nation only 150 years ago, and since then has survived numerous wars, external political manipulation, and internal power struggles, all of which have taken time and attention from the question of national definition. Still, there has existed a stubborn retention of custom, culture, and language, even though the Greek roots being preserved may actually be imbedded in foreign soil. The time seems ripe for such self-examination, and there is great concern that the "Greek reality" (whatever it is or turns out to be) is being presented with whipped cream distortion.

There is a backlash of hostility toward the "musical comedy" treatment of Greek folklore. Michael Cacoyannis' ZORBA THE GREEK and Jules Dassin's NEVER ON SUNDAY are the most successful (and therefore the most "shameful") examples. This criticism may not be as legitimately motivated as it sounds; the Greeks are far from shy about delivering critical opinions. Anyone or anything enjoying success is considered fair game in open season. In some defense of the Cacoyannis and Dassin films, it should be pointed out that the Greeks are not guiltless in the matter of converting folk art into commercial expressions, even for internal consumption. The shrieking electronic bouzouki, in comparison to its origin, is a disastrous corruption. By comparison, ZORBA THE GREEK appears as authentic as a detached documentary. Even the much-loved popular music of Mikis Theodorakis, Manos Hatzidakis, and Stavros Xarhakos is musically rooted in a past folk art, but the essence is an expression of another time, another musical treatment. They have refined rembetika, making it highly palatable, granted, but it is really a tasteful, musical comedy treatment of the original. *

The Cannes Film Festival is a frequent setting for the Greek musical comedy. Greek dancing, originally an interaction between an internal feeling and an external expression, and thus not extended to an audience, is now performed at parties for finger-snapping, ouzo-drinking viewers. ** Piles of smashed plates add to the forced gaiety, although original reasons (loss of self-containment) for the custom are now distorted into audience-pleasing curiosities. The Greeks themselves sponsor these exhibitions, and, in fact, offer similar thrills at a heady price in Athens nightclubs, having lured

---

*The popularity of rembetika music, brought from Turkey in the 1920s, has inspired musicologists to great lengths of research to link the music to Byzantine Greece. Though that may actually be the case, the drama of the situation is the seeming compulsion to make it of Greek derivation.
**Sometimes performed by "Zorba the Greek" himself--actor Anthony Quinn, who happens to be Mexican!

the tourist to Greece with musical comedy TV commercials.
Ghastly reproductions of exquisite art pieces clutter the tourist shops, which not only insult both buyer and seller but
also diminish appreciation of the originals.

An interesting extension of this is that artists of the
1950s (especially the composers) are now considered the lost
Greek culture, time having conveniently erased the part they
played in altering the Greek culture that came before them.
Voulgaris, in particular, mentions the music of Hatzidakis
when speaking of lost tradition. He is hardly alone in his
concern for defining "Greekness." Dimosthenis Theos
searches for a pure Greek model on which to base film language; Angelopoulos admits the continuing importance of
Greece in his creativity; Psarras is completely insulated na-
tionally in his subject interests; Ioannis Lintzaris' work thus
far is exclusively dominated by a surface content of Greek
rural-to-urban migration; Maranghos is openly critical of the
commercial cinema for not having been Greek; and even
Panayotopoulos is called upon to state that every product
coming from Greece is Greek, a fact that apparently has to
be verbalized in identity-conscious Greece. A quite intelli-
gent woman at a screening one night defined Greekness thus:
"The West thinks we are East. The East thinks we are
West. But, of course, we are neither. We are Greek."

Cinematographer George Panousopoulos seems the
most clearly attuned to this subject. "I want to know myself. And if I am Greek, then I have to know what that is."
Since the 1930s, political circumstances have encouraged the
Greeks to group together for strength and protection. The
necessity to relinquish individual independence in favor of
group alignment has, no doubt, invited a search for self-
definition through external association. Perhaps that is why
everyone seems so concerned about answering "What is
Greek?" rather than "What am I?" It may all lead to the
same answer in the long run; it's just a matter of emphasis.
Costas Sfikas and Thanassis Rentzis, of all the Greek filmmakers, seem the least involved with the question of defining Greek. Sfikas, with many years behind him of feeling
that his artistic desires and possibilities have been stunted
and victimized by livelihood necessities, is concerned about
the damage to him that condition may have caused. Rentzis, concerned with exploration of the language of film,
shows little concern for self-definition through being Greek.
He is a Greek whose primary interest is film, and that is
that.

After a lengthy stay in the United States, filmmaker George Tsemberopoulos makes this summation: "The meaning of being a Greek is something you find when you are not in Greece. You have to take your distance. Being anything, you have to take your distance to get it in its proper dimensions. Only after being here do I find out how much and what kind of a Greek I am. In Greece, we take the definition for granted. You mentioned that though the Greek filmmaker wants to hit the international public, he takes no real notice of it. The Europeans know something about Greece, but here in the United States no one knows anything about the Greeks, except that they run the luncheonettes. So I am very alienated here. No one knows my point of reference when I talk. By wanting to explain, by wanting to communicate on this basis, I check myself out. And this can only be done by being in this alienating environment. Always, in my mind, I am back there. I cannot imagine making a film that has nothing to do with Greece. And it is there I want to work. But I need some time for myself. In Greece, I feel compelled to focus on special things, but here I am less so. I focus, but they don't touch me so strongly, so I am free to be myself. Of course, one can question one's self no matter where. But the alienation I feel in New York causes me to question myself about everything. I don't have points of reference."

It is worth mentioning that the Greek traveler is allowed to take very little money when leaving the country, which clearly inhibits the possibilities of exploring self through alienation. Furthermore, the limited access to the world surely must insulate the Greek filmmakers psychologically from alignment with the current reality of international cinema.

It is understandable and proper that artists explore their known world. In the case of the cinema it is a costly exploration if the end result is of such an intimate nature that only the few who are "in" on the message can find the results of interest. With the overthrow of the junta, Greek filmmakers went wild in their new-found freedom to talk openly to one another, especially about the taboo subject of politics. In the cool light of film history it becomes obvious that films too insulated in their appeal can contribute little to the expansion of an "industry." Films like Nicos Kavoukidis' EVIDENCE and Maranghos et al's STRUGGLE may have many virtues, not the least of which is excellent execution. But it may come as something of a shock to them

to learn that a large part of the world doesn't know that
Greece had a junta, let alone that it was overthrown! The
annual festival is littered with shorts which examine various
internal problems which are of little or no interest to the
outsider. Psarras' film THE REASON WHY, a dandy primer
on how to organize a union, may be of interest in underdeveloped countries, but it would have limited appeal, if any,
in countries where unions have long existed, effected profound
social changes, even manifested their own expressions of corruption and exploitation. Likewise, his MAY would seem to
have limited appeal, aside from its stylized-to-a-fault execution, in that its historical reference is not targeted to an outside audience. Manoussakis' VARTHOLOMEOS is so personal
that the audience is frequently ignored. There are visual
references an outsider--and possibly many insiders--couldn't
hope to grasp. Considering that the Greek audience for Greek
films is a threatened species, Greek filmmakers simply must
learn to see beyond their Greekness. Or better still, must
absorb their Greekness, which will help to demolish the wall
that keeps them separated from the world film community.

There are a number of intriguing "Greek" subjects
that have not as yet been attended by the '70s Greek cinema.
In THE HEAVY MELON Pavlos Tassios hints at the idea that
all of Greece is becoming a tourist mecca, with no room left
for Greece or the Greeks. Unfortunately his film sidetracks
to a far more routine story and leaves this provocative subject unexplored. Greece is so full of antiquity, for which
there is great respect (and much commercialism), that the
edifices of the past centuries are ignored and left to decay,
or are destroyed and replaced with ugly, repetitious modern-
ity. Voulgaris is particularly concerned with this destruction
and a film from him about it would have great potential.

Manoussakis' POWER investigates competitiveness,
power-seeking, and corruption--but on a grand scale. It
would be interesting to see an exploration of this subject as
it applies to a day-to-day existence. Frequently the Athen-
ians behave as though who enters a bus first were a life-or-
death situation; queues are unknown; to resolve a simple business transaction is to take on a battle of no small proportions. This kind of filtering down of power-orientation to
daily life is as yet unfilmed. (This may not be an exclusive "Greek" characteristic, but it is unquestionably pertinent.)

The Greek manifestation of such subjects as parental

authority, attitudes toward marriage, the educational system
(embracing its extreme competitiveness in Greece), repressive sexual mores, socio-political manipulation (that is,
"use" and "get used"), and many more, has only rarely been
tested in film. The world cannot turn to Greek films of the
1970s to discover any exploration of the family ties which,
to some outsiders, may seem constrictive and stunting. No
explanation exists for what appears to be gross indulgence of
the Greek child. Sexual mores remain in cinematic darkness,
including any detailed references to the suspiciously homosexual camaraderie between males who "love their buddies
and fuck their girls. " This descriptive vulgarity is used even
by those who claim a knowledge of the difference between the
selected word and "make love with. " The "quick-change" aspect of the Greek character goes unexplained on film. The
hate-you-today-love-you-tomorrow expression of this quality
is a mystery unsolved by film. The role of the Greek woman
has not been cinematically explored. The socially obligatory
marriage (with the still-existing dowry problems) is ripe for
film treatment.

It is not for lack of subject matter that the 70s Greek
film output has flirted with political monotony. Even within
the political framework, one could welcome a film concerned
with victimization by a powerful outsider (currently the United
States) if it were handled in a constructive way rather than
in the cry-baby manner of those that have touched on it.

No one has questioned cinematically how a country
which tenaciously survived for centuries as a conquered people, capped by a majestic and victorious struggle for independence, can then produce two dictatorships within a half-
century. There is sad irony in overthrowing foreign oppression and replacing it with a native one.

The Future of Greek Cinema

George Arvanitis on the future of Greek cinema:
"Black! There is no money for financing. The existing
producers do not look for an outside market. The producers
of the commercial cinema made films for the Greek market,
and every year the films were exactly like those of preced-
ing years. The producers made much money; some spent it
on big homes, some lost their money. But the level of the
cinema stayed the same. In fact, it stayed at the level
where television is now. If you see Greek television now,

you will know what was the level of Greek cinema before it
collapsed. Now it is a problem of scripts. We must find
scripts that reach out to a foreign market. We must make
films that show less folklore and more the Greek reality.
Many of the problems we experience are problems that exist
everywhere, so there is no reason not to make films which
can be shown outside Greece. "

Any prediction about where the Greek cinema goes
from here is obviously speculative and personal. Most members of the new wave will continue making films when possible, for they are truly committed to the medium. Angelopoulos alone has found his way to European recognition (he
is still comparatively unknown in the United States). Voulgaris will undoubtedly break the national boundaries in the
not too distant future. Panayotopoulos has the talent if he
can find the strength to go his own way without being unduly
influenced by attitudinal pressures around him. Many other
filmmakers in the ranks have ability and, given time and
development, might quickly follow.

The major problem for the Greek filmmaker is simply
money, but at this juncture it is not just a question of financing (an overwhelming problem in itself) but one of monetary
returns which can be reinvested. It is imperative that the
filmmakers replace the emphasis of their concern; financing
is not inexhaustible. It is not enough to have made a film,
even though this is a phenomenal accomplishment in Greece.
They must now think in terms of making a film that will in
turn make money. This is not to advocate artistic prostitution, but it does mean that self-indulgence can no longer be
supported.

To find money the filmmakers now turn to advertising
or television. TV is in its infancy in Greece. There are
two channels, both under the control of the government.
Situation comedies, melodramas and soap operas reign, which
hardly inspires the filmmaker to devote too much time or effort to the medium. On the other hand, were they to commit themselves to raising the standards of the medium with
the same ferocity they brought to their films, startling results might soon be seen on television.

Television and cinema can obviously be rewardingly
compatible. Given less snobbery on the part of the filmmakers and a greater sense of quality within the television
organizations, there could be a mutual exchange of talent and

outlet, not to mention the rewards of using TV as a medium
for re-educating the Greek audience to Greek film. The
state-owned TV is not eager to serve as medium for the
cinema's politically subversive message, but as the films
turn their attention to other topics, it is intriguing to imagine
the possibilities of a TV responsive to Greek films. A TV
rescreening of the annual festival, giving all of Greece a
chance to attend the festival, is a fascinating idea. A retrospective series based on the "best film" festival winners
would not only be a pleasant nostalgia trip for a formerly
active Greek cinema audience, but a chance to contemplate
and/or discover the changes that have occurred. Spotlighting
a director or a performer for a film series could be, as
always, a rewarding experience.

TV is ideally suited to documentary film. Assuming
the filmmaker is given freedom to create within the scope of
acceptable compromise between the two interests, it seems
that TV-commissioned documentaries could siphon this less
internationally-saleable form from the cinema scene, giving
it a useful and lucrative outlet, and possibly also giving the-
ater-targeted film a "mainstream" image.

Whatever the success and direction of the mating of
film and TV in Greece, it appears that it must come, and
it may as well be attended with respect and dignity. A
modest study of American TV history should reveal the pitfalls of a war between the media, and the rewards of peace
and cooperation. In fact, it is now frequently impossible
here to establish the parent of a product. Films made for
television are released to theaters; films made for theaters
get initial screening on television. The media quite literally
often meld indistinguishably.

New directors have joined the basic ranks--either
from the streets of Greece or returning from studies abroad.
(Some of them are acknowledged in the "Who's Who" section
which follows.) They bring new ideas, new talents, and new
competition into the scene, making the structure more complex in ways both positive and negative. With the strength
that could be found in their growing numbers there may be
a possibility of the filmmakers themselves giving some attention to internal distribution. Perhaps a theater in Athens
can be found which will feature Greek films. Assuming they
were sub-titled, it is not inconceivable that such films could
attract the massive tourist influx which looks for local color
to enjoy and experience. The Greek audience, formerly

highly supportive of Greek films, might be courted into the theaters again, given the opportunity.

The most crucial need, however, in order to solve their financial problems, is to make films which can be exported. An external success can often result in the local community discovering what it has in its own backyard. There is some indication that the filmmakers are at long last giving this matter serious thought. In 1977 one emerging trend was to search for money outside Greece, and to use international actors--all on the theory that it is just as easy to find $50,000, assuming the possibility of a return on the money, as to find $10,000 in Greece, where the money can be written off as a contribution to the cause. This truly represents a broadening of attitude which is a small ray of hope within an otherwise gloomy atmosphere.

Greek history is a demonstration of the tenaciousness of its people. Greek cinema, too, will hang on despite the overwhelming odds.

Chapter 13

A SELECTED FILMMAKERS WHO'S WHO

Despite the negligible after-the-fact rewards for making film, it remains a competitively sought-after expression in Greece. A large percentage of people working in film, regardless of capacity, voice a future desire to make film. The Who's Who which follows is representative of the filmmakers who have been successful in this quest.

Some of these filmmakers actually predate the independent movement of the first half of the 1970s, having started their careers during the commercial cinema. Others were out of the country working or studying during the major thrust of the new wave. Returning to Greece, they have integrated into the mileau, contributing to it and, in most cases, advancing it. Others are included because they have retained their Greek affinity, despite the fact that they are currently working outside of Greece.

FERRIS, COSTAS

Costas Ferris was born in Cairo, Egypt, in 1935, of Greek parents. He has been involved with film since 1958, during which time he has worked on more than 80 films, both Greek and foreign. He has assisted the work of such notable directors as Nicos Koundouros, Michael Cacoyannis, Jean Daniel Pollet, Richard Sarafian, James Neilson and Andrew Marton. He directed his first short film in 1961. He lived in Paris during the junta and there co-scripted (with Pollet) the film BLOOD, wrote the book and lyrics for "666, " a rock opera, and directed and co-authored "Birds Opera, " which was staged at the Lyon Opera House in 1971. He also wrote the libretto for Stavros Logaridis' ballet, "Akritas. " Prior to leaving Greece he directed the 1965 feature, SOME GIRLS LIKE IT WITH SOLDIERS.

COSTAS FERRIS.

Following the downfall of the junta, he returned to
Greece, and since then has directed two feature films as
well as two serials for television. His first feature of the
post-junta period was THE MURDERESS (1974), based on an
astounding story by Alexandres Papadiamantis about an aging
woman, so demoralized by her role as female slave in a
male-dominant society that she begins to murder female in-
fants to save them from the bitter life she has experienced.
Tinged with religious mysticism, the end result is part grand
tragedy, part gothic horror. The mood of the story has a
delicate equilibrium, and to transfer it successfully to the
screen demands not just technical proficiency, but a feeling
for the inherent complexity of the original. Ferris has a
goodly degree of the former, but falls considerably short on
the latter. He is further plagued by a broad performance by
Maria Alkeou in the title role. The role is innately grand
and dramatic, calling either for underplaying or a thorough
grounding in cinematic acting. Ms. Alkeou is stage-bound
throughout the film and the end result of her performance,
so crucial to the whole, is one of over-statement, for which
she can be held only partially accountable. It was a dream

Maria Alkeou, star of Costas Ferris' THE MURDERESS.

of the marvelous Katina Paxinou to film this story, and it is tempting to imagine what she might have done with it. Mr. Ferris is so irresistibly enamored of the pyrotechnics of his craft that he repeatedly steps away from the straightforward potency of the story to show what he can do. On the plus side is Stavros Hasapis' photography, despite the story's artistic begging for black and white, rather than color. This is a chilling horror story emerging from a routine atmosphere, somewhat comparable in mood to Shirley Jackson's THE LOT-TERY. It would be interesting to see what Alfred Hitchcock, Orson Welles or Michael Cacoyannis might do with this story.

Ferris' second Greek film in the 1970s might be called pretentious were it not so unintentionally funny. PROME-THEUS SECOND PERSON SINGULAR is an outrage of direc-torial stunts, and confirms the eagerness to display his tech-nical vocabulary which was hinted at in THE MURDERESS. The film may be most kindly described as "artsy": a chorus of dancers, in what appear to be bird masks, flap endlessly, repetitively and unimaginatively between sexually caressive shots of a young man lashed to a western wagon wheel perched precariously on a mountain top. Meanwhile an in-compatible and unnecessarily loud rock score crashes away in the background, further contorting the amateur gyrations of the ill-trained dancers. Sensual but repetitive camera-work (again by Stavros Hasapis) adds a slick sheen, partly disguising the egotistic shallowness of the whole.

Ferris has now made amply clear that he is an ac-complished technician. It is still a question whether or not he can convert his craft into art. There are those who dis-agree with this evaluation and Ferris has a few trophies to prove it. THE MURDERESS won the best director award at the 1974 Thessaloniki Festival, as well as a best actress award for Maria Alkeou. PROMETHEUS SECOND PERSON SINGULAR garnered a Best Music award for Stamatis Span-oudakis at both the 1975 Thessaloniki Festival and the 1976 Cairo Festival.

KOLLATOS, DIMITRIS

Dimitris Kollatos was born in Athens in 1940. His father was killed during the December 1944 civil war; his mother was supportive of his artistic aspirations, manifesting

DIMITRIS KOLLATOS, with arm outstretched.

her support by financing his first book and film. In 1956 he
published a collection of poems and a year later formed The
Pocket Theater, where he directed and acted in plays by
Ionesco, Beckett and Pinter, whose plays had until then not
been performed for Greek audiences. His non-film activities
have continued: he owns a theatre in Paris which serves as
outlet for his own plays ("The Last Emperor," "A Love
Story under Fifth Democracy," "A Greek Today"--a musical
revue). He has lived in Paris since 1971, but maintains an
affinity with his home country.

FILMS

ATHENS XYZ (1962). (11 minutes). A French tourish looks
    with critical, satirical, and admiring interest at con-
    temporary Greece. Won Best Short award at 1962
    Thessaloniki Festival.

THE OLIVE TREES (I ELIES) (1964). (24 minutes). Won
    Best Short at 1964 Thessaloniki Festival.

ALEXANDER'S DEATH (O THANATOS TOU ALEXANDROU)

(1966). (85 minutes). Script by Kollatos and Aristides
Carydis Fuchs. Edited by Renee Lichting. Music by
Yannis Markopoulos. With Dimitris Kollatos, Arlette
Bauman, Dora Volanaki, Costas Carayorgis, Nelli
Riga, Haroula Angelousi, Menia Papadopoulou, George
Salpigidis, Panos Vasiliadis. Produced by Lia Kario-
tou & Kollatos. Reviewed by Cinématographe, Feb/
Mar. 1974; Revue du Cinéma, Oct. 1974; Cinéma 74,
Jan. 1974, all in French.

SYMPOSIUM (1971). Script by Kollatos, based on his short
story. Photography: Michel Kelber. Edited by
Madeleine Gug. Music: Yannos Spanos. With Kollatos, Arlette Bauman. Filmed in Paris.

LE BANQUET (1975). See Revue du Cinéma, Oct. 1975 for
review (in French).

LINTZERIS, IOANNIS

The universal concern with the question of how much
the individual is manipulated by his environment, or how
much freedom of choice he has within it, is particularly dynamic in Greek films. The dimensions of this question get
explored repeatedly, from a social position, from a political
position, and THE COLORS OF IRIS even touches on it as a
philosophical question isolated from a relative framework.
In practically every answer to this questioning, the responsibility for behavior is skewed toward environmental control.
Yet, to meet these filmmakers is to belie their message.
They have emerged through a thankless maze of negative circumstances to practice their art, and have done so solely
(in the final analysis) on the strength of their own personal
belief in themselves, even if their conclusion is one of self-
denial. The emphasis of their message is on the external
difficulties they have faced, rather than the remarkable ingenuity they have exercised in wading through or overcoming
those difficulties.

The excessive debilitating pressures that have been
exerted upon these artists throughout most of their lives is
not to be de-emphasized. Obviously victimization exists, but
to examine one's alternatives--to make a choice--to accept
self-responsibility--is an approach to the question which has

IOANNIS LINTZERIS.

rarely been explored in Greek films. Melina Mercouri
touches on this in her autobiography. Despite her passionate
anger at Greece's position of victimization, she is able to
say, "... In the final analysis, who is more guilty, the ex-
ploiter or the exploited? Those who rule by terror, or those
who are intimidated?"* This kind of objectivity, even if
short-lived, is rare indeed in Greek cinema.

Ioannis Lintzeris' film EXODUS garnered small attention at the 1976 festival. The original story by the filmmaker and his sister is about a young man returning to his
village following his servitude in the army. The period of
adjustment the film subsequently examines reveals his growing awareness that he cannot simply pick up his life again.
The "old way" is dead to him. Despite the pain his departure
may bring to his parents who want and need him, he leaves
the village to make a new life, having used a romantic in-

---

*Mercouri, Melina. I Was Born Greek. New York: Dell
Publishing Co., 1973, p. 286.

Simeon Triantafillidis and Antigone Athanasiou in EXODUS.

volvement with a widow as pretext for his escape. The romance has been socially rejected, and he, feigning romantic dejection, departs.

Lintzeris' story is rather youthfully overstated, as though he is afraid his audience will not perceive its intent. On the surface, it appears a modest beginning and provides few clues as to the potential of its maker. It does have effective mood, an obvious concern for the characters, and there is no question that Lintzeris is serious about making film; that is, he is not merely using film as an ego outlet, as many first efforts do.

The importance of EXODUS is a "second-level" message which threads its way throughout the film and which, within the context of the 1970s Greek cinema, is very nearly unique. Though it says little about Lintzeris as developed filmmaker, it hints at a new direction, a new message, which may be filtering into Greek consciousness.

Thodoros Angelopoulos' success has inspired considerable imitation (whether conscious or not) in Greek cinema. After four films, his message continues to be that the individual is subservient to "something bigger, " be it system, dogma, or history. His characters are rarely seen in closeup; they are always somewhat insignificant compared to their environments. The emphasis is upon the lack of individual choice.

Lintzeris' EXODUS is the first film overtly dealing with this question which reaches another position, despite the subliminal pronouncement of the conclusion.* Rarely do we see the characters within the framework of their environment, the literary content to the contrary. They talk a lot about the conflicts they feel imposed by their environment, but these are not shown. Visually, Lintzeris' "emphasis on individual" message is telegraphed repeatedly. Constantly he works in closeups. The young lovers of his story are both extremely physically attractive, in itself a detraction from the surroundings. The son helps the father in the fields,

---

*A major exception to this statement is Thomopoulos' ALDE-VARAN, but Thomopoulos spent several years living in England, inevitably absorbing different viewpoints. Lintzeris' film is the first indication of this concept from a "home-grown" base.

Simeon Triantafillidis in EXODUS.

but is not overcome by the size of the field, nor the hard work, nor the heat, nor any other environmental factor. What one remembers, instead, are the flecks of grain that cling to his sweating chest. He is the focal point, and the environment clings to him and accents his worth.

Lintzeris did not accept this analysis of his work. His conscious intent was to "... show the individual as a small part of the whole. This individual was taken as a sample of a given social framework, " but then he added: "... he would find a pretext to escape. In this particular case, the pretext was the love affair. " The basic dichotomy within the film, i. e. , the literary context of environment only as framework for the individual, is further verified as Lintzeris explains: "His acquaintance with the widow is the decisive element which obliges him to choose.... " We may indeed be obliged to choose, but the confusion in this film is whether the emphasis is on the obligation or the choice.

Still, for the first time in the 70s Greek cinema there is a hint that some future film content may concentrate on what the individual does with the pressures of the environment rather than what the pressures of the environment do with the individual. Both are legitimate, but the latter position has received very nearly exclusive attention and Lintzeris' EXODUS becomes memorable as an indication that another position may be explored in the future.

Although not literally autobiographical, EXODUS has autobiographical overtones. Lintzeris was born in Mani and lived there until he was 13. "Mani has retained its customs from years ago. The customs are very strict, the society is very closed. I have a cousin, George Manos, who was born in the United States and has become a well-known orchestra conductor. He has been an influence in my life. It was the awareness of him that helped me gain courage to go against the customs of Mani--to make my own small revolution--because it is not very easy to accomplish this. Just knowing that someone from Mani has made a success in the 'outside' world was an aid to my own behavior. "

Altering the course of direction established by one's environment during the formative years is difficult in any circumstance. To tackle the demands presented by the customs of Mani is a mark of the degree to which individual courage and commitment to self can be effectively tapped. Lintzeris' positions were aggressively opinionated, suggesting

a healthy determination to attain his goals and an almost bel-
ligerent pride in their attainment. "I will now expose something I believe to be very strong and immovable, and I have
the arguments to support it. Work is the most important
thing in my development. I believe in something Marx said
--20 per cent of your development is personal talent, and the
rest is a result of work and effort, support of ideas, etc.
From this point of view I express my art and thought."

Lintzeris is a handsome, large-framed man who gives
the impression of consuming space with deliberation, as
though he has earned the right even to it. It is no wonder he
films in close-up--he presents himself in close-up.

His future as filmmaker is unpredictable at this point,
but EXODUS is a hint of something new in Greek filmmaking.
There is little indication that Freud-or-after has taken root
in Greek film. The "thinkers" are philosophical, the "feel-
ers" are sociological. The only films with psychological
emphasis have been made by filmmakers who have spent considerable time out of the country and have brought home
with them another way of thinking. EXODUS may present a
new and fertile ground leading to a home-grown psychological
harvest.

BIOGRAPHICAL BRIEF

Ioannis Lintzeris was born in Mani, 1948. Moved to Athens
at age 13. Passed university examination with intent to study
law, but switched to cinema at last minute because of a love
for photography. Went directly to second-year studies as reward for winning a competition. EXODUS produced with savings from job in advertising, with aid of family. Co-scripted
the film with sister, Veronica. Married, lives in Athens.

FILMS

SILENT CRIES (Short).

EXODUS (1976).

MANIATIS, SAKIS

Born Massini, 1944. Studied filmmaking in Paris and

Scene from MANI.

in Athens. Since 1969 has worked as Director of Photography in films and television. In 1972 began working on his
first film as director. MANI was not completed until 1975.

George Tsemberopoulos on MANI: "Maniatis went to
Mani for several years to make the film. He would run out
of money, come back to Athens, make enough for another
shooting trip. Maniatis' film views Mani from various viewpoints. One is historical--an outline of Mani's history, ac-
centing what people think, as well as what he thinks is important in Mani's history. Greek films do not enjoy the luxury of having money to back up a thorough film investigation.
But Maniatis waited until he had the money to pursue his
subject with depth. He went to Corsica where there is a
Greek community of people from Mani who settled there as
a result of a quarrel between two leading families of Mani.
This happened around 300 years ago, and the descendents of
the Corsican family still live there. Some of them speak

Greek. The people of Mani are quite different, peculiar. It is important to view them outside the environment. How are they in Corsica? How are they in Germany? When they become immigrants, do they retain their customs from Mani? How can you call it a finished film until all conceivable avenues are explored? So why call the film finished until 'there is enough money to finish it? For me, MANI is the first complete example of an ethnological/sociological film made in Greece by a Greek. "

MANI took a Special Prize at the 1975 Thessaloniki Festival. While making MANI, Maniatis shot and co-directed (with Tsemberopoulos) MEGARA in 1974. It took First Prize at the 1974 Thessaloniki Festival, as well as a prize given by the Greek Critics, and the FIPRESCI Prize at the Berlin Festival in 1974. See Chapter 14 for more on MEGARA and Maniatis.

FILMS

As Cinematographer (including films for television):

PARTITA (1969). (Dir: Y. Maris).

MYCONOS (1971). (Dir: M. de Barsy). (For French TV).

BLACK & WHITE (1973). (Dir: T. Rentzis & N. Zervos).

ATTILA '74 (1974). (Dir: M. Cacoyannis).

THE BIRDS (1975). (Dir: M. Couyoumtzis).

SONGS OF FIRE (1975). (Dir: N. Koundouros).

PERSIANS (1975). (Dir: M. Couyoumtzis).

KAROLOS KOUN (1976). (Dir: P. Voulgaris).

ACHARNIANS (1977). (Dir: M. Couyoumtzis).

EASTER (1977). (Dir: P. Voulgaris). (6 films for TV).

FEMMES GRECQUES (1977). (Dir: C. Castagno and C. Djidou). (For French TV).

THE VILLAGE'S PHOTOGRAPHER (1977). (Dir: A. Voyazos). (16 films for TV).

As Director

MEGARA (1974). (Photographed and co-directed).

MANI (1972-1975). (Directed, photographed, produced, edited).

MARKETAKI, TONIA

The most important female filmmaker currently working in Greece. Born in Andravida in 1942, Ms. Marketaki studied film at IDHEC (Institute of Higher Studies in Filmmaking) in Paris. She served her apprenticeship as editor in England for one year, and spent time in Algiers working on educational and agricultural films.

In Greece, she served as production manager for three films, and worked as a film critic from 1964 to 1967. In 1967 she wrote and directed her first short film. Her full-length feature, VIOLENT JOHN, came in 1973 and collected the Best Director, Best Script and Best Actor awards at Thessaloniki. Since then she has worked primarily in television as program advisor and director. In September 1977 she was directing a film for television in collaboration with cinematographer George Panousopoulos.

Unfortunately VIOLENT JOHN was unavailable for viewing during the researching of this book, but it seems to belong with those films which serve as core to the new wave film movement occurring in the early 1970s in Greece. She has announced preparation of a second theatrical film, THE LOST MAN, but it has not yet been realized.

FILMS

JOHN AND THE ROAD (O Yiannis kai o dromos). (Short). (Director, Screenplay, Editor).

VIOLENT JOHN (Ioannis O Viaios) (1973). (Director, Screenplay, Editor).

ALDEVARAN (1975). (Editor).

NIKOLAIDIS, NICOS

Nicos Nikolaidis was born in Athens in 1939. After studies in theater and film he made his first short film in 1962 (LACRIMAE RERUN), followed by UNCONDITIONAL (1968). He works in advertising and has made nearly 100 commercials for television.

He made his initial feature entry in 1976 and won the Best Director·award at Thessaloniki that year. EURIDICE BA-2037 is one of the few Greek films of the '70s which is psychologically rather than sociologically or politically based. A woman waits in her apartment for an order to move. An unidentified group of people threatens to break into her privacy, and there are sounds of gunfire and explosions. The victim panics, and the remainder of the film is an hallucinatory nightmare.

Actually the film has political implications; the internal exploration of the subject was highly unusual among the outburst of political films following the junta. The film is grim and bleak. It would be unfair to accuse it of being influenced by the work of Roman Polanski; still the comparison --especially with Polanski's earlier work--can be drawn. There is throughout a sense of doom, of hopeless movement, as though to struggle is only to become mired deeper in a nightmarish quicksand. Some of the sexual symbolism is so obvious as to be a cliché. This is no doubt due in part to the strict censorship, which disallowed sexual reality, but it also suggests a cocoonish lack of awareness of what the rest of the cinematic world was doing in 1976.

George Panousopoulos' silvery black-&-white photography makes a major contribution, giving the end result a kind of '30s film noir look. If the film is at fault it is in its naiveté rather than in the overall conception or the mechanics of its execution. Nikolaidis shows considerable ability, daring and, given the film's historical reference, a highly individualistic reaction to environment. The whole, however, does not measure up to its best parts.

PAVLIDES, STELIOS

Stelios Pavlides was born in Athens in 1938. He was an actor in the theater before becoming interested in film. He studied at the Film Akademie and Max Reinhardt Seminar in Vienna. Until 1976 he lived in Germany, where he had an active career in television. He began directing theater films in 1968.

His first film after returning to Greece was an adaptation of Jean-Paul Sartre's short story "The Wall," which re-

Director Stelios Pavlides, above, and below, Vassilis Diamadopoulos and Christos Tsangas in THE WALL.

flects both the theater and television background of the director. Utilizing one set and depending heavily on the abilities
and charisma of the actors, it is executed proficiently and
has the look of a stage play photographed for serious television. Intended as a film, it immediately sold to television,
along with the provocative idea of doing a series of similar
films based on short stories from around the world. Thus
THE WALL served as an unintentional pilot for a television
series. THE WALL was filmed in nine days and represents
a business-like approach to filmmaking without undue sacrifice of artistic standards. Mr. Pavlides shows no desire to
be a martyr and is a welcome breath of practicality (elected
rather than enforced) on the Greek filmmaking scene. Whether such an attitude can find a functional outlet in Greece is
a matter for conjecture at this point.

FILMS
(First three films produced in Germany)

OCCUPATION (1968). (Directed).

LIVING AND LOVING (1971). (Wrote and Directed).

CALL COLLECT (1975). (Wrote and Directed).

THE WALL (1977-Greek). (Adaptation, Screenplay, Directed).

TASSIOS, PAVLOS

Pavlos Tassios was born in Polygyros, Chalkidiki, in
1942. He studied cinema at the Stavrakou Film School in
Athens, and served as assistant director to several directors
at Finos Film Studios. He is one of the few directors working in the commercial cinema during the 1960s who moved
comfortably into the independent structure of the 1970s, in
terms of the mood and spirit of Greek '70s filmmaking. As
a director, his career extends back to 1966, but he really
caught the public's attention with his 1967 film, THE RIVALS.

His initial entry into the '70s scene was EVERYTHING
IS IN ORDER, BUT ON THE OTHER HAND ... (1972), which
took a best screenplay award at Thessaloniki in 1972. A
man brutally murders a girl who has not submitted to his

PAVLOS TASSIOS.

sexual advances, and threatens to commit suicide by jumping
off the roof of a building. A reporter attempts to dissuade
him.   The film evolves as a succession of flashbacks showing the potential suicide's life as a series of personal and
sociological frustrations.   Even his victim was a girl who
was attracted by abnormal sexual games, which tends to
further establish audience empathy for the murderer.

In 1977 Tassios took the Best Film award at Thessaloniki with THE HEAVY MELON.   Had there been any doubt,
this film makes it quite clear that Tassios is professionally
at ease with the craft of making films.   The conservative
camera talks only when it has something constructive to say.
The sound is particularly good, and contributes in establishing
mood as the character moves from country to city.   A traditional beginning-middle-end storyline reminds one that Tassios spent his apprenticeship days in the commercial cinema.

THE HEAVY MELON traces the plight of a small businessman who sells his coffee shop when a large tourist hotel

moves in and ruins his business. He moves to Athens, hoping to establish a small business in the city, but his money is soon eaten up by the expenses of getting settled, his lack of any real skills, and a marriage. He cannot cope with his growing awareness that he is likely to be a waiter the rest of his life; his resistance to this fate even erodes his successful marriage. In the end he realizes he has very little choice and accepts his future, somewhat joylessly.

Actually there are three stories in THE HEAVY MELON and the film's confused intent weakens its impact. Tassios' contention that Greece is developing for the foreigner-- that soon there will be no room in the country for the Greeks --could indeed be vital subject matter for a film. Though this is initially the direction of the film, it quickly develops into a love story which subsequently runs into problems because of the hero's inability to find a professional niche. The hero is shown mostly at odds with his life. He stews, and complains, and even strikes out in anger at his position, but we do not see him make any constructive thrusts to overcome or change his position. Perhaps there is nothing for him to do, but we are not allowed to discover even that.

Filming THE HEAVY MELON.

Tassios seems to be somewhat detached from his character, as though he is merely watching the experience rather than feeling it. The camera peers in windows, down air shafts, etc.; it is the outsider looking in. This dispassionate approach evokes a cool response from the audience, which doesn't so much feel sympathy for the character as wonder why he doesn't take more positive steps to resolve his problems. Further confusion arises when the hero finally does accept his waiter's profession: is it because he has really resolved his internal dilemma, or is it because he wants his wife (particularly well-played by Caterina Goghou) to return, in which case the dilemma may resurface? His joining the waiter's union at the end of the film is also handled ambiguously: is he truly committed to purpose at this point, or is this act merely an acceptance of the line of least resistance?

The Best Film prize awarded to THE HEAVY MELON is indicative of a conservative, "safe" mood in 1977. Certainly the film is professionally made, deftly directed, even if flawed by confusion of intent. Tassios is a skilled, knowledgable director from whom many a more passionate director could learn much.

THE HEAVY MELON also captured the Best Director and Best Screenplay awards at the New Directors Festival in 1977, as well as being named Best Film by the Panhellenic Union of Critics.

FILMS

ILLEGAL PASSION (1966).

LOST HAPPINESS (1966).

THE RIVALS (1967).

EVERYTHING IS IN ORDER, BUT ON THE OTHER HAND...
(1972).

THE PROTECTORS (1973).

THE HEAVY MELON (1977).

THOMOPOULOS, ANDREAS

Andreas Thomopoulos was born in Athens in 1945.

ANDREAS THOMOPOULOS.

He studied theater and film in England from 1963 to 1968, and remained in that country during the majority of the junta years. He worked with film and television, but became primarily interested in music in the early 1970s, composing and performing his own songs. Perhaps the fact that he did not personally suffer through most the oppressive junta period explains, at least in part, the mood and subject matter of his primary feature film made in Greece in 1975.

ALDEVARAN was the anomaly of the 1975 Thessaloniki Festival. This was the year following the overthrow of the junta, and the year's film output was almost completely political. Gloom, struggle, protest and bitterness are understandably characteristic of the '70s Greek film; lyricism is a rare commodity. Along with the work of Pandelis Voulgaris, though, ALDEVARAN ranks high on the debit side of the lyric ledger. Compared to Voulgaris' films, ALDEVARAN is more conscious of the joy of living, but the repeated verbalizing of that joy tends to erode the message. However, no criticism of the film can alter its unusual, positive position within the context of the new wave Greek cinema.

The film is constructed around an event and the characters' responses to the event, rather than following a more
traditional plotline. A poet discovers he has only two years
left to live. His closest friend, a musician, leaves--we don't
know why--for an extended, wandering trip through the world.
The poet's girl, a casual, part-time prostitute, continues living with him, with no apparent change in attitude toward him.
He continues his work, though his poems begin to be meaningless gibberish, a mere exercise in sound. The pivotal scene
in the film is one in which the poet brings home another girl
with whom he intends to make love. The "civilized, modern"
attitude which has typified their life together collapses when
the poet's girl, whom he expects to tolerate this infidelity,
throws the poet and his new girl out of the apartment, and
by so doing declares her real commitment to the love she
feels for the poet. The characters throughout the film have
treated their lives, and life in general, with a kind of satir-
ic acknowledgment of the meaningless of it all. Even the
poet's impending death, on the surface at least, has been
accepted rather casually. This declaration of love symbolizes
the collapse of the armor with which the lovers have warded
off the investigation or recognition of "meaning" and "value"
in their lives. Their hippie facade has represented their rejection of middle-class values. The poet's writings have
voiced his rejection of known values, with no search for al-
ternatives. And though the poet and his girl are shown in
tender sexual involvement with one another, they accept her
prostitution as a material necessity. We never see them
searching for meaning, and it is only when their love is
finally declared that we realize that their breezy, cynical
posturings have been only a shelter from values accepted by
others which they view as a trap.

There is much humor in the film, despite the rather
humorless character of the poet. He is played with sullen
self-indulgence which, in early retrospect, seems to work
against the film. The fact that he is facing death, however,
necessarily adds an introversion to the character and even
he, finally, does fit correctly into the whole. There is a
satisfying lack of cliché in dealing with his impending death;
in fact, his death has little to do with the real content of the
film, which is an investigation of personal defenses and acknowledgment of their destruction. In this case, death is
only a timely catalyst.

Thomopoulos repeatedly proves himself a very knowledgable director from a technical point of view. Camera

movement and positioning, lighting, staging, all contribute
subtly but importantly to character delineation. The absence
of the negative aspects of the '60s hippie movement gives
the film a '50s beatnik mood in a '70s physical setting. This
adds a non-real quality to the film, mirroring the non-real
feelings the characters have about life. Even the opening
line of the film accents this unreality: "Once upon a time
there was a Poet living here, in our town. ... " But the
"play-acting" atmosphere of the film is really a result of the
characters' inability to find their own sense of reality in life.

Within the '70s Greek cinema, ALDEVARAN is particularly unusual from two points of view: it is about people
attempting to govern their own lives, not lost in their environment, not feeling victimized by an external power; and
it investigates love and sex as a tender, joyful expression.
The latter point may not sound so unusual to most filmgoers
but the '70s Greek cinema has been preoccupied with the subject of power, and even the minimal sexual expression that

Scene from ALDEVARAN.

has found its way to film has emphasized power-orientation; there has been little that has portrayed sex as an expression of love.

ALDEVARAN is a quiet film. It avoids proselytizing. Even its message of "searching youth" and "disenchanted drop-out" is handled with self-mockery. Like Panayotopoulos' THE COLORS OF IRIS and Voulgaris' THE GREAT LOVE SONGS, it was tossed off by audiences as a pleasant but comparatively unimportant movie. That may not be a totally accurate assessment, since it did receive the second highest number of votes for best screenplay at the 1975 festival. But that was the year of big-gun political statements, and ALDEVARAN generally got lost in the pressures of the moment. Some future retrospective of Greek films may discover its delicate but enduring worth.

Since ALDEVARAN, Thomopoulos has been working in television. Marriage, a home, and creature comforts have motivated a more practical attitude toward his work. He has continued writing music, and may soon re-enter the film scene with a new project written with Orson Welles as model (and hoped-for star). It is a thriller involving the kidnapping of an international film star which turns out to be a publicity stunt. Again he will structure his story around the reactions of the characters to an event. Thomopoulos was not a part of the initial new wave movement, but he is indeed a talented, expansive addition to it.

FILMS

IT'S ALRIGHT, MA (14 minutes) (1967). Starring the guitarist Mike Farren.

PIRATES (30 minutes) (1968). A documentary about the radio pirates of the international waters between Holland and England. During filming the British Labor Party legislated against the legality of radio pirates; thus the film was completed in Holland, and the showing of it was banned in England.

ON YOUR OWN (50 minutes) (1969). Produced by Peter Whitehead with the actors of the theatrical group, Freehold Co., an off-shoot of the La Mama Troup. Played the Edinburgh and London Underground Film Festivals. Made the rounds of the "underground" film circuit in London.

ALDEVARAN (1975).   Produced, written and directed by
        Thomopoulos.

TSEMBEROPOULOS, GEORGE

Born Athens, 1950.   Extremely active in the '70s
Greek cinema in various capacities.   Co-director of MEGARA
(with Sakis Maniatis), which took a Best Production prize at
the 1974 Thessaloniki Festival and a Special Mention at the
Berlin Festival.   Directed a 5-minute short, KNOTS OF
R. D. LAING.   Leading role as actor in BLACK & WHITE,
minor roles in several films.   Served as Assistant Director
on several films, most recently Manoussakis' POWER.

"I had three interests, and decided to pursue one by

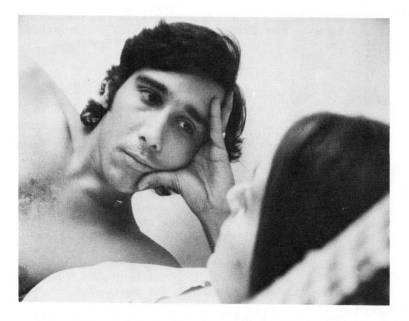

George Tsemberopoulos in BLACK & WHITE.

a flip of the coin. Economics won out and I entered the university. It was the first year of the dictatorship and most of the professors had been dismissed by the junta, and the studies seemed too meaningless to me. I had no interest at all. For years I had been fond of taking pictures. Because I was so disinterested in my studies, I had much more time to pursue this hobby. So I drifted, quite naturally, into photography. This was my main occupation for four or five years. Still I always felt there was something missing, and the missing elements were, of course, movement and sound. I was never shooting just one shot, but several; then I could never pick one or two, but fifteen, putting them in a row, creating film. I drifted into filmmaking by volunteering my services and since have worked in many capacities: actor, assistant director, assistant cameraman, director. I would like to do a fiction film. I need some of the luxury of time and distance which are ingredients of fiction film, even though it seems easier for me to make a documentary. My credits are in documentary filmmaking, and here (in the United States), why would I be chosen to make a fiction film when there are so many from whom to select, and my past has been in documentary?"

At this writing, Tsemberopoulos is studying filmmaking in Los Angeles. (See Chapter 14 for more on Tsemberopoulos.)

VOUDOURI, HELEN

Helen Voudouri was born in Athens in 1950. She took a B.A. in English Literature at Pierce College in Athens, then graduated from the Stavrakos Film School. Her first short was a 3-minute, color, fiction film called ANIMA. After two years of research, she made her most important entry into the Greek Film world with her 75-minute color documentary, KARGHIOZIS, which investigates this popular shadow theatre and its relation to the history of modern Greece. It won Special Mention at the 1975 Thessaloniki Festival, where it was cited for its ethnological research. The film has since been shown at Bologna, Italy (1975), and at a festival of women's films in Brussels in 1976. It subsequently sold to Germany and Italy for distribution.

Since KARGHIOZIS, Ms. Voudouri has concentrated on television work. She has made two 30-minute documentaries,

HELEN VOUDOURI.

From Voudouri's KARGHIOZIS.

THE CHILDREN'S DAY CARE CENTERS and THE PROB-
LEMS OF THE COUNTRY UNIVERSITY STUDENTS. In 1977
she made a film on Greek-Cypriot children called THE CHIL-
DREN AND THE WAR and a 60-minute film on various forms
of popular theater in Greece.

        Ms. Voudouri has yet to display an interest in "main-
stream" filmmaking. An increasing number of short films
by women surface at the Festivals.   The success of Ms.
Voudouri and Tonia Marketaki indicate that the doors are
open to female filmmakers in Greece, despite the male dom-
inance of the society.

Three Well-Known "Non-Greek" Greeks

MICHAEL CACOYANNIS, COSTA-GAVRAS, JULES DASSIN

        The three best-known Greek directors in the interna-
tional cinema world are Michael Cacoyannis, Costa-Gavras
and Jules Dassin, none of whom is Greek, nor are they members of the new wave movement examined in this book.
Michael Cacoyannis has spent the bulk of his life and career

in Greece, currently lives in Athens, and has utilized money provided by the Greek government for his latest film, IPHI-GENIA. But the identity-conscious Greeks, who frequently slip dangerously close to chauvinism, are quick to point out that Mr. Cacoyannis is a Cypriot. Greek-born Costa-Gavras became an ex-patriot in 1956, at which time he became a citizen of France, where his entire film career has been headquartered. Jules Dassin is an American who, caught up in the Joseph McCarthy inquisition, also moved to France. There he eventually met his wife, Melina Mercouri, returned with her to Athens and shows little indication of leaving.

It is probably safe to say that the world's image of modern Greece is largely a product of the work of two of these three directors. Dassin's NEVER ON SUNDAY and Cacoyannis' ZORBA THE GREEK have contributed greatly to the fantastic tourist business which threatens to turn all of Greece into a playground for a non-Greek population. It was certainly not the intention of either of these gentlemen to in-stigate such consequence, but the success of their films has not only introduced (or at least developed) a kind of folksy abandonment to irresponsible sensual pleasures, but has in-spired imitation and perpetuation of that image as a selling gimmick to a world weary of a 9-to-5 way of life and in search of a two-week spree.

NEVER ON SUNDAY was not Jules Dassin's initial en-try into the Greek subject. Having left the United States, he settled in Paris; but the tentacles of McCarthyism reached out even there and he remained unemployed for a time even in Europe. Finally he managed to make another film, RIFIFI, which was a huge success and reactivated his career despite the blacklist. RIFIFI represented France at the Cannes Film Festival in 1954, and there Dassin met Melina Mercouri, who was attending the festival in conjunction with Michael Cacoyannis' STELLA. Dassin was planning a film based on Greek novelist Nikos Kazantzakis' Christ Recruci-fied, which became the film HE WHO MUST DIE. Dassin fell in love with Greece during the planning and making of this film. When he later married Ms. Mercouri, he adopted Greece as his home, and has been an active part of the Greek cinema world since.

NEVER ON SUNDAY is the story of a naive American who attempts to impose his will and way upon those around him--in particular in this case, a dynamic prostitute from the red-light district of Piraeus. Instead of enlightening and

Jules Dassin, the late George Tzavelis, unidentified man, and Melina Mercouri, 1976.

enriching her life, he succeeds in making everyone unhappy; finally admitting that he too desires her body, he packs up and leaves her to her customers. It's all presented with great charm, including Ms. Mercouri's marvelously lusty performance as the happy Greek hooker, and Mr. Dassin as the innocent American; and it's aided and abetted mightily by the infectious musical score by Manos Hatzidakis. *

---

*Original score recording is available on United Artists UAS

One cannot take seriously Mr. Dassin's innocent American, any more than one can Ms. Mercouri's prostitute
Greek. Or, if we are to take one seriously, we must necessarily accord the other equal consideration. It would hardly
be unexpected for Mr. Dassin to feel some hostility for his
own country, and to give vent to it. But NEVER ON SUNDAY
cannot be taken other than as a gentle spoof on a pedant, expressing his narrowmindedness in an effort to maintain his
own precarious equilibrium. No such moral, esthetic, or
psychological judgments are brought to bear on the prostitute.
If one assumes that Mr. Dassin's character in the movie was
meant to be other than just an isolated individual--that is, if
he was meant as a symbolic American, the Greek audience
might indeed have been amused at the references to the innocent and disruptive Americans. But acceptance of this view
necessitates a view of Greece, symbolized by Ms. Mercouri,
as a prostitute who is not only for sale, but enjoys the selling.

NEVER ON SUNDAY is such entertaining froth that one
must assume it has no such devastating message. It is a
little amoral, perhaps, but without destructive intent. Off
the record, however, repeated references were made to the
film as being representative of a kind of film which has ultimately contributed to the irresponsible, non-serious, and
childish image held of Greece by the world. That the world
doesn't necessarily support this conclusion is of little consequence to the serious young directors who are eager to be
taken seriously by the world. And before Mr. Dassin's
NEVER ON SUNDAY gets too maligned, it is important to
reiterate that very frequently success in Greece reaps con-
tempt!

Melina Mercouri shared the Best Actress Award with
Jeanne Moreau (MODERATO CANTABILE) at the 1960 Cannes
Film Festival. NEVER ON SUNDAY figured prominently in
the 1960 Academy Award race: it was nominated for Best
Picture, Best Direction and Screenplay (Dassin), Best Ac-
tress (Mercouri), Best Costumes (Deni Vachlioti), and Manos
Hatzidakis won the Oscar for Best Musical Score.

Jules Dassin and Melina Mercouri have collaborated

[cont.] 5070. The three later collaborated on a kind of
Turkish remake of RIFIFI--this time heisting a treasure
from the titled museum in Istanbul; Hatzidakis' score for
TOPKAPI was recorded on United Artists UAL 4118.

on three more Greek-subject films since the world-wide success of NEVER ON SUNDAY: a modern-setting version of PHAEDRA; THE REHEARSAL, a documentary on the injustices and horrors imposed by the Greek junta government--which has had minimal release due to the overthrow of the junta around the time of film completion (see filmography for further details); and A DREAM OF PASSION, a modern version of MEDEA with Ms. Mercouri and Ellen Burstyn which represented Greece in the 1978 Cannes Festival competition. (For further details on the Dassin-Mercouri film collaboration, see I Was Born Greek by Melina Mercouri, Dell Publ. Co. , 1971.)

Ms. Mercouri has now found a formal way to act out her lifelong interest in politics, having been elected to Parliament. Mr. Dassin may be safely defined as a permanent resident of Greece and it will be of interest to see the direction of his career without the intermittent collaboration of his wife, assuming that she maintains cinematic inactivity. It should be noted that they have worked together in the theater as well as in films, their most recent joint effort being a production of THE THREE PENNY OPERA--which unfortunately did not get recorded.

Michael Cacoyannis was "new wave" in Greece when some of the young directors were too young to go to the movies alone. Had they gone, they could have seen some early efforts of Mr. Cacoyannis which even now would serve the younger directors well as models to guide their filmmaking. A specific case in point is the modest but highly satisfying film, THE GIRL IN BLACK, Mr. Cacoyannis' third film, made in 1956. Using a Greek rural locale both as backdrop and as influence upon individuals' behavior, he strikes a happy balance between people deciding their fates and acting on their own decisions, and people being manipulated by social expectancies and prejudices. Aided by a still-exquisite performance by Elli Lambeti and memorable photography by Walter Lassally, Mr. Cacoyannis' film remains even now a personal and socially moving statement.

Two more Cacoyannis films could easily be moved forward in time to become part of the current new wave of independent filmmaking, at least if one considers the financial modesty and imaginative execution with which they were made. STELLA, a melodramatic but moving film, might well enjoy a revival today in the wake of women's lib. Stella,

Michael Cacoyannis on location during filming of IPHIGENIA.

a nightclub entertainer, so cherishes her freedom that she
refuses to relinquish it even to marry a man she truly loves,
because she would have to assume "wifely" and other duties
expected by a rigid society. Her lover (George Foundas), a
celebrated sportsman, cannot understand her rejection and
murders her, motivated both by his love for her and desire
to "possess" her, and to avenge his loss of face in the community, as well as his damaged male ego. As Stella, Melina
Mercouri, in her first film, gives what may still be her best
film performance. Jules Dassin met Melina Mercouri shortly
after seeing STELLA, a fact which further enhances the suspicion that STELLA was at least a partial inspiration for
NEVER ON SUNDAY.

The emphasis in THE GIRL IN BLACK and STELLA
is clearly on the principal characters and their situations
within a social framework. None of the new wave directors
has assumed a like position with the major exception of Voulgaris in THE ENGAGEMENT OF ANNA and, to a lesser degree, Panayotopoulos in THE COLORS OF IRIS and Angelopoulos in RECONSTRUCTION. In fact, had these five films
emerged as a movement, the current new wave would likely
have gone in a different direction, one in which people would
not have been lost in the shuffle of more grandiose but lesser
statements. Despite some current hostility from the young
directors toward Mr. Cacoyannis' presence in the Greek film
scene, they would do well to look again at these early films,
which have much to offer their current endeavors.

Michael Cacoyannis may point with umblemished pride
to a third film: ELECTRA (1961), which gave Irene Papas
to the cinematic world (although she had made films before
this) and which remains a superb example of cinema created
from another medium. Little interest has yet been displayed
by the new directors in adapting film from the wealth of their
literary inheritance, both ancient and modern. In fact (and
again off the record) there were scornful remarks at Mr.
Cacoyannis' "old-fashioned" following of the classics. Youthful nonsense? Jealousy? Perhaps, but most likely they are
merely registering their frustration at the difficulties they
have in obtaining financing for their films, while Cacoyannis
is awarded the lion's share of government-supplied money
for making films. (This is detailed in the discussion of the
Greek Film Center in the Producer section.) To date, only
Costas Ferris' THE MURDERESS was adapted from a literary source, though one hopes it is only a question of time
before the young directors take advantage of the abundance of
Greek writing for inspiration for their films.

Along with NEVER ON SUNDAY, Mr. Cacoyannis' ZORBA THE GREEK receives credit for inspiring a "plastic" folkloric presentation of Greece to the world. Zorba, him-self, is a bit of a folksy-philosopher who can wear thin rath-er quickly. Like Hatzidakis' score for NEVER ON SUNDAY, the effervescent score by Mikis Theodorakis (original score recording available on 20th-Century Fox Records #T-903) makes no small contribution to the feel-it-but-don't-think-about-it "profundity" of Zorba's message. Despite the Greeks' antipathy toward the Cacoyannis film, ZORBA THE GREEK was a major commercial success, reaping awards as well. The film won Oscars in the United States for Best Photogra-phy (Walter Lassally), Best Supporting Actress (Lila Kedrova) and Best Art Direction (Vassilis Fotopoulos). Cacoyannis re-ceived Oscar nominations for Best Directing and Best Screen-play, and the film was nominated for Best Film.

Again, it is not with unadulterated objectivity that ZORBA is criticized in Greece. Cacoyannis comments on the Greek tendency to denigrate success: "Obviously there are enormous advantages that one derives from fame. But I think that one knows that people would be delighted to see you slip. First of all you verify it every day because you are exposed to the press. And the press is ready to jump. I mean, if you were to have an accident or a public row, or anything like that ... look, let's face it, if you are a failure, they are delighted. Whenever I have worked outside Greece and had 70% good reviews and 30% bad, the 30% bad are the ones that are imported first. I've developed a thick skin. " (From a 1976 interview with the author.)

Cacoyannis' IPHIGENIA has been a success with both critics and audiences, and shows strong indication of bringing profit to the Greek Film Center which produced it. The film was nominated for an Academy Award in the Best Foreign Film category in 1978, and Variety reported a gross box of-fice of $340,774 in the United States alone, as of May 3, 1978. The young directors may begrudge Cacoyannis the money which they themselves would have liked, but to bring in a profit for further investment is the stated purpose of the Greek Film Center and IPHIGENIA was surely the best business risk presented them. Furthermore, Michael Cacoy-annis' career obviously is not over. Even if he contributed nothing else to the new wave Greek cinema, he introduces it to solid, professional competitiveness--which is a reality the new wave directors must face if they hope to confront an in-ternational market.

Costa-Gavras was born in Athens in 1933, of a Russian father and a Greek mother. He went to France to study in 1951 and became interested in film. He became a French citizen in 1956. "Z" is his only Greek-oriented film. Based on a novel which in turn took its inspiration from a true incident in Greek history, the film engaged Greek actors, and was scored with music by Mikis Theodorakis (original score recording: Columbia Special Products #AOS-3370), who was a political prisoner at the time. But the film was not actually set in Greece, and certainly not filmed there (the junta was in power). Costa-Gavras obviously has nothing to do with Greek cinema, and the only reason he appears here is to make just that point, in contradiction to the frequent references to him as a Greek filmmaker.

Much has been written about Cacoyannis, Costa-Gavras and Dassin. A selected list of sources is appended here for the convenience of those who wish to read more about these filmmakers.

Michael Cacoyannis

Cacoyannis, M.   "The simple approach; filmmaking in Greece, " International Film Annual, 1:49, '57.

"Michael Cacoyannis on a matter of size, " Films & Filming, 6-4:13 Ja. , '60.

Stanbrook, A.   "Rebel with a cause, " Film, 24:16, Mr/Ap '60.

Manus, W.   "Michael Cacoyannis, " Films in Review, 13-10: 638, Dec. '62.

"Personality of the month, " Films & Filming, 9-9:19, June '63.

Cacoyannis, M.   "Greek to me, " Films & Filming, 9-9:19, June '63.

Dallas, A.   "Michael Cacoyannis, " Film Comment, 1-6:44, Fall '63.

Biography.   Current Biography, 27:5 May '66; Current Biography Yearbook 1966, 34, '67.

Lerman, L. "International movie report, " Mademoiselle, 64:117, Feb. '67.

Robbins, F. "Director Michael Cacoyannis and his Trojan Women, " Show, 2-8:29, Oct. '71.

"Biographical note; filmography, " Film Dope, 6:6, Nov. '74.

Georgiadou, M. "Director of the year; filmography, " International Film Guide '76.

Schuster, M. "Euripides guides the camera; interview, " Hellenic Journal, May 4, 1978.

Costa-Gavras

Georgakas, D. "Costa-Gavras talks, " Take One, 2-6:12, Jul/Aug '69.

Austen, D. "Pointing out the problems; interview, " Films & Filming, June '70.

Semprun, J. "Interview, " Film Society Review, Jan '71.

Davis, M. S. "Agent provocateur of films, " New York Times Biographical Edition, March 21, '71.

Berman, B. "A conversation with Costa-Gavras; filmography, " Take One, 3-12:23, July/Aug '72.

"Interview, " Cinéaste 6-1:2, '73.

Klemesrud, J. "Not anti-American, " New York Times Biographical Edition, April '73, p. 569.

Solinas, P. "Interview; filmography, " Cinema (Beverly Hills), 34:35, '74.

"Biographical note; filmography, " Film Dope, 8:21, Oct '75.

Jules Dassin

Ferrero, Adelio. Jules Dassin. Parma: Guanda. 1961. 142 pages. A study of his career. Includes interview, filmography, bibliography. In Italian.

Lane, J. F. "Interview," Films & Filming, Sept. '58.

Grenier, C. "Interview," Sight & Sound, Winter '57/58.

Bluestone, G. "Interview," Film Culture, 4-17:3, '58.

Alpert, H. "Greek passion," Saturday Review, 41:14, Dec 20, '58.

"Talk with a movie maker," Newsweek, 56:130, Oct. 24, '60.

Hammel, F. "A director's return," Cue 31-10:11, Mr 10, '62.

Nolan, J. "Jules Dassin; filmography," Films in Review, 13-9:572, Nov '62.

Gow, G. "Style and instinct; interview," Films & Filming, 16-5:22, Feb '70.

Biography. Current Biography, 32:18, Mar '71.

"Biographical note; filmography," Film Dope, 9:35, Ap '76.

Chapter 14

DOCUMENTARIES

A high percentage of shorts made in Greece in the
past four years have been documentaries. To the outsider,
documentaries present a special problem because the language
barrier becomes accentuated; commentary is frequently a
soundtrack appendage and is therefore less immediately connected with the visual. This difficulty, combined with the
large number of short (and feature-length) documentaries produced, gives the impression that the documentary genre is
prolific in Greece.

To the beginning filmmaker it might seem that documentary is a less demanding genre than most in which to
work. Obviously it is less expensive, in that the salaries
of a cast and crew are obviated, as well as the need for
sets, costumes, props, etc. Furthermore, "handling" a
cast and crew--their psychological and physical needs--is a
rather threatening responsibility to the apprentice. It is
understandable that the tyro should seek to gain experience
through the documentary. Alas, the form has qualitative requirements which cannot be met simply by passion for subject. This is a severe obstacle in Greece, where many of
the volatile young filmmakers are so enthusiastically imbued
with their subject that they lose sight of the theatrical requirements of filmmaking. The result is seemingly endless
footage of interviews--a hand-held microphone capturing opinions which verify the filmmaker's preconceived position on
the film's subject. Not only are these films highly subjective
(a flirtation with propaganda), they are quite simply boring.
It is not the subject that bores, but rather the presentation.

George Tsemberopoulos, co-director (with Sakis Maniatis) of the documentary MEGARA, seems ideally suited to
the genre. He freely admits to being more of an observer
than a participant; expresses a somewhat overdeveloped interest in objectivity; obviously takes great satisfaction in the
learning process. To say that he lacks a sense of "fun" is

Tsemberopoulos and Maniatis (MEGARA).

not to be specific, for, in general (with the major exception
of Nicos Panayotopoulos), this seems to be the case throughout the Greek film world. Tsemberopoulos seeks conclusions,
and presents the ones he has found, with perception, thor-
oughness, and awareness of correctable limitations. His major thrust of attention is on career, a position which demands
and receives unflagging energy, resourcefulness and ambition.

Tsemberopoulos speaks English with a penetrating ac-
curacy and it seemed opportune to ask him to serve as spokes-
man for documentary within the Greek film world. Although
he agreed, he was most concerned that he not be presented
as "a critic" or "an authority." He constantly softened his
opinions with "to my knowledge," "in my opinion," or "as I
see it," and the elimination of those phrases in the following
should in no way distort the fact that Tsemberopoulos is highly conscious of reaching for the objective while repeatedly re-
minding of the subjective. If he was openly hostile to a film
or filmmaker, he either turned off the tape recorder, or re-

quested that such opinion be edited from the tape.   He thus
expressed his desire that his dissertation be more revealing
of the subject at hand than of himself.

Documentary Films in Greece*

There are three kinds of documentaries, not just since
the collapse of the commercial cinema, but that is when they
manifested themselves.   One is the travelogue, then comes
the ethnological documentary, lastly the overtly political.
Let's forget the tourist documentaries and discuss ...

The Ethnological Documentary

Until ten years ago there were more ethnological documentaries on Greece made by non-Greeks than by Greeks.
Within the last decade we have started to make our own ethnological documentaries.   However, these films have all used as
a springboard, a particular event.   The filmmakers have
shown the event, and possibly even some of its history, but
they fail to examine its possible origin.   They don't investigate the meaning of the event to those persons involved in or
affected by the event.   The filmmakers are very sure of their
points of view.   They say, "This is the event, this is how it
happened, and this is what people think of it. "   They don't
question the persons involved; they don't question themselves
as to why; they don't take into consideration all the possibilities.   They are not interested in giving their subject all the
possible dimensions it might have.   They are not willing to
learn while filming or investigating.

There is another kind of ethnological film which records in the conventional way the different customs of different regions, which are very interesting customs.   But when
I see them, I say, what is beneath them?   I'm not interested
only in seeing all the beautiful dresses, or how fancy or
peculiar everything is.   I want to know what's behind them:
why? for how long?   How do the customs affect the people?
What do persons who don't believe in the customs think of
them?   How do they interpret them?   Is it only a minority

---

*The remainder of this article is adapted from an interview
with George Tsemberopoulos, conducted in May 1977, in New
York City.

who live the customs? Is it a tradition that is dying? I
don't think that today people need films that glorify their
subjects or answers--making them more beautiful than in
reality they are. I want to see the beauty, but within its
correct proportions to its other ingredients. After all, life
nowhere has 100% of beauty or 100% of ugliness. I want to
see all the ingredients, and I believe this is what audiences
should get. They should get what is available to them should
they actually go to a place.

The Political Documentary

Now we come to the overtly political documentary.
Up to 1949 there had been some newsreel material shot, but
after that time there was nothing. There was no Greek filmmaker who was aware of the possibility of making a piece of
cinema direct; to film the action of the political life and
events that were occurring. Of course, from 1949 until the
end of the dictatorship, everything was subjected to heavy
censorship. Not just films, but literature, journalistic re-
portage--everything. During this "blackout" period there occurred a major event in Greece which has affected the lives
of the entire population--the civil war. Even during a period of comparative freedom just prior to the junta, the civil
war was still a taboo. Many of the people who were more
liberal in the late 1960s were the conservatives during the
civil war. This represents a kind of role-switching that is
better left unspoken of. Also, whatever newsreels were shot
during the civil war were done by the British. The forces
against the government had no cameras, and thus the existing
film coverage is from a single point of view. For years
even these films have been secret. Only now have they become available. At the time there was simply an absolute
lack of information, and what did exist was completely distorted, even in school books. Until the collapse of the junta,
there simply has been no accurate information about this period of history. There was only the official point of view,
which was one of complete distortion. Immediately following
the junta, the big taboo was over, and suddenly there was a
flood of books and articles on the period. Sudden freedom
frequently results in a sentimental rush of expression. Time
will allow for a more proper dimension of investigation.
This is background for the documentaries that were made immediately following the junta. Suddenly the filmmakers could
say anything, and, of course, anything is not the way to do
it. Freedom naturally calls for self-control.

MEGARA (Tsemberopoulos and Maniatis).

Let's look at them very briefly. With what do they
deal? All of them deal with a major event. The first was
GRACE OF GREEK CHRISTIANS, which was a motto during
the junta. I think it was shot between 1968 and 1970. As I
said, each of these films deals with one subject or event.
This one has as its subject the dictatorship and its absurdity
in manifesting whatever they were thinking. Whatever the
dictators were thinking of their country and their way of rul-
ing.

And then there was MEGARA, also dealing with a major event: the expropriation of land, which caused much public trouble in this area--political and social, ecological, and
every kind of trouble for these people. This expropriation of
land combined with the polytechnic, which was such a big
event, and finally it deals with the dictatorship. So it was
referring to a major event.

There is an in-built dynamic in documentary filmmaking. In mainstream filmmaking, that is, with a script, selecting actors, re-enacting the story or event, there is a kind of long-range commitment. But when living within a situation where immediate events drastically change or mold one's life, there are events which occur which demand immediate attention. One feels an urgency about commenting on the event. And when such events are occurring, more traditional filmmaking is viewed as something for the future. At the time of the MEGARA incident, we said, "This is now! It will not happen tomorrow! Someone has to report this. We have to let the people know!" So we started shooting. Where we were going, we had only vague ideas. But we were moved to action by the event.

When the pressures of the moment are relieved, there then is time and distance to allow one to sit down and deal with slices of life. But when there are daily outrages against one's freedom, and even personal safety, it is not possible to just sit down and let one's mind and imagination flow. Even filmmakers like Nicos Koundouros, Michael Cacoyannis and Jules Dassin, all of whom had a past in theatrical filmmaking, were moved to make documentaries when moved by events which they personally found irresistible to ignore within the immediacy.

Two more examples of political documentaries are STRUGGLE and THE NEW PARTHENON. The latter refers to the same island depicted in HAPPY DAY, which was a concentration island. Both deal with major events. They don't go to a village, say, and view the lives of the villagers and find out, through minor events, the political situation there, and extend their investigation--a combination of ethnological and political. Instead, they deal with an event, with something really major. And, of course, there is EVIDENCE, which I find the most extraordinary footage from the period of the dictatorship. It refers to the dictatorship and the first year after its collapse.

I give all these examples to make a point: that I hope the time is now ripe to make documentaries not exclusively based on major events. They now are free to make investigatory, in-depth films which are free from a particular event.

EVIDENCE (Nicos Kavoukidis).

MEGARA*

In the summer of 1973 I was working with Sakis

*Synopsis: "In 1973 the shipowner and banker S. Andreadis has
200 hectares of fertile soil, together with 7,000 olive trees, destroyed by his excavators in Megara, near Athens. The film
shows the fight of the inhabitants, peasants of Megara, against
the unconstitutional expropriation and, running parallel to it, the
latest political developments in Greece: the expropriation and
destruction of the soil, the attitude of the Megarians, the social,
economical and ecological consequences of this expropriation,
the demonstration in Megara (the first since dictatorship was
established), the protest march of the Megarians to the Athens
Polytechnic where they united with the rebellious students, the
military intervention which caused 140 dead, the second putsch,
the outcome of the whole affair." Quoted from the program notes
accompanying screening of the film.

[Maniatis] on four different films. We were moving from one
site to another and passed this site where we saw all those
beautiful, alive olive trees being uprooted. When we saw
this, we remembered the whole case which, because of censorship, had been reported on the front pages of the newspapers, but in very small detail. We agreed we wanted to
return and record what we saw on film. Our intention was
to just return and capture the spectacle on just one roll of
film and keep it in our private archive, that might in the future combine correctly into another film. We returned a
couple of days later with our one roll, and started to film.
As we filmed, I saw an old man, and I went to him and
started to talk with him. This was during the dictatorship
and we were used to people who, when you asked them something about dictatorship or about their lives--especially outside of Athens--were not willing to answer you. Even if you
knew them, they would say little more than just to let you
know they were against it. The old man was a shepherd,
and when I spoke to him, he gave me a political-sociological-
ecological-philosophical speech. The most complete I ever
heard! I simply said, "Tell me baba (old man), what happened here?" and he spoke for five minutes, in anger.

As a journalist I wanted to learn more about this case,
so I went to the somewhat liberal newspaper that existed. I
was interested in the whole area, for there were something
like eight expropriations of land in order to build factories
of various kinds. I was given names of people in the various areas who might tell me what was going on. I took my
tape recorder and went back to Megara. I hid the tape recorder, as sometimes one has to play tricks in order to do
something honest. Then I talked to Sakis, and he said we
must not let this thing drop. Let us make a film. And so
we sat down and began to plan it. From this point on it is
impossible to say other than "we, " because though I was supposed to be making the film, with Sakis on the camera, from
this point on it was impossible to determine who did what.
We made the film. This didn't become an issue until the
very end when we began to compose the credits. At that
time, of course, we put a film by both of us. There was
no way of saying who did what.

But anyway, in the beginning I was the initiative and
he was supporting me. We thought we would be doing a 20-
25 minute film, because in the beginning there was a dead
period. That is, the factory was not yet being built; the
peasants were awaiting an answer from the supreme court,

so there was no action. We thought we would make a film
showing these people's point of view, some facts on the whole
case, and maybe some very scientific speeches on pollution
and expropriation of land, and all that. Although we didn't
really discuss it at the time, we thought maybe we would
show the film before the trial and hope that it had some influence, or maybe send the film abroad in hopes of creating
some talk about the whole subject.

And so we started shooting, while being engaged with
another film. Although we were very busy during the summer, I had a few free days to go to Megara with the tape
recorder, establishing contacts with the people there--meeting
the people, making relations, rather than acquaintances. Although they seemed to be willing to speak, they couldn't understand why we would make a film. They knew that films
cost money; they knew they had no money and that I had no
money, and so I must be really doing some work for the
other party. So they were rather suspicious. On the other
hand they could see we were nice guys. We knew how to
deal with them. We knew how to talk with them. So little
by little we gained their confidence and trust.

When we decided to buy two or three rolls of film,
we began to consider the amount of money we had available.
Then we found out we had to buy much more film than that.
At the time I had a small, old car. But cars are very expensive in Greece, so I sold it for $3,000. Sakis owned a
camera, so the necessity to rent equipment was minimal.
Still, this money was finished very soon, and the Megara
story continued. The story seemed endless, but the money
was not. We began to borrow from individuals. And other
people began to lend whatever they had--cars to go to the
shooting, equipment. All of this contributed to a low cost
of the film--plus the fact that Sakis and I were the entire
crew. We did everything from producing to distributing. I
mean, I'm still distributing.

Finally we had to realize that even six or seven rolls
of film was only a beginning, so we just decided to shoot and
let whatever was to happen, happen. We didn't have the
money to buy all the film we needed in color, so we bought
half in color and half in black & white. It was a question
of economy, not artistry that decided us to shoot the interviews and demonstrations in black & white and the environment and ways of life in color. This was hardly a "heavy"
artistic demonstration--merely a financial solution.

We started shooting with the old man with whom I had first talked. If one knew nothing about the subject, his eight-minute spontaneous speech was all one ever needed to hear on the subject, it was so thorough and knowledgeable. He became so enthusiastic with his subject that he couldn't stop talking while we reloaded the camera, so I had to use some of his speech, obtained only on aural tape, at other places in the film. * Although many of the people were reluctant to

MANI (Maniatis).

---

*Author's Note: Actually, this was a disguised blessing for no matter how interesting or animated, visual interest in a filmed interview can be sustained only so long. Furthermore, Tsemberopoulos' excitement over this old man's philosophy and willingness to express it allows for an intriguing unexplored comment. At one point the old man establishes that he does not really blame the exploiters of the situation, but rather a government which allows for the exploitation. He

speak publicly, it was point zero for them. Their homes
and lives were being threatened. These were people who had
worked all their lives and had by now obtained ownership of
small pieces of land. Some even were able to afford employees to help them work the land.

By tradition, they were conservative, even blindly so.
To say "right wing" or "left wing" in Greece is considerably
different than what you have here in the United States. The
people believe blindly in the leader of the party, and who he
chooses to help him govern is of little concern to the people.
We have no such thing as a liberal Republican or a conservative Democrat. It is RIGHT, CENTER, and LEFT. And
when I say these people were traditionally right, I mean that
they have never questioned that political philosophy. It was
their party which was not only not protecting them, but actually attacking them. It was their first occasion to question
their own beliefs. They felt betrayed. One said, "It is un-
believable. Twenty years ago they threw a rifle in my hands
and said go out and kill people, you have to protect your
family and property. Twenty years later, because it doesn't
suit them, after I have killed people, they tell me you are a
bastard. And they deprive me of my home and property. "
This man left the country and moved to the United States because of this situation. But something you should know is
that this is the first time a government has acted against its
own supporters. People who were right-wing found themselves in the middle because there were others more right
than they. The junta acted against even those who supported
the right-wing philosophy, which means that ultimately practically the entire population turned against the junta.

Ninety-five per cent of the film was shot with hand-
held camera, and it was shot non-synch, which means no
connection between camera and tape recorder. In the cutting
room, Sakis synchronized the sound, word by word. He took

[cont.] implies that given the opportunity, he would behave
the same as his "enemies. " This suggests that ethics or
morality are not really in question, but just that he happens
to be the victim. Given the chance, he would behave with
equal unconcern for the next guy. The brief comment was
an opportunity to expand the film momentarily beyond its subject immediacy, further fulfilling Tsemberopoulos' stated pre-
requisite in making a documentary: the investigation of the
"why" as well as the "what. "

out or added the sound after every frame. Non-Greek speaking people believe the film to be shot in synch. To our awareness, there are no more than two or three spots in the film where the synchronization is not absolutely accurate.

Finally, after all these years, the film has made a little money. But after four years of work, the small amount we have made, you would not believe! (Author's Note: ME-GARA won a Best Production award at the 1974 Thessaloniki Festival.)

Question: Do you think that as television grows in Greece along with its potential news coverage, the "event" documentary will lose its value? Its necessity?

I do believe you have excellent news coverage in the United States, but I don't believe that any of that coverage exhausts the possibilities of the investigation. Let's say that television at its best--in the United States--is not geared to reach the internal of the event. It is not able to reach the

STRUGGLE (Maranghos and company).

maximum dimensions of an event. It is very frustrating to see a show--the excellent 60 Minutes for example--exhausting a subject in 20 minutes. I feel frustrated; I want to know more. Even in an ideal television situation, there is no time to explore in depth; therefore, television does not obviate the need for feature-length documentaries. But one can't hold television's failings as exclusive self-blame. Audiences, the kind of lives we lead--television serves our needs. The audience itself allows a given amount of time for information intake. It wants to be informed, nothing more. Greek television is a long time off from becoming as American television. Nobody is interested in objectivity in Greece. Any public servant in Greece can call the news media and tell them to write or not write something. So Greek television is serving, and will serve for many years, the government that is in power. This is not only news, this is throughout the programming. This is true of both of our television channels. Television comes within the control of the Ministry of Culture, so whatever political force might be functioning has control over the television medium.

Christos Palyanapoulos (top) and Lefteris Xanthopoulos.

Chapter 15

SHORT FILMS

Perhaps it is an illusion that the number of would-be filmmakers in Greece is greater than anywhere else, still, cinema is indeed a hot medium there. Each year introduces a goodly number of new names to the cinema world, though given the inaccessibility of money and the severe competition for the little that can be found, many of these aspiring film- makers drop by the wayside or quickly find their way into television in some capacity or other.

Making a short is obviously a comparatively inexpen- sive way to alert the audience to a new talent. Many shorts are screened during the Thessaloniki Festival, which provides an immediate showcase for the filmmaker's product. Thodoros Maranghos holds two awards for shorts; Nicos Zervos, Pan- delis Voulgaris, Dimosthenis Theos each reaped honors for their shorts before moving on to features. Most of the other directors made their initial entry into the cinema world via shorts.

A review of the award-winning shorts through the years makes it quite clear that a registered success with a short does not automatically pave the way for easy entry into feature filmmaking. Many names which are heralded as fu- ture hopes unhappily fade into distant memory as economic difficulties and lack of commitment take their toll.

A Capsule Look at Greek Short Films*

CHRISTOS PALYANAPOULOS

Christos Palyanapoulos was born in Agrinio in 1942. After finishing conventional schooling, he studied film in

---

*Quoted material is from various issues of International Film Guide.

Last shot in Takis Davlopoulos' COINCIDENCES ON A TROL-
LEY.

Athens for three years. He graduated from film school in
1963 and worked as an assistant director for Finos Film on
25 films. He produced and directed his first short in 1968
--DEPARTURE, which played the 1968 Festival. In 1973 he
made a 15-minute short (TESTIMONIAL), based on a real
event. A mother sells her new-born child to save her other
children from starvation. The film investigates the legal and
ethical problems of the situation without exploiting the melodramatic potential. In 1975 Palyanapoulos filmed the La
Mama Company's production of ELECTRA. He has made
four films for television, and has worked in the production
crew of Angelopoulos' RECONSTRUCTION and THE TRAVEL-
LING PLAYERS, and Voulgaris' THE ENGAGEMENT OF
ANNA.

LEFTERIS XANTHOPOULOS

Born in Athens in 1945. Xanthopoulos took a second

prize in 1976 for his short, GREEK COMMUNITY CENTRE
IN HEIDELBERG, as well as earning the vociferously demonstrated approval of the audience. The film was a 30-minute
documentary on the migrant Greek workers' problems in Germany. Many scenes with children produced a rare commodity in Greek films--humor! The film was produced, directed
and edited by Xanthopoulos, photographed by Mihalis Rokos.
Xanthopoulos co-founded the Students Film Club in 1963; attended both the Athens University School of Law and the London Film School. He is also a poet of growing reputation,
having won the Panhellenic Student Poetry Competition in 1966,
and produced two collections of poetry (1969, 1972). He currently lives in Germany; plans to continue his involvements
with poetry and film.

COINCIDENCES ON A TROLLEY (directed by Takis Davlopoulos) "... translates in rather cheap but very effective satirical terms the opposing political currents and the strong anti-
American feelings which were the daily bread of the man-on-
the-street immediately after the return of democracy." This
film ends with a close-up of a small boy taking aim with his
pea-shooter at the emblem adorning the U.S. Embassy in
Athens. This David-and-Goliath image enchanted the audience
at the 1975 festival, and they reacted with enthusiastic identification with the child's magical efforts to solve an adult
problem.

COMMUNICATION (written and directed by George Lanitis)
"... was the best short of the year ... a fascinating, moving, and disturbing tour of a deaf-mute children's school in
Cyprus."

THE EDGE (directed by Dim. Benisis) is an intriguing study
of the moment of development or deterioration, at which time
action is necessary, either to continue (over the edge) or to
change direction. The success of the film is largely due the
sense of theatre which guided the construction of the film in
the editing room.

THE LADY AND THE COWBOY (produced, written and directed by Costas Papadopoulos) won the Best Short Award
in Thessaloniki in 1970. It is a "... wild, nonsensical, and
very witty satire of the star system in Greece's Hollywood."

νυχτες

μια ταινια του γιωργου κατακουζηνου
σε μουσικη γιαννη ξενακη

Poster for Katakounzinos' NIGHTS. Opposite, from Velissaropoulos' OPERA.

LAST REHEARSAL (directed by Nicos Koutelidakis) "... tells
of a real event, an accident--a schoolboy was shot dead by
his comrade during the rehearsal of a patriotic play--that
took place two years ago in a small provincial town. Koutelidakis displays a remarkable assurance in the satirical approach of his characters ... but the tragic end, given in a
rather rhetorical tone, does not match well with the reportage style of the narration. "

LINE (animation by Yannis Koutsouris and Thanassis Mirmiridis) "... is a well-drawn, at once very funny and merci-
less, satire in cartoon form about the use and abuse of the
technological and other 'miracles' of this age of prosperity. "

MINUS--PORTRAIT (directed by Leonidas Papadakis). More
theatrical in concept than cinematic, this film is more memorable for the cleverness of the idea rather than for its imaginative execution. A bare stage adorned only with a flag of
Greece is, piece by piece, inundated by objects thrown from
off-camera which slowly and chaotically engulf the symbolical
country of Greece. The objects include commercial, political and cultural symbols which, so stated, become unswept
litter.

MY USUAL DREAM (produced, written, directed, and starring actress Niki Triantafillidi) is "a semi-autobiographical,
satirical portrait of a young woman, haunted by the fantasies
of her peculiar artistic ambition. "

NIGHTS (directed by George Katakounzinos) is a visual setting of Yiannis Xenakis' musical composition "Nuits. " Set
in a prison camp, it quickly captures the loneliness of isolation, the debilitating quality of limited creature comforts,
the claustrophobia inherent in the absence of freedom. The
recurring fantasies (or memories) of the woman in the prisoner's life is a conceptual error within the limited time-frame
of the film, but the relentless sun beating down on the

Opposite: (Above) Nicos Zervos' censored short, CATCH
'76. (Below) Dimosthenis Theos' short HUNDRED HOURS
OF MAY, based on the murder of G. Lambrakis, the same
incident on which Costa-Gavras' film "Z" was based.

gloomy prison, the fascinating patterns of shadows captured by the camera, and the visual complements to the disturbing music remain in memory long after the minor faults of the film have slipped away.

OPERA (directed by Andreas Velissaropoulos). A speeded-up tape-recording serves as audio for chattering, bare-breasted women. The camera captures the dramatic lighting glorifying the beauty of the naked male. Bits and pieces of opera recordings accompany the somewhat corny proceedings. This film has some of the dated quality of certain experimental films in the United States from the 1950s. But frontal nudity and obvious unbiased visual references to homosexuality, new in Greece as a local product, subsequently created a minor scandal at the 1976 festival.

SIGN HERE PLEASE (directed by Lambros Papadimitrakis) "is a humorous but also depressing account in memorable cinematic terms, of a moment of crisis in the life of a young student. "

THE TAVERN (directed by Takis Papayannidis) "... is by turns a sad and funny fable, attempting to put the blame on socio-economic progress and the introduction of foreign styles for the decline in authentic Greek life in the big cities. "

Chapter 16

CINEMATOGRAPHERS

Giorgos Arvanitis, Stavros Hasapis, Giorgos Panousopoulos

Inadequate financing is the basis of problems confronting Greek cinematographers in the development of their art and craft. Like the entire cast and crew, they are underpaid. The greater the financial demands on the personal life of the individual, the greater the compromises made within the art. Stavros Hasapis, married with two children, says: "We are obliged to accept any offer. We might know in advance it will be a bad film." Giorgos Arvanitis, currently single, can (modestly) afford to be more selective: "The money I earn must go for living expenses, and even that doesn't make for an easy life. But I don't want to just shoot any job that comes along. I want to choose. I was offered a job with a Greek-French co-production for television, a 90-minute program in color. I asked for 50, 000 drachmas (approximately $1, 500), and they went out and found someone for 10, 000. You have to remember that even 50, 000 is not much. After all, a 90-minute film will take at least a month to shoot."

Although the personal problems of the cinematographers parallel those of all other artists and technicians within the Greek film "industry, " lack of adequate financing takes a unique toll on the art of the cinematographer. "For instance, " says Hasapis, "if we start shooting under given light conditions but are not finished as the light changes, we simply have to go on because there is not enough money to disband and continue the next day in comparable light. If the photographer complains, or refuses to resolve problems over which he really has little control, we simply are not hired the next time. The producers think only money, not quality. "

Hasapis continues: "We also have problems in the laboratory. There is no quality control at all. One roll of film may be processed today with a given result. But tomor-

Giorgos Arvanitis (at top) and Stavros Hasapis (at camera, below) with director Tasos Psarras, filming MAY.

row the variables are not the same, so the film can end up looking different from reel to reel. There are accidents in the laboratory too, that can destroy very valuable footage, and there is no money to reshoot the lost footage, so we have to salvage what we can, or restructure the film to accommodate the loss. " Arvanitis adds: "They don't want to do anything they consider out of the conventional way. They say the laboratory has a good name only when the pictures have very faithful colors. They don't want to do anything imaginative. Red MUST be red; green MUST be green. "

"Another problem, " continues Hasapis, "is that we have very little equipment. In fact, the cinematographer in Greece must have his own equipment; there is none for rent. Therefore, one of the criteria for selecting a cinematographer for a film is the equipment he owns. If you need, for instance, a zoom lens, you have to find a cinematographer who owns one. The fee the cinematographer can ask for is not necessarily reflective of his qualitative worth, but rather depends on the equipment the production calls for and whether or not he owns it, and it is available. "

The three cinematographers most prominently on the scene in 1976 were George Arvanitis, Stavros Hasapis, and George Panousopoulos. * Hasapis affirms there were "many good ones from the commercial cinema days, but they all work in advertisements. This older generation of cinematographers do not find work in the current cinema because the new generation of filmmakers naturally turn to their own generation for cooperation. " Arvanitis adds: "There are some younger people who are good, but the problem is whether they will survive because of all the problems. There is no organization where a person needing a photographer can go to find out who knows their job. Therefore, there are a lot of young people in Greece working as photographers who really know nothing about it. They will work for very little money. They are simply interested in the money, not what they are doing. "

GIORGOS ARVANITIS has photographed about 70 films,

---

*A fourth important cinematographer is Sakis Maniatis who is actively moving into the role of filmmaker (or director). Further information on him and his work can be found in the Director's Who's Who section and in the interview with George Tsemberopoulos concerning documentary filmmaking.

Giorgos Panousopoulos on location for POWER.

Giorgos Arvanitis (with cigarette) talking to actor Pierre Clementi.

having worked for Finos Films for eight years, making up to six films a year. He currently is enjoying an artistic rela- tionship with Thodoros Angelopoulos, having worked with the director on each of his three films. Given the collaborative creative framework of filmmaking, it is impossible to say at this point how much of Angelopoulos' success may be accred- ited to Arvanitis' camera, or to what degree the Arvanitis "look" is in response to the requests of Angelopoulos. Nev- ertheless, the partnership is a personal and creatively happy one. "My first problem is communication with the directors. With Angelopoulos there is no such problem. There is no need to talk with him, no need to say anything. We have the same direction. We are as one. Outside the technical prob- lems, which are mine, I want to collaborate with the director, know what they are doing, what the film is about, and think about how I would do it because the film is the certain way it is. The result will be something that comes from me. An- gelopoulos gives me this freedom to create."

Above, DAYS of '36; below, THE TRAVELLING PLAYERS, both directed by Angelopoulos and photographed by Arvanitis.

Arvanitis was 15 when he saw his first film. "I don't remember the film, but I remember the magic. I came out with a fever! I had no parents; lived with an uncle outside of Athens, and we were very poor. Sometimes there was only a piece of bread, so cinema was out of the question. I worked for ten years as an assistant in the commercial cinema. I began watching the light from the first time I was behind the camera. There were many times I did not agree with the photographer, so I would go work with another one, and then another. I learned that all photographers of the period used light as a technical tool, to light the shot, but not as a means of expression. I tried to forget what I had learned and to evolve my own way. I wanted to make films about which people would not say, 'Oh, this is an Arvanitis film,' but rather that it projects the character of the film itself. It is not always a success, but it is what I try for.

IPHIGENIA, directed by Cacoyannis and photographed by Arvanitis.

"During the commercial cinema days I always tried to do some experimenting in each film. And always during the film there would be one shot that was really mine. There was a scene in a commercial film set during the German occupation. The house was empty, no furnishings or any- thing, because the Germans had taken everything. There was no food, so the people were all hungry. I wanted a par- ticular light to make the walls of the rooms look cold, and the faces of the people hungry, with shadows under the eyes. The director said, 'You can do all that, but you must put a baby spot on the leading actress!' "

Arvanitis is divorced, lives in Athens. His favorites among his own films are THE TRAVELLING PLAYERS and DAYS OF '36. "I have been very much helped by the painter Ioannis Tsarouchis, not by saying things to him, but by study- ing the works by him. When I was making THE TRAVEL- LING PLAYERS, I kept this book of his paintings with me. " (Arvanitis owns an original Tsarouchis, autographed: "To Arvanitis, the teacher of the painters. ")

"I love Greek cinema. I know the struggle of the peo- ple and the cinema. I wouldn't like to leave, but I would like to work outside Greece without leaving it; but I have no connections outside of Greece. The new Angelopoulos film and Cacoyannis' IPHIGENIA will be shown at Cannes. Per- haps that might result in some connections for me. Mean- while I wait for proposals. I know in the near future in Greece there can only be one or two. Perhaps I will have to go out to find work. I am ready to do anything providing I can be faithful to my art. "

* * * * *

STAVROS HASAPIS has photographed 11 features and 42 shorts, including his own THE LABYRINTH, which took a prize at the Thessaloniki Festival. Hasapis had photographed so many of the films at the 1976 festival that it was prac- tically a one-photographer show. The jury had less trouble deciding who was to get the photographer's award than which film to give it to. Of the three photographers, he is the most practical and matter-of-fact about his craft. He has no stated desire to be a director, nor does he voice any overly sacred yearnings toward creativity. He simply per- forms his function with technical know-how, not only making real the visions of his young directors who depend on him to know how to realize their desires, but often fulfilling a mere unformed idea.

PROMETHEUS SECOND PERSON, SINGULAR, directed by
Costas Ferris, photographed by Stavros Hasapis.

Hasapis was studying mathematics in a school in the
provinces in France when François Truffaut came to the
school to present some of his films. Hasapis abandoned
mathematics and went to Paris to study film. "I really discovered film in Paris. I had seen many films in Greece,
but we had the star system, and everyone really went to
the films only to see Vouyouklaiki. "

Hasapis lives in Athens with his Swedish wife and
two children. "When I first returned to Greece I was so unhappy and disappointed about the situation that I wanted to go
away. But now I feel that Greece needs all of us who are
working in the cinema. I will not go away. When the film
world passes me by, I will probably do as other older cinematographers have done, move to television. "

*   *   *   *   *

GIORGOS PANOUSOPOULOS really thinks of himself

less as a cinematographer than as a director: "Of the 20
films I've worked on, at least 18 were the first film by the
director. This means I had one eye on the camera and one
on direction. I would like to direct, but I also like to work
with directors--something more than just holding the light
meter. I'm not really complaining. I would work with whom-
ever. I don't want to change anything to my way, but my
problem now is if I have a 'my' way, because I have worked
with so many different people. I don't know, do I have a
style? When I do direct a film, I don't know how it is going
to be. I feel as a director, or to be more precise, I never
feel as a cameraman. I feel uneasy when people talk about
Greek cinematographers and they mention me. I don't accept myself as a cinematographer.

"EURIDICE is my best work. The only absolutely acceptable work I've done. If anyone says my work is good,
I accept that positive criticism only for EURIDICE and partly for HAPPY DAY. All over the world--well, at least in
Europe--photographers like to think of themselves as some-

HAPPY DAY, directed by Pandelis Voulgaris and photographed
by Giorgos Panousopoulos.

thing more than photographers. They work with hand-held
cameras a lot. They work indirect lighting--like, you throw
some light on a white ceiling or a wall, and then you shoot.
At one time that was an imaginative way to light, but now it
has become the easy way, the result of which is that all
films look alike. In EURIDICE I decided to use the old style
of lighting, with projector lights not used anymore. The people who rented me these lights thought I was crazy. They
said they hadn't rented them for 20 years. This was the
first time I really felt like a photographer. We would have
to work sometimes two hours to set the lights to get the effect that was desired.

"When I worked with Savopoulos* in HAPPY DAY, I
asked him if he had seen EURIDICE. He said, 'Yes I did.
I didn't like the film at all, but I liked your work.' 'Why
and how?' I asked him, because he doesn't know movies.
And he said something I will never forget. 'I could see that
you worked hard, and I could see it on the screen.' For
me, if I can see that someone has worked hard, even if I
don't like the results, I respect the work. It is the only
thing I can respect with no doubt. If I see something that
would take someone two days to do which someone else could
do in five minutes, the one that took two days has to be more
beautiful and more important. Even if it's a style or product
that I don't like. I admire effort. The satisfaction I have
gotten from most of my work is more from having ideas,
rather than extending effort. Everything seems to be too
easy. That's why I'm never too enthusiastic about myself.
Maybe this is a weak point, everything is too easy. I'm
still looking for a director to really give me a challenge.
Generally speaking, if it is too easy, it is not worth doing.
Well, there are exciting ideas, but actually I don't respect
ideas as much as I respect work. This has come as I have
grown older. I started very young. At the age of 22 I was
already the director of photography on a French production
here in Greece. It was a big thing and I thought I was God
in those days. And still people in Greece recall my name
as a good photographer, but I think they were more impressed by the noise I made in those days than they were
with the work. I would say to my friends, 'Whatever I do,
they will like it,' which is really stupid."

*Dionisis Savopoulos is a currently popular composer. He
did the score for HAPPY DAY, the first score written for a
"new wave" film by a "major" Greek composer.

The Cinematographers Talk About The Directors

Panousopoulos: "Greek filmmakers don't know shit about making films! We are still in the process of learning how to express ourselves through film. And if you want to know my opinion, all Greek films, let's say 'new' films, that have been made in the last 15 years, should have been made in 16mm. None of these people have ever experimented. They never spend time experimenting to learn their craft. We want to go directly to the big screen, which is wrong. We don't give ourselves time to learn the language we call movies. We learn by spending millions when we could learn spending thousands. That's why the directors don't really ask too much of the technicians, because they don't know what to ask. Whatever they get they are happy with. Whatever you are going to be, you have to learn from the ground up. A director should start with an 8mm, choose his own sets, costumes, stories, actors. Do his own editing. The end result is not important. What is important is that he learns while doing it.

"By the time you are ready to be a director, you can ask your collaborators to do what you want, because you have learned what it is you want and know something about how it can be obtained. Angelopoulos is the only one who knows exactly what he wants. It doesn't matter whether you think it's good or bad, the point is he knows what he wants. He worked as a critic; he saw a lot, thought a lot, and had the time to formulate his ideas about this language.

"Just for fun sometimes I will make a suggestion to a director. I'll say, 'would you like the camera traveling here?' And he will say, 'Yes, that's a good idea.' And then I say, 'well, actually, I think something else would be more effective,' and he'll say, 'yes, that's a good idea.' An exception was a German director I once worked with. He didn't always know what he wanted, but at least knew what he didn't want. I'd say, 'then, what do you want?' and he'd answer, 'I don't know.' Voulgaris was somewhat this way in HAPPY DAY. He knew what he didn't want, but not always what he did want."

Arvanitis: "What is very important is that there are no new directors in Greece. There are many young directors with a copy of Brecht under their arms, and they sit in Kolonaiki Square all day and talk and talk and talk, but when they

Director Manoussos Manousakis lends a helping hand to photographer Giorgos Panousopoulos during filming of POWER.

come before the camera, nothing happens. Our hope is Voulgaris, Angelopoulos, and I don't know who else. I believe Voulgaris is very talented, and will go far.

"Cacoyannis and I collaborated well during IPHIGENIA, but there was always the problem of trying to understand one another because it was the first time we had ever worked together. It was a different way of working because Cacoyannis had not worked in Greece for some time and he is used to another way of working. He was used to foreign people, and I am used to Angelopoulos, so we simply had different methods of working.

"Angelopoulos will ask me to do something, but basically we work together. After a decision has been reached, he leaves me alone to do my job. Angelopoulos is willing to wait two, even three days for the light to be just right for a shot. Not because he is interested in a pretty picture, but because the shot is an integral contribution to the whole.

"Cacoyannis would ask that I do something and I would do it. I didn't face any unusual problems because there was always no wind and plenty of sun. There were one or two shots that were a little different, and we discussed them. At first Cacoyannis was not convinced that things were going the best way. For instance, there was a shot--a difficult shot, and Cacoyannis asked me how long it would take to light the shot and I said I needed some time. After about 20 minutes I said I was ready, but Cacoyannis said, 'Oh no, it is not possible!' because with his previous working experience he knew such a task would take some three-four hours. Cacoyannis was very anxious to see the results, saying that perhaps it would have to be done again.

"Well, I'm not playing the star. I could have said I need some time to think. People do that. But I'm not thinking of myself, I'm thinking of the film. There are times when I have put bad lighting in a shot because it seemed right for the film. I never think of myself, but always of the film. This makes people suspicious sometimes.

"The major difference between Cacoyannis and Angelopoulos is that Cacoyannis works always thinking of the editing. Angelopoulos thinks of the whole as it is being done."

At top, THE REASON WHY; below, MAY. Both films were directed by Tasos Psarras, photographed by Stavros Hasapis.

Hasapis: "Many of the directors are very good at their technique, but in essence they have nothing to say. Others are real artists, but cannot find the opportunity to express their artistry. It's difficult for me to explore this idea further, because I collaborate with all of them. I worked on three of the six feature films shown at Thessaloniki in 1976. It's not because I'm the best, it's because they socialize with me, they know me. There is not enough work for everyone. And there simply is no money for anyone to do their jobs. We have to produce in a minimum amount of time with a minimum amount of film, whatever it is we produce. I am eager for you to understand that what we do accomplish is miracles!"

BIOGRAPHICAL BRIEF

George Arvanitis

Born in a village near Lamia, February 1941. Moved to Athens age 8. Worked in commercial cinema. Divorced, lives in Athens. Favorites among own films: THE TRAVELLING PLAYERS, DAYS OF '36. Worked on approximately 70 films. Awards (all from Thessaloniki Festival): 1970, Best Cinematography, RECONSTRUCTION; 1972, Best Cinematography, DAYS OF '36; 1973, Special Award, THE GREAT LOVE SONGS; 1974, Best Cinematography, THE TRAVELLING PLAYERS.

PARTIAL FILMOGRAPHY

LE FILS DANS LE MORT. (Dir: Jean-Jacques Andrien). (Filmed in Belgium).

ABUSE (1969). (Dir: Stavros Tsiolis).

HIGH TREASON (1970). (Dir: Panos Glykofridis).

WHAT DID YOU DO IN THE WAR, THANASSI? (Dir: Dinos Katsouridis).

RECONSTRUCTION (1971). (Dir: Thodoros Angelopoulos).

ALIKI DIKTATOR (1972). (Dir: Takis Vouyouklakis).

PRISONERS OF HATE (1972). (Dir: Nicos Foskolos).

A MATTER OF CONSEQUENCE (1973). (Dir: Petros Lykas).

VIOLENT JOHN (1973). (Dir: Tonia Marketaki).

THE GREAT LOVE SONGS (1973). (Dir: Pandelis Voulgaris).

CRANIUM LANDSCAPE (1973). (Dir: Costas Aristopoulos).

THE TRAVELLING PLAYERS (1975). (Dir: Thodoros Angelopoulos).

THE PROCEEDINGS (1976). (Dir: Dimosthenis Theos).

ASSAULT ON AGATHON (1976). (Dir: Laslo Benedek).

IPHIGENIA (1977). (Dir: Michael Cacoyannis).

THE HUNTERS (1977). (Dir: Thodoros Angelopoulos).

A DREAM OF PASSION (1978). (Dir: Jules Dassin).

BIOGRAPHICAL BRIEF

Stavros Hasapis

Born 1942 in Valeousta, a village near Agrinion. Grew up in Athens. Studied mathematics in France. Switched to film, studied in Paris. Lives with wife and two children in Athens. Has worked on over 40 short films, including his own 22-minute short, THE LABYRINTH. Awards: 1969 Thessaloniki Festival, Prize for First Work of a New Director for THE LABYRINTH; 1976 Thessaloniki Festival, Best Photography, THE OTHER LETTER. Among the 11 feature films on which he has collaborated are:

FILMS

THE REASON WHY (1974). (Dir: Tasos Psarras).

THE MURDERESS (1974). (Dir: Costas Ferris).

PROMETHEUS SECOND PERSON, SINGULAR (1975). (Dir: Costas Ferris).

THE DOUBT (1975). (Filmed in England).

THE ROBOT (1975). (Filmed in France).

THE OTHER LETTER (1976). (Dir: Lambros Liaropoulos).

CYPRUS (1976). (Dir: Thekia Kittou, Lambros Papademetrakis).

MAY (1976). (Dir: Tasos Psarras).

BIOGRAPHICAL BRIEF

George Panousopoulos

Panousopoulos started working in film in 1961, becoming a cinematographer in 1965. Has done about 20 films, including three in Germany. Written and directed two shorts. Has ambitions to be a director. Divorced, two children. Lives in Athens. His photography for Manoussakis' POWER received an Honorable Mention at the 1977 New Director's Festival. His films include:

FILMS

BLOKA (1965). (Dir: Ado Kyrou).

THE GREAT LOVE SONGS (1973). (Dir: Pandelis Voulgaris). (Photography mostly by George Arvanitis. Panousopoulos did additional photography and edited).

DEATH HAS BLUE EYES (1974). (Dir: Nicos Mastorakis).

KIERION (1974). (Dir: Dimosthenis Theos). (This film was made in 1968 but not premiered in Greece until 1974).

EURIDICE BA-2037 (1975). (Dir: Nicos Nikolaidis).

ALDEVARAN (1975). (Dir: Andreas Thomopoulos).

HAPPY DAY (1976). (Dir: Pandelis Voulgaris).

POWER (1977). (Dir: Manoussos Manoussakis).

In 1977 he was working on a TV film being directed by Tonia Marketaki.

Chapter 17

PERFORMERS

The routine day-to-day life of the average Athenian is
led with a boisterous openness; it is theorized that this refreshing lack of self-consciousness, along with a tongue-in-
cheek self-glorification, contributes to the existence of a remarkable number of accomplished performers in Greece.
The most insipid television serials are littered with highly
skilled actors. Theaters are more plentiful than audiences.
After exposure to this superior level of competence, one re-
grets even more that Greece has not made a larger contribution to the growing international pool of acting talent.

Any opportunity to see Greek films from another decade quickly reveals that quality acting has always been available in Greece. Many of the performers from the films of
the '50s remain active on stage and television in the '70s--to
the mutual rewarding of themselves and their audiences. Why
so few have found their way to international fame remains a
mystery.

The young directors of the '70s have not as yet crossed
a generation gap to work cooperatively with these seasoned
performers. Perhaps it is simply a question of money, for
they do not have much money to offer their performers--in
most cases, no money at all. The established professional
actors are likely disinclined to work for a token payment.
Even should they be willing, there is the stated position of
the young directors that they prefer to use performer-spokes-
men from their own generation. Their films are usually on
"now" subjects, with no place for the older performers.
Furthermore, a large percentage of the films either use no
actors at all, or use them in such a way that they really are
incidental. Of the seven films shown in competition at the
1976 festival, three used no actors. The only film with sizable roles for actors was Lintzeris' EXODUS, and even he
used amateurs. The other three (Voulgaris' HAPPY DAY,
Theos' THE PROCEEDINGS, Psarras' MAY) so integrated

actors into the overall purposes of the film that the jury declined to give individual acting awards.   HAPPY DAY may be somewhat of an exception in that Voulgaris is very people-oriented and even within a large cast such as that of HAPPY DAY, each individual does get isolated attention.

Some of the directors observe that the Greek actors are theater-trained and find it difficult to move comfortably from one medium to another.   There is probably some truth to that, but aside from the slim financial pickings for the actor in film, there simply are two few roles in cinema for the Greek performers to grant much attention to film as a possible career.   Television is providing performers an opportunity to work before the camera, bridging the gap between the technical differences of stage and film acting.   When the directors are ready to use performers, the performers will be ready to make cinematic contributions.

There certainly have been highly successful exceptions to the generalization that the directors are not using actors. Angelopoulos' films abound with brilliant performances, despite his claim that he does not feel comfortable with actors. Voulgaris' THE ENGAGEMENT OF ANNA was cast entirely with theatre-trained actors who never for an instant give any clue that they have not always worked in front of the camera. Panayotopoulos shows promise of being an actor's director, and also is the only '70s director to show any interest in working with a previous generation.   In THE COLORS OF IRIS there is a set piece wherein a retired chanteuse is allowed a musical number which has nothing to do with the forward movement of the film (but is a delightful contribution to it), and in September 1977 he was negotiating with former film-star Elli Lambetti to make a guest appearance in his new film.

MELINA MERCOURI

Despite this cache of quality performers, the number who are known outside Greece is pitifully small.   Unquestionably the best-known is Melina Mercouri, who burst on the international scene in 1960 as the beloved hooker in Jules Dassin's NEVER ON SUNDAY.   Ms. Mercouri had made her screen debut in 1955 in Michael Cacoyannis' STELLA, playing a role which may have inspired NEVER ON SUNDAY. STELLA is an early women's lib film (before it had a verbal identification), Stella being a nightclub entertainer who so

Melina Mercouri in STELLA (Director: Michael Cacoyannis).

loves her freedom that when she has an option to marry a
man she truly loves, she rejects the marriage bonds and
faces death at the hands of her suitor.   The film captures a
period when the influence of the rest of the world was being
felt in Greece, and Stella's dressing room is arrayed with
pictures of Hollywood movie stars.   Even her nightclub act
rejected the accepted forms and was cheaply and pathetically
modeled after the plastic glamor of Hollywood films.

NEVER ON SUNDAY is a "musical comedy" treatment of STELLA, but it resulted in an international awareness of a dynamic screen personality which remains un-
dimmed.   Ms. Mercouri was the first Greek actress to break
through the national boundaries since Katina Paxinou, who
acquired recognition and prestige in Hollywood's FOR WHOM
THE BELL TOLLS in the 1940s, but whose career was full
and respected throughout her life.

In 1977 Melina Mercouri was elected to parliament in
Greece. This may mean the end of an acting career, or may
be merely a hiatus. She has been actively political most of
her life. Prior to her election she completed a film with
Jules Dassin, co-starring the American actress Ellen Burstyn,
so there is at least one more Melina film to which one can
look forward. Her screen projection has always been aggressive and thrusting, and with time it has become even more
so. The voice has moved from baritone to bass; the gestures
are more operatic; what was once subtle is now grand. But
there is no doubt that she was and is a star!

IRENE PAPAS

Michael Cacoyannis played a role in the introduction
to the world of a second great actress: Irene Papas in 1961's
ELECTRA. ELECTRA is a model of screen adaptation from
another source, and Ms. Papas in the title role is a presence
to inspire awe. In fact, her presence is so commanding that
in image if not in fact, she has been limited in the roles
available to her. One doesn't think of Irene Papas so much
as an actress, but rather as one of the basic elements.
Both Mr. Cacoyannis and Hollywood are contributing to this
projection, but on distinctly different qualitative levels.
Cacoyannis has cast Ms. Papas in four films; in each case
there is at least one shot (if not more) of Ms. Papas that
freezes in memory and, though it remains an indelible pleasure, it also undermines both Ms. Papas' performance and
the films themselves. One remembers the shot, much as
images of film stars are created by still photographs rather
than their film roles. In ELECTRA, the primary introduction of the character is a closeup of Ms. Papas' face slowly
emerging from the severely contrasting shadows. It is so
memorable that the film suffers as one searches for the repeated magic. (This is an exaggeration; ELECTRA is a completely successful film and the excess is only allowed because
this is a stunning moment within it.)

Ms. Papas gets the Cacoyannis treatment again in
ZORBA THE GREEK when we first see her as the widow,
hanging on the clothesline her symbolically immaculate sheets
which flap in the wind, allowing quick, framed glimpses of
her marble face. And again, in THE TROJAN WOMEN, as
the caged Helen, pacing back and forth like a black panther
with just the searching eyes darting through the bars.

Irene Papas in IPHIGENIA (Director: Michael Cacoyannis).

Along with the Cacoyannis glorification has come the uni-dimensional use of her in her Hollywood films. She was seen by Hollywood as a Mother Earth who suffered and survived, but rarely talked or acted. She simply was, like the Acropolis or the Pyramids. It is thus no wonder than when Cacoyannis turned her loose in THE TROJAN WOMEN, it came as a marvelous surprise to some to learn that she could act. It wasn't that she hadn't acted before (after all, there had been ELECTRA), but that the composite had been one of presence rather than actress. It was daring of Cacoyannis to cast her as the beautiful Helen, for despite Ms. Papas' personal magnificence, she is not beautiful in the mold of such women as Hedy Lamarr, Elizabeth Taylor or Ava Gardner. In the embodiment of Ms. Papas, Helen becomes not simply a legendary beauty for whose sake a ten-year war was waged, but a force which might indeed have inspired a holocaust.

In IPHIGENIA (Cacoyannis, 1977) Ms. Papas pulls out all the stops and delivers a full range of histrionics. It is not excessive, in that the characters are real within a modern psychological framework, despite the mythological unreality of the story. Ms. Papas proves herself an actress of major proportions. She is aided this time by the timing of Cacoyannis' inevitable (and by now demanded) shot of her, since this time it comes at the end of the film, allowing us to deal with her up to that point as an actress rather than the Papas presence to which we have become accustomed. The final shot of the film is a closeup of her face which remains on-screen during the running of the credits. It is an expression of hatred, repulsion, lust for revenge, which sets the stage for an understanding of the character of Clytemnestra when next we meet her following the Trojan War in ELECTRA. *

Ms. Papas, one hopes, has many films in her future. She, too, has not worked with any of the new directors, despite the fact she is the aunt of Manoussos Manoussakis.

---

*It is trivial amusement to reflect that Irene Papas has played practically the whole family: Electra, Clytemnestra and Helen. Since Electra came first, she has thus played her own aunt, and then her own mother.

ELLI LAMBETTI

Two other actresses not now working on-screen are deserving of attention: Elli Lambetti and Aliki Vouyouklaiki. Ms. Lambetti starred in Michael Cacoyannis' first film, and in three additional ones thereafter. THE GIRL IN BLACK (1956) is a marvelous example of Ms. Lambetti's projection. Her characterization combines the "feminine" warmth of Simone Signoret in ROOM AT THE TOP; the wounded vulnerability of Olivia de Havilland in THE HEIRESS; and Sophia Loren's yielding to fate yet surviving in TWO WOMEN. Despite these comparisons, Ms. Lambetti has her own unique qualities. Why did she not attain broad international recognition?

America was fascinated with "ladies" in the 1950s.

Elli Lambetti in THE GIRL IN BLACK (Director: Michael Cacoyannis).

We had a bevy of talented but rather bland actresses on the
screen: Vera Miles, Dina Merrill, Diane Baker, Diane Var-
si, Eva Marie Saint--and the queens of the professional vir-
gins, Grace Kelly and Doris Day. It wasn't that these actresses didn't have talent, or that time proved them all considerably more dynamic than the '50s led us to believe; they
were just representative of a period when there was a movement to re-establish the male-female role-playing which had
been disrupted by World War II.

All of this is to theorize why Ms. Lambetti did not
find a larger audience. There were already many actresses
voicing her message (despite her considerable talent). A
star from another culture was only welcomed when she was
an "exotic" presence which could be accepted on its own
terms: the mother wolf of Anna Magnani, the fair princess
of Audrey Hepburn, the voluptuous challenge of Sophia Loren.
Ms. Lambetti was simply too much like the girls back home.

Fortunately she has had a successful and lengthy career in Greece where her delicate and developed talent has
been greatly appreciated. She continues to appear on stage,
making a personal success in 1976 of "Miss Margarida's
Way" at least a year before the American production starring
Estelle Parsons. To my knowledge, she is the first of the
major female screen stars of earlier years to be seriously
approached to make a film with the new directors. Unfortunately, Ms. Lambetti has declined the role in Panayotopoulos' THE INDOLENCE OF THE FERTILE VALLEY.

ALIKI VOUYOUKLAIKI

Who or what is Aliki Vouyouklaiki? Take a pinch of
Debbie Reynolds energy, a touch of Doris Day steeliness,
lace generously with Brigitte Bardot child-womanliness, season with the committed ambition of Joan Crawford. Stir
vigorously while adding Julie Andrews, Gina Lollobrigida,
Lana Turner, Ruby Keeler and Shirley Temple. Bake for
15 years under a perpetual spotlight and voila! Aliki Vouyouklaiki! But know that the ingredients only combine to
make a new and quite phenomenal element, unique and more
than the ingredients.

The December 1974 issue of The Athenian carried a
vivid portrait of her, signed S. E. To quote: "What ex-

Aliki Vouyouklaiki as cover girl on <u>Romance</u> magazine.

actly is the Vouyouklaiki magic? ... It has first of all to do
with the rapport she creates with her audience, which is almost tangible. Her appearance arouses in her spectators an
inexplicable urge to raise and sing the National Hymn.... It
is not just that ravishing wink she gives us every now and
then, it is the whole manner ... here, down stage center we
have Aliki playing straight out to her admiring public. It is
the most honest of hoaxes. Once this is established ... we
can sit back, relax and enjoy the many-sided subtleties of
her performance. We have seen most of it before: Aliki,
the winsome comedienne; Aliki the rejected woman (beware!);
Aliki, the grande dame; Aliki, the ethnic champion.... She
scans the auditorium with the utmost familiarity. It is after
all, hers.

"Women admire Aliki more openly.... A single man
she sees through quite easily--but to what?--another man?
Other men? ... Note her curtain calls: how she brusquely
throws her supporting actors forward for their applause, dis-
posing of them as if they were infinitely recyclable.... "

Apparently Ms. Vouyouklaiki tends to view herself as
recyclable also. She treats time as though in suspended animation, presenting herself with little consideration for the
changes that may have been wrought within the past 15 years.
Another 15 years promises a continuum. Given the severity
of Athens air pollution, one suspects that she may outlast
the Parthenon.

Ms. Vouyouklaiki claims to be willing to make a film
with a new director, but it is hard to imagine the possibility.
Like Betty Grable or Jeanette MacDonald, she belongs to the
commercial cinema. Were she in THE TRAVELLING PLAY-
ERS, her bags would have been Gucci. Were she in THE
ENGAGEMENT OF ANNA, her aprons would have been imported lace. Were she willing to play herself, Panayotopoulos could create another Margo Channing or Norma Desmond
for her--a most unlikely eventuality.

Meanwhile Vouyouklaiki goes on her successful, campy,
charming, talented, and phenomenal way, the former film
queen of Greece, the current stage and television queen.

A Selected Who's Who of Greek Film Performers

Despite the minimal number of films which provide an

opportunity for performers to express their art, given the chance the performers have risen to the occasion with memorable effectiveness. Considering Greece's long, long history and tradition of theatre, it is not surprising that there is excellent acting training available. Unfortunately for cinema, the training is all stage-oriented and the actors talk about their difficulties in making the media transition.

Natural talent abounds, however. Dimitris Poulikakos is a prime example. Poulikakos is a composer and singer of popular music who drifted into acting in response to an opportunity. The opportunities continue to present themselves; he is now playing an important role in Panayotopoulos' new film THE INDOLENCE OF THE FERTILE VALLEY. His credits include POWER (Manoussakis), HAPPY DAY (Voul-

Stavros Kalaroglou and Dimitris Meletis in HAPPY DAY (Director: Pandelis Voulgaris).

garis), ALDEVARAN (Thomopoulos). He's a good character
type with considerable humor.

A second example of the effective "non-actor" is
Dimitris Meletis who, so it is rumored, wants to be a director. (But then, in Greece, who doesn't?) Off-beat handsome, Meletis has a "modern" quality--a kind of cross between James Dean and Dustin Hoffman in appeal. Given en-
viable on-screen time in Voulgaris' HAPPY DAY as the singer of "Folk Singer" at the "happy day" musicale, he moved
on to an even more memorable specialty number in Manoussakis' POWER, doing a particularly erotic strip tease at a
drunken party. Meletis could play leads, especially in mod-
ern-youth-struggles stories, assuming his directorial ambitions allow.

Obviously technique is only an ingredient in acting--
presence is often more important. Takis Kilakos, who plays
Judas in Aristopoulos' CRANIUM LANDSCAPE, may indeed

Takis Kilakos as Judas in Costas Aristopoulos' CRANIUM
LANDSCAPE.

Simeon Triantafillidis (above) and Antigone Athanasiou, both in Ioannis Lintzeris' EXODUS.

be a knowledgeable actor but what one remembers is his presence, dynamic enough to evoke a positive understanding of Aristopoulos' interest in making a film about Judas. Caterina Goghou, in Tassio's THE HEAVY MELON, is outstanding as "embracing woman" confused by the modern changes and external influences confronting her. Ms. Goghou won the Best Actress award for the film in 1977. Her screen credits also include Katsouridis' WHAT DID YOU DO IN THE WAR, THANASSI? (1971).

Another actress of interest is Helen Maniati. Her uninhibited sexuality in ALDEVARAN is that of a modern woman who feels tenderness and compassion for her sexual partners, but never to the point of servitude. Ms. Maniati also appears as the royal matriarch in Theos' THE PROCEEDINGS, but the director imposed a detachment on the actors in that film which detracts from interest in the performers.

Simeon Triantafillidis and Antigone Athanasiou, in Lintzeris' EXODUS, both succeed in difficult roles, although neither is a professional actor. Tatiana Papamoskou in the title role of Cacoyannis' IPHIGENIA, with no training at all, outshines the theatre-trained males in the cast. But these examples are not given to imply that theater performers are ineffective on screen. Anestis Vlahos in Theos' KIERION and Vassilis Diamadopoulos in Pavlithis' THE WALL make it powerfully clear that such is not the case. The depth of these older actors stirs the imagination ... what if Voulgaris were to work with George Foundas?* How about Aleka Katseli** in a Panayotopoulos film?

A comprehensive who's who of Greek cinema performers would certainly provide enough material for a separate book. Those discussed here are selected arbitrarily and by availability, and should be considered as merely representative.

---

*George Foundas appeared in many Cacoyannis films, most memorably as Melina Mercouri's lover in STELLA. He is currently very active in television.
**Aleka Katseli played Clytemnestra in Cacoyannis' ELECTRA. She is active on stage, an older, but remarkably handsome woman.

All About Eva

- EVA KOTAMANIDOU -

Eva Kotamanidou has a very good chance of being the next Greek actress to transcend the inhibiting national boundary. Film being the medium most likely to lead to international recognition, the Greek performer's opportunities are practically non-existent, considering the small number of films being made, and the small percentage of these which employ actors (perhaps only about two or three films a year). Ms. Kotamanidou, therefore, has overcome fantastic odds by making her film debut in Thodoros Angelopoulos' THE TRAVELLING PLAYERS, the most internationally successful Greek film of the 1970s.

As Electra in THE TRAVELLING PLAYERS, Eva Kotamanidou projects a character somewhat combining the silent, enduring strength of Irene Papas in her American films and the accelerated force of Katina Paxinou. The structure of the film invites these comparisons: there are numerous sequences where the scraggly theatrical troupe must simply, silently survive; there are also scenes more intimately involved with the characters. In some of these latter scenes, Ms. Kotamanidou has long speeches, delivered directly to camera, which are a grueling test of her ability to hold an audience. Without aid of cuts, camera movement, or other help from the medium, she makes triumphant use of these opportunities.

Eva Kotamanidou was only one of many actresses being considered for the role. "Angelopoulos called many girls, took some pictures, then took a month to make his selection. When he chose me I was very pleased because it was a new job, something I didn't know. I was afraid, but excited too. I was also surprised he selected me because he had not seen me in the theater and I had only worked television once, in a one-act play done very quickly, and in my opinion, very bad.

"In essence, I had never worked with the camera. I was fortunate in that Angelopoulos begins all his films with the easier scenes. The first scenes in THE TRAVELLING PLAYERS were those scenes with the troupe and all their luggage outside the railway station. The camera is far away, so it was very easy. I could ease into it. When the scenes

Eva Kotamanidou models a dress she made, having learned
to knit during the filming of THE HUNTERS.

came when the camera was closer, I was used to it by that
time. And, you see, his work is a little distant. You never
have the camera so close. Sometimes I had the feeling I
was in the theater. You might have a scene of 20 minutes,
or eight minutes or six minutes, and you feel some continuity.
That made it easier. And, of course, not having continuity
in playing a film role is the real difficulty in acting for the
camera.

"At first I was afraid. We were filming during the
junta and Angelopoulos did not give us the complete script,
which increased my anxiety as a performer. But, little by
little, I began to understand the whole character. I knew,
of course, that I was Electra, which gave me some knowledge of my relationship to the other characters in the story.
When we would do a scene, Angelopoulos would say the scene

Eva Kotamanidou during filming of THE TRAVELLING PLAY-
ERS (Director: Thodoros Angelopoulos).

goes before or after another scene we had already done, so
I began to piece the role together.

"Even at the end of the film I had never seen the complete script. We stopped filming during the summer, and
during that time I spoke with him many times, so I had put
it all together. When we resumed filming, I knew everything.
It was much easier then, of course.

"At first I would make mistakes. Sometimes I would
laugh when everyone else did, only to discover that I was not
supposed to. There was the scene near the sea when the
English make us play for them. Then the English come and
invite us to dance. As we rehearsed, some Englishman
came and asked me to dance, and I began to dance because
I didn't know Electra hated the English. And then Angelopoulos said, 'Oh no! You do not dance.' So, you see, at the
beginning there were things I didn't understand."

The strength of Eva Kotamanidou's performance in
THE TRAVELLING PLAYERS creates the illusion that she
is a tall, sturdy woman; I was quite unprepared for the
rather mousy impression I had when I unexpectedly met her.
This impression soon changed also, and she became a charming little girl with a tendency to giggle--many steps removed
from Electra of THE TRAVELLING PLAYERS. I began to
sense that Eva Kotamanidou has a chameleon quality, and so
I was not surprised when at our next meeting she was quite
bewitching in a smart costume, exaggerated sun-glasses, and
a kind of Lizabeth Scott casual hairdo. The total effect was
that of a glamorous actress. During our exchange she effectively convinced me that she was naive, sophisticated,
hopeful, determined, grateful, calculating, youthful, mature,
shy, aggressive, humorous, serious, docile, ambitious--and
above all, a startlingly versatile actress.

A few days later we met accidentally. She was in
slight disarray, on a break from some domestic chores.
Since she didn't look like any of the other Eva Kotamanidous
I had seen, I was convinced this one really was Eva Kotamanidou, and looked forward to observing the ease with
which she would alter her appearance, which she did with
a ready smile. I stood to greet her and the coffee shop of
the Athens Hilton was transformed into a stage on which I
happily played a scene with Greece's most important "new
wave" film actress.

Eva Kotamanidou has been working in the theater for over ten years. Her entry signalled exceptional talent from the very beginning: an audition for the famous school of Karolos Koun, whose theater, during the last few decades, has been in the vanguard of progressive and quality theater in Greece. Of the 60-70 hopefuls auditioning for the three-year course at the Koun school, ten were selected, four of whom were released after a year. Among the remaining six was Ms. Kotamanidou.

"I played in the theater while going to school. My first part was in a Greek play called "The Fair." It was not successful: in 20 days it was finished! After completing school I stayed in the theater, where I played from 1964 to 1971. We played Greek plays and foreign: Ionesco, Beckett, Williams, Brecht. We did the ancients too: Electra, Antigone, Lysistrata, The Frogs. My face changes, so I was able to play many parts. For example, I have played a 100-year-old woman, and I have played a 16-year-old girl. This may keep me from being a star, because stars, especially film stars, adapt the role to themselves, rather than themselves to the role.

"But I have always wanted to do a film. Since I was a little girl I have gone to the cinema. I liked them very much. I have seen all those American films with Tyrone Power and Errol Flynn and Ava Gardner and Joan Fontaine. I went to the cinema two or three times a week. In fact, I began to like theater from my love for the cinema.

"Theater is, in a way, more difficult because there is a contact with an audience while you are playing. But film stays. The performance in the theater is there, and then it is over. It's like the wind that blows and then it is gone. I like it. But now that I have made a film, I realize it will stay. You can see it again after ten or 20 years. It's very important.

"Of course films can make you more popular. Many people came to the theater when I was playing THE THREE PENNY OPERA and they would come backstage to see me and say what a good performance. Then I would discover they were speaking about THE TRAVELLING PLAYERS. I had been in the theater for ten years and they didn't know me.

"The capacity of television to reach so many people at one given time is why so many actors switched to television

Eva Kotamanidou on stage in THE THREE PENNY OPERA,
directed by Jules Dassin.

when TV first came to Greece. They were famous from one minute to another. During the junta there were actors who starred in a TV series. Now they have earned much money and can afford to be directors of their own theaters.

"I am in rehearsal for a television play. This is the second time they have called me. I want to work on television, but of course, to do some interesting work. There are an awful lot of silly roles and it is a shame to play them. But I want to do some good work, like in the theater, like in films. I have only a small role in this show, but I didn't want to say no when they called because I want to know something about television when something more serious comes my way. When I did my first TV play, I noticed the other actors did not speak to each other. They spoke to the camera. When they had a conversation with me, they were not talking to me at all, but to the camera. They knew very well the camera would see only their face, and not the other actor. I didn't know that, so throughout the show you can't see my face.

"THE TRAVELLING PLAYERS has opened a few doors for me. Many actors and directors who didn't know me before, know me now. Working with the Koun theater is a little closed, because he will not permit his actors to play television or outside theater. We had repertory and were always rehearsing or playing. We had no time to meet other artists or craftsmen. But after THE TRAVELLING PLAYERS, they called me to replace Melina Mercouri in THE THREE PENNY OPERA. I don't think they would have done that before. It's not really that I am a better actress now, but that they know me. And perhaps now they trust me more. In the theater of Koun it is often said that we are not good actresses or actors, but that it is Koun who makes us appear so. I don't think that is true. He always says, 'If you can do it, do it. If you can't do it, I can't do it for you.'

"I would like to work with some other film directors. Lena Voudouri approached me for a film, but she was unable to find the money. I went to the Koun school with Costas Aristopoulos who has since become a film director, and many times we have talked of doing a film together, but he too has never found the money."

Ms. Kotamanidou won the Best Actress award at the 1975 Thessaloniki Festival: "I was pleased, of course. But

I don't think the prize at Thessaloniki has much meaning. I have known many actors and actresses who have won this prize, and then they disappear. The award? It's not in my house yet. It's in the office of Mr. Angelopoulos. The important thing to me was not the award, but that the people liked the film. "

In November 1976, Eva Kotamanidou starts a new film with director Angelopoulos (THE HUNTERS). "I have a good role. I am about 45 years old and throughout most of the film I am quite repressed.* But at the end there is an explosion. She is from the aristocracy, and they think about the king and all the power they have lost. It is a New Year's scene, and when the lights go out at midnight, she thinks she sees the king open the door and come inside. She dances with him, flirts with him, and in the end makes love with him. It is a fantasy and he is not actually there. But she must give the impression to the audience that he is there. It is difficult and I'm a little nervous about it. "

Perhaps the language barrier is a major reason for the insulation of Greek actors. Maybe the comparative smallness of Greece effects a comforting security. Whatever the reasons, the world knows few of Greece's many talented performers. Eva Kotamanidou speaks French and English, and there is a strong possibility that her name may follow that of the shamefully small list of Greek performers known internationally: Paxinou, Mercouri, Papas. The current focus of attention is on actors rather than stars, which means that the time is ripe for Eva Kotamanidou. And even if the star time reappears, I suspect "star" is one of the roles Eva Kotamanidou can play very well.

"If I had the opportunity to play outside of Greece I would not say no. This does not mean that I want to leave Greece. But it would be easier in Greece after having a big success outside. When our artists are working in Greece, frequently no one pays any attention to them. But if they go out and get recognized, when they come back they are 'someone'. "

* * * * *

---

*To add some definition to her character, Ms. Kotamanidou learned to knit, which she does throughout the film. She became so proficient that she now makes some of her own clothes.

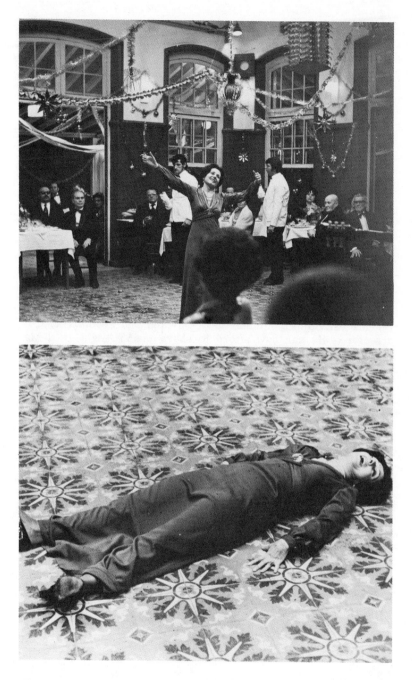

Eva Kotamanidou in Thodoros Angelopoulos' THE HUNTERS.

1977 UPDATE: Although she is on-screen throughout THE HUNTERS, Ms. Kotamanidou is only one of an ensemble cast. Each player has a scene, though, which allows for emergence from the group, and when it is Ms. Kotamanidou's turn, at nearly the end of the film, she grabs the opportunity. It is an incredible scene, shot in a single take, in which she dances and makes love with the fantasized king. Angelopoulos shows great daring as a director, and faith in Ms. Kotamanidou as an actress for allowing the scene to play out its allowed time. In solitary mime, the actress greets her nonexistent partner, dances with him, then lies on the floor and copulates with him. The character is a conservative middle-aged woman, and Ms. Kotamanidou projects a particularly incisive delineation of the character when, during the actual copulation, she mimes the act by moving only the upper half of her prone body, thus capturing the repressions and rigidity of the character as well as adding to the unreality of the scene. To thus play the scene was Ms. Kotamanidou's idea, and Angelopoulos wisely allowed it. It is obviously time for Mr. Angelopoulos to write a film to star Ms. Kotamanidou. He has established himself as a talented and accomplished director. He can now afford to share the spotlight, and Ms. Kotamanidou has made amply clear in THE TRAVELLING PLAYERS and THE HUNTERS that she is ready to handle anything.

BIOGRAPHICAL BRIEF

Born Athens, 1943. Parents came from Smyrna in 1922. Three sisters, none in theater. Studied in the school of Koun; played in Koun theater from 1964 to 1971. Some television. Single, lives in Athens. Best Actress award, 1975 Thessaloniki Festival, for THE TRAVELLING PLAYERS.

FILMS

THE TRAVELLING PLAYERS (1975). (Dir: Thodoros Angelopoulos).

THE HUNTERS (1977). (Dir: Thodoros Angelopoulos).

Vangelis Kazan, above in Hermes Vellopoulos' CLOSED WIN-
DOW; below, in Angelopoulos' THE HUNTERS.

Never a Husband--Always a Lover

- VANGELIS KAZAN -

Vangelis Kazan is one of Greece's most prominent and talented film actors. He is also a happening! Throw away your list of questions and turn him loose; he is uncontrollable anyway, so relax and enjoy the performance. Vangelis Kazan says he speaks Italian and "a little Greek" and then launches into a two-hour nonstop verbal marathon, most of which I was able to understand because his ideas were not just talked out, they were acted out.

He played tragedy, comedy, Victorian melodrama, dignified mature artists, little boys, wise sages, and, but for the absence of an orchestra, would have no doubt offered a complete musical revue, singing and dancing all parts. Had it been an audition, I would have hired him on the spot. Had it been any semblance of an interview I would have asked him a few questions; I even attempted a few in a rather half-hearted manner, recognizing my folly even in advance. (There are no paragraphs below--he didn't leave room for a paragraph break.)

Behind the dramatic performance of Vangelis Kazan in THE TRAVELLING PLAYERS is a vaudevillian. Behind the tragicomic Vangelis Kazan in GET ON YOUR MARK is a one-man show. Behind Vangelis Kazan, literally, is a trail of happily exhausted interviewers who once asked some stimulating opening question like: "How many films have you made?"

"I don't know. About ten features and shorts. I made a film in the 1960s in the commercial cinema called DIHASMOS. It was the first film in which I got recognition. I played a German and they said it would be a problem because I didn't speak German. But then they saw the first scene, they decided not to dub me. It was shown in Cannes. No, no photographs full face. I never look at the camera, because I want to be natural. It is a respect for the camera, because the camera is the eyes of the public. All the eyes of the world are in the camera. The camera is very strict. It doesn't forgive anything. Then I did TREACHERY, directed by Costas Manosakis. I played a policeman. They said I was very good and they wanted me to play a policeman all the time, but I refused, and never played a policeman

again. Every time I played a role this happened. If I played
a fisherman, they would call me to play another fisherman.
I said, 'No. I am going to play only one fisherman, and one
policeman. But not two fishermen nor two policemen.' And
every time there would be a battle between me and the director and the producer. They would say, 'Kazan as a fisherman? No! He is a priest!' and I would reply, 'Let me try
it. You will see whether or not I can be a fisherman.' And
after doing it, they would say, 'Aha! That is what you will
do from now on.' THE TRAVELLING PLAYERS is merely
a sample of what I can do. I always believe I can do something more. This is a modest expression of my immodest
beliefs. But anyway, it is not that I am modest or immodest, but every time I have taken an award I say, 'I didn't
deserve that,' meaning that I think I have so much more to
give, and I suppose from a certain point of view that can be
thought of as egotistic. When THE TRAVELLING PLAYERS
started, I knew only the theme of the film, the general structure of my role. Angelopoulos had told me there were many
ups and downs in the role, that it was a very complicated
role. Knowing little more than an outline of the role, I became very anxious about it. I had worked with Angelopoulos
in DAYS OF '36 and knew I could trust him. It wasn't a
question of not having confidence, but I like to know the whole
of a role--the beginning, the development and the end. It
was during the junta period and the subject matter was very
dangerous. Angelopoulos said that should something happen,
he wanted complete responsibility, and to pay for it himself.
Therefore the actors were not to know anything about it.
He asked that we have confidence in him and said that perhaps later he would tell us more about our roles. Meanwhile he would show us the right direction to take. When we
went out on location, Angelopoulos noticed I was quite anxious
and asked what was the matter, and I confessed it was the
same problem. I told him I wanted to know what happens to
my role so I could connect what I had done with what I was
doing. Angelopoulos then took the leading actors aside, and
said, 'Do you want me to tell you about the development of
your roles, and if you don't want, just tell me now.' We
had to decide whether we wanted this responsibility. Some
of them declined to know. They said they trusted him. I
trusted him too, but I wanted to know for myself, not as a
show of lack of faith in Angelopoulos. Finally he agreed to
tell me about the role. We went into a room and searched
it to make sure it was not bugged. It was one of my best
experiences, because I felt great relief that I would soon
know what the role was all about. After this experience

Angelopoulos and I became good friends. There were difficulties during the shooting, but always we remained very
warm and very close. Because of THE TRAVELLING PLAY-
ERS I am known as an actor. I have received clippings
where I have been mentioned in the reviews and there have
been job offers. From the roles I have done it is among the
best. Angelopoulos liked my work in the film very much.
But I'm really pleased that the young filmmakers write roles
for me. I believe in them, even those not very experienced.
All of them have something, and I'm pleased that they want
me. If I don't accept all the roles they offer, it is simply
a question of not having the time to do them all, and also
that I don't want to do roles too similar. I always see the
director, no matter whom, as a child sees his father or with
the respect of a student to a teacher. I always have this attitude, even when I know that I know more than the director.
I don't take into consideration the age of the director, who
may indeed be younger than I, or less experienced. From
the time I accept him as a director, I leave myself in his
hands. But I must add that when I think I can offer something above and beyond what is asked of me, I do not stay
indifferent to the shooting of the film. When I find that because of my experience or instinct, that I can make a further
contribution, I try to do it in a very discreet way. I make
no suggestions in front of the rest of the cast or crew because, after all, there is the ego of the director to consider,
and besides, cinema is a group achievement. It is conceivable that someday I will direct a film. If I do, I will ask
each individual in the entire crew to offer his suggestions,
because from their experience and intuition, they may offer
something that I do not see or know. Before even signing a
contract, the director and I discuss the role. I am a very
enthusiastic person and I believe what is said at this time,
so with joy and happiness I start the work. I always feel
that it is my first job, my first film. I want to feel in love
with what I am doing. I never want to feel that I am a hus-
band--always a lover. There are times when they don't keep
their promises, mostly at times when their egos are involved.
But the results frequently show the truth of the matter. I
always try in a very indirect way to make suggestions to the
other actors or the directors. Sometimes I have to say,
'But don't you remember when we first started discussing
this, you said such and such?' and the director says, 'No,
I never said any such thing.' I'm not interested in who did
or did not say what, I am only arguing for the good of the
film. The result is what counts. The cooperation between
Angelopoulos and me has been one of my best experiences.

If he has anything to say to me, he never says it in front of the other actors, but takes me into private where it can be discussed without other considerations. That's the task of the director. The director must employ a different approach to each actor, depending on the needs of the actor. Were I to be a director I would try to know every minute of the day what is in the mind and the lives of my actors. This the directors don't do, usually. I like a very friendly ambience when I work. If there is any violence or bad words going on, I can't work. I will accept it only if the director uses those as a tool to make me angry because it is called for to be shown in the film. I will use Angelopoulos as an example. He says to me, 'I have great confidence in you. Develop the role. Play the role as you see it. ' The words 'confidence in you, develop the role as you see it' give me the wings to fly upward. There are many who think I am made for comedy, and I tend to agree. I have done much comedy on stage. Angelopoulos had come to see me in the theater before I made a film for him. At the beginning of the play he sat as though to say, 'O. K. , let's see what you can do. ' But as the play progressed, his position changed and his interest in what was happening caused him to lean closer and closer to the stage. When the play was over, Angelopoulos came to me, embraced me, kissed me, and this is something Angelopoulos is not known to do freely. He offered me the role in DAYS OF '36. I am asked why I work so much more in film than in theater. I think my responsibility is much greater on stage. The director's role is more that of placement. The actor is in direct contact with the public. What I give is very much my own. I want much rehearsal--about six months is ideal for a role, and even then the opening night is not the completion of the role's growth. When Angelopoulos admired me in this performance, I knew it was only about 30% of what I could give, and as the play went on I watched the role grow. In film I am merely a member of the orchestra. I play the fiddle and I try to play it as best I can. But the director is the conductor of the orchestra. It is his job and his responsibility. Well, I said I played the fiddle, but actually I don't play the fiddle at all. I play the piano, accordian and guitar, but not the fiddle. I also like dance. I studied ballet for three years. When I used to see Fred Astaire and Gene Kelly dancing and singing, I impersonated them, and the whole neighborhood would come to see me. I am very unhappy that I haven't had an opportunity to be in a play where there is music and dancing. I have supported cinema during this period of film by being good at my work, during a period of crisis and transition.

Without being immodest I believe I have made a worthwhile contribution to the cinema. Television is also in a period of transition. Eventually people will return to the cinema because it offers a different ambience to that of their homes. With this belief I have gone on within the cinema framework. It is a quite different thing to stay in one's home and watch a film, or go outside the home and watch a film. Even if you don't want it or know it, you communicate with the other person sitting near you. This capacity of the cinema to make the public communicate through the film is very important, and as a result film will not die or be replaced completely by television. I was born in Nafplion in 1938 and came to Athens when I was 18. I left home without telling my family. I hitchhiked to Athens in the back of a tomato truck. When I returned to Nafplion for the showing of THE TRAVELLING PLAYERS, the mayor presented me with three awards. It is my dream to make a theater in Nafplion. I never participated in theatricals when I was in school. No one knew that I wanted to be an actor except my best friend Petros. I used to spend a lot of time telling stories to children, though, and once Katina Paxinou's grandson heard me tell a story, and he is now writing a script based on the story. When I came to Athens I studied for six months at the National Theatre, then with a private teacher. I supported myself as a carpenter's assistant and I passed out advertisements on the street. Elia Kazan is also from Nafplion. I believed that we were related and when I met him I was very warm toward him because I admire him as a director. Mr. Kazan accepted my adulation, but denied relationship to me, suggesting that perhaps we were merely neighbors. I had expected a little warmth, even if we were just neighbors, because after all, we had the same name: Kazantzoglou. Furthermore, he had come to the theater, I had not sought him out. Anyway, I found occasion to tell him that I had seen most of his films, some more than once. I asked him to do me a service, and the barriers went up as though he were afraid I was going to ask for money, or sponsorship to the States, or at the very least a role in a film. I asked for his permission to use Kazan as my stage name. He does not speak Greek very well, but in Greek he granted his permission most enthusiastically because he said I would be a reminder of his name in Greece. So I said, 'Thank you very much, ' and left the stage before he did. Eventually he offered me a role in AMERICA, AMERICA but I had been so disillusioned with our meeting that I chose not to collaborate with him. I did go to Montreal during the Olympics to make a film. We made a documentary about athletics, because I am a sports fan. I was the director.

Kazan with Gogo Anztoletaki (above) in Hermes Vellopoulos'
CLOSED WINDOW; (below), Kazan with unidentified actor in
the same film.

It was an ideal collaboration with Costas Smaragdis, and we hope to have it ready for release sometime around November. It is a feature-length documentary and I am credited as the director. The film was sponsored by an athletic association. Already we have received interest from Japan and the United States. But I don't want to work outside of Greece. I love my country and I love the people I work with, even though sometimes we don't see eye to eye....

BIOGRAPHICAL BRIEF

Born Nafplion, 1938. At 18 hitchhiked to Athens in back of tomato truck to study acting at National Theatre and with private teacher. Active on stage and film. Single, lives in Athens. Awards: Special Award for GET ON YOUR MARK, 1973; Best Actor for THE TRAVELLING PLAYERS and THE CELL ZERO, at Thessaloniki Festival, 1975.

FILMS

DIHASMOS (1966).

TREACHERY. (Dir: Costas Manosakis).

A LAW-ABIDING CITIZEN. (Dir: Errikos Thalassinos).

METAMORPHOSES. (Dir: Yannis Kokolis).

DAYS OF '36 (1973). (Dir: Thodoros Angelopoulos).

GET ON YOUR MARK (1973). (Dir: Thodoros Maranghos).

THE COLORS OF IRIS (1974). (Dir: Nicos Panayotopoulos).

THE FLAW (1975). (Dir: Peter Fleischmann).

THE TRAVELLING PLAYERS (1975). (Dir: Thodoros Angelopoulos).

THE CELL ZERO (1975). (Dir: Yannis Smaragdes).

MAY (1976). (Dir: Tasos Psarras).

THE HUNTERS (1977). (Dir: Thodoros Angelopoulos).

CLOSED WINDOW (1977). (Dir: Hermes Vellopoulos).

KALAROGLOU, STAVROS

Stavros Kalaroglou was born in Thessaloniki in 1944.

Stavros Kalaraglou as the gentleman caller in Voulgaris'
THE ENGAGEMENT OF ANNA.

He attended both the National Theatre and the Pelos Katselis Schools. Despite the formal stage training, his two performances on film establish him as eminently suited to the more intimate requirements of screen acting. In Voulgaris' THE ENGAGEMENT OF ANNA, he plays the shy gentleman caller, giving the character a timid vulnerability, but demanding admiration for his willingness to reach out for greater security. In HAPPY DAY (also Voulgaris' direction), he is the resister whose determination to act out his convictions brings him death, but his "survival" is established through the inspiration he offers to others. In two roles, Kalaroglou has effected a distinctive image of a silent, internal man whose strength is in survival; whose weakness is a vulnerability to insensitive externals. The character possibilities within this range are limitless and ageless, opening doors to a potentially lengthy film career for him. He is currently continuing his studies in Berlin at the Cinema and Television Academy. Received an Honorary Distinction for HAPPY DAY at the 1976 Thessaloniki Festival.

STATHOPOULOU, TOULA

Toula Stathopoulou is included as representative of the natural acting ability of the Greeks. She portrays magnificently the murderess in Angelopoulos' RECONSTRUCTION, despite her lack of training. She was a seamstress in real life before she filmed RECONSTRUCTION and DAYS OF '36 for Angelopoulos; later she did a short film entitled THE RICHES OF MIDAS (1973) for Panou Papadopoulos. Her portrait of the joyless, desperate, but surviving villager in RECONSTRUCTION is a tribute to presence over developed skill. Angelopoulos claims to be unsure of himself with actors, and thus surrounds himself with knowledgeable and imaginative performers who bring their own ideas and capabilities to his scripts. The lingering memory of Toula Stathopoulou in RECONSTRUCTION suggests either that Angelopoulos minimizes his ability to work with performers, or that Ms. Stathopoulou has an innate talent which here had its brief moment in the sun. She has returned to private life with either no desire or no potential to continue as a professional actress. She won the Best Supporting Actress Award for RECONSTRUCTION at the 1970 Thessaloniki Festival.

Toula Stathopoulou as the murderess in Angelopoulos' RECON-
STRUCTION.

TSAKIROGLOU, NIKITAS

Nikitas Tsakiroglou projects a happy blend of star
charisma and developed talent. Within the framework of the
1970's Greek cinema, he has displayed the strongest potential of becoming a film star. Not classically handsome, he
has the kind of appeal of French actors such as Jean Paul
Belmondo or Jean-Louis Trintignant. In fact, he looks a bit
like a mature Jean Pierre Leaud.

Born in Athens in 1938, he is a graduate of the National Theater School. He has played both classic and modern in the theatre, and has been a regular in many television
series during the 1970s. He has supported the new Greek

Nikitas Tsakiroglou, hero of Nicos Panayotopoulos' THE
COLORS OF IRIS.

cinema with his presence since very early in its movement.
He was particularly effective in the leading role in Panayotopoulos' THE COLORS OF IRIS, revealing a multi-faceted
ability, with a welcome emphasis on lightness and flippant
comedy. Panayotopoulos has also cast him in his 1977 film,
INDOLENCE OF THE FERTILE VALLEY. He has worked
with Tonia Marketaki and Pavlos Tassios in the 1970s.
Without suggesting a type-casting or a limit to his range,
one director with whom Tsakiroglou has not yet worked but
for whom he seems highly suited is Andreas Thomopoulos.

FILMS

OPERATION ISADORA

THE PROTECTORS (1972). (Dir: Pavlos Tassios).

VIOLENT JOHN (1973). (Dir: Tonia Marketaki).

THE COLORS OF IRIS (1974). (Dir: Nicos Panayotopoulos).

THE INDOLENCE OF THE FERTILE VALLEY (1978). (Dir: Nicos Panayotopoulos).

VAGENA, ANNA

Anna Vagena was born in Larissa in 1947. She is a graduate of the National Theatre School in Athens and played in several films during the commercial cinema. (She prefers not to list them.) She is one of the founders of the Thessalikou Theatre, which is headquartered in Larissa. The troupe tours Thessaly, playing even in barns when no other stage is available.

Anna Vagena in title role of Voulgaris' THE ENGAGEMENT OF ANNA.

Ms. Vagena appeared in Pandelis Voulgaris' THE
GREEN LOVE SONGS, and in Tasos Psarras' MAY, but it is
in the title role of Voulgaris' THE ENGAGEMENT OF ANNA
that Ms. Vagena fulfills her real promise as a screen actress. Her portrayal of Anna is introduced as one of empti-
ness and melancholia. Until Anna's date with the gentleman
caller, which occurs during the second half of the film, Anna
is a dull, colorless, hard-working girl for whom we feel
sympathy but not a greal deal of interest. It says much for
Ms. Vagena's presence that interest in the character is sustained until other dimensions of Anna begin to be revealed.
The character is then laced with timidity, tenderness, curiosity, anguish, anger--we begin to see all the layers of a
personality buried under the plodding facade. In the early
part of the film, Anna seems only to be a pivotal character
without personal development. But as events suggest other
possibilities to her, her reactions reveal a strength, a secret life, unknown or even suspected by the people with whom
she lives. Ms. Vagena's performance keeps the secret, even
from the audience, giving no hint of the depth of the character until it is time to reveal them. It is a carefully and
beautifully modulated performance which ranks high among
acting contributions to the Greek cinema in the 1970s. Ms.
Vagena won the Best Actress award for the role at the 1972
Thessaloniki Festival.

As there are so few roles (thus far) for performers,
it is difficult to project Ms. Vagena's film future. Until that
future reveals itself, there is always the beauty of her Anna
to look back on.

TZOUMAS, KOSTANTINO

Costas Tzoumas was born in Piraeus in 1944. "I
have been fascinated with films since I was a child. But
Greek families have different ideas about film-acting, acting
in general. So years passed, during which I kept my interest in acting a secret." Tzoumas is a tall, thin, very ex-
pressive man. He saw a performance by the Alwin Nikolais
dance company in Athens and was so intrigued that he followed the company back to New York to study with Nikolais,
eventually appearing with the company. He met Pandelis
Voulgaris socially in New York, and Voulgaris eventually offered Tzoumas the role of the priest in HAPPY DAY. Voulgaris claimed that the priest was the only character in his

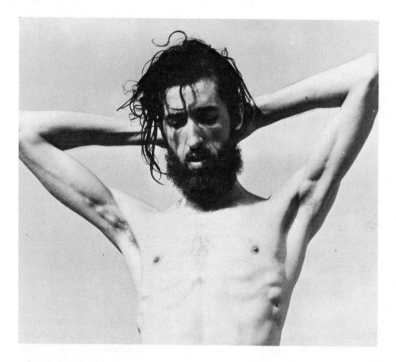

Kostantino Tzoumas as the enigmatic priest in Pandelis Voulgaris' HAPPY DAY.

film that he didn't understand--and therefore Tzoumas seemed
right for the role! Tzoumas returned to Greece to do the
film, remained, and has been actively employed in various
capacities since. His only other film role to date is that of
the elegant diplomat in Manoussakis' POWER. His training
with Nikolais opens doors to him as a kind of resident authority on movement. His personal presentation suggests
versatile casting suitability: he has a balletic grace curiously
combined with lanky clumsiness; his range of potential projec-
tions includes the poetic, weak, evil, power-driven, puff,
neurotic, stuffy, humorous, tragic--in short, he is a highly
versatile character type. Divorced, he lives in Athens. He
won an Honorary Distinction for HAPPY DAY at the 1976
Thessaloniki Festival.

Chapter 18

MUSIC, ART DIRECTION, SETS & COSTUMES

Just as in the United States, some of the "classic" popular songs produced in Greece were written for films. The "golden age" of film composers is either over or suspended, but music is an active ingredient in the everyday life in Greece, and it is simply taken for granted that the music which finds its way into contemporary film is selected with thought and perception. It is regrettable, though, that the musical creativeness of the 1960s is not part of the current film scene. Fortunately, much of the work of the best-known composers is available on record, as a memento of one of the better ingredients of the commercial cinema.

Particularly favored during the period were the works of Stavros Xarhakos, Manos Hatzidakis, and Mikis Theodorakis. All three live in Athens and are still active, in various capacities, in the Greek musical scene. * Xarhakos has expanded the scope of his compositions beyond songs, although they are still vocally oriented. Hatzidakis hit international fame with his score for Jules Dassin's NEVER ON SUNDAY, followed by TOPKAPI and the Broadway musical ILYA DARLING; he continues to produce new arrangements and compositions, but is more active in the administrative end of the musical scene. Theodorakis' political involvements have had many repercussions, not only upon his life but also upon his music. His prolific output runs the gamut of form and content; to discuss Theodorakis it is necessary to define which Theodorakis is the point of reference.

None of these three artists has played a substantial role in the '70s Greek cinema. The Nikos Koundouros' documentary, SONGS OF FIRE, cinematically recorded the occurrence of two concerts staged to celebrate the collapse of the junta, in which much music by these and other com-

---

*Xarhakos is currently studying at Juilliard School of Music in New York City.

posers was played. The audience response in this film, and the sustained support at frequent subsequent concerts, attest to the continued popularity of the music of these composers. Some of their music is used occasionally, but thus far they have not contributed any new material to the new directors' films. Theodorakis did the score for Cacoyannis' IPHIGENIA, but that film figures in the new movement only insofar as it was produced by the Greek Film Center, the establishment's contribution to '70s cinema.

Just as the directors have turned to their own generation for performers and technicians, so they have done with their choice of music and composers. Particularly effective has been the use of folk and popular song to enhance or provide commentary on the visuals. Prime examples of this augmenting use of music are Angelopoulos' THE TRAVELLING PLAYERS and Psarras' THE REASON WHY.

Occasionally directors turn to their composer friends or acquaintances for musical contributions. Payment for any kind of film work is rare, so it may be assumed that the aspiring composer welcomes the opportunity to be heard as a kind of payment. ALDEVARAN uses music by Dimitris Poulikakos, a singer-composer who also plays the role of a musician in the film. * The director, Andreas Thomopoulos, also composes and sings, but is not credited with having used his own music in the film. In the composer-as-friend category, the most significant score encountered was Fivos Ekonomidis' politically poetic songs which added much to the documentary STRUGGLE. These songs were performed at a concert in 1977 in Athens, but unfortunately have not been recorded. Ekonomidis has continued his pursuit of music, but has not been involved with any other film to date. Born in Athens in 1948, he graduated from the Law School of Athens University and currently studies Political Science in Paris, but maintains an active interest in music.

A hit song behind the opening credits was almost obligatory at one time in American cinema. Manoussakis makes strong use of this gimmick in VARTHOLOMEOS, using a song by the well-known composer Yannis Markopoulos. BLACK & WHITE uses music by the equally well-known composer, Manos Loisos. ALDEVARAN is thickly laced with

---

*A recording of Dimitris Poulikakos singing his own compositions is available on EMI, #2J 062-70262.

contemporary popular music from both Greece and the world further west. Classical music gets limited attention; the most notable exceptions are Bach in ALDEVARAN, Saint-Saens in METROPOLIS, Villa-Lobos in THE COLORS OF IRIS. Andreas Velissaropoulos' short, OPERA, utilizes snatches of many operas, and George Katakounzinos created a highly memorable short inspired by the Yiannis Xenakis composition, NUITS.

The closest thing to a musical has been Panayotopoulos' THE COLORS OF IRIS. There are two musical numbers which make it clear that the director has an instinctive (or developed) affinity for the genre and that he may have a musical in his future. Angelopoulos also gives time and attention to a musical number in THE HUNTERS, and though he indicates less facility here, he nevertheless makes a contribution to the idea that time and attention may be devoted in film to such "frivolity." The respect accorded him in Greece may evoke like creative behavior from other, less daring directors. To suggest that a musical number is daring is to underline the overwhelmingly leaden approach to subject and style which has characterized the '70s Greek cinema. (Psarras' MAY even has a scene which intimates that serious music is a money-wasting diversion of the indulgent bourgeoise!) The occasional attempts at lyricism (most notably THE GREAT LOVE SONGS, THE COLORS OF IRIS and ALDEVARAN) have not met with enthusiastic support.

In general, however, the contemporary Greek cinema is well-attuned to music as an important and contributing ingredient. Two films in particular are worthy of closer examination for their use of music. Both happen to be films by Pandelis Voulgaris.

THE GREAT LOVE SONGS

Obviously Voulgaris is greatly attuned to music, in refreshing contrast to most film directors who, regardless of nationality, are generally apathetic or misguided about the quality of the music in their films. THE GREAT LOVE SONGS was actually inspired by music and the visual responses to the songs that comprise the film are occasionally set in a recording studio where we see the composer, Manos Hatzidakis, overseeing a performance of the songs by singers Flery Dadonaki and Dimitris Psarianos.

Singer Flery Dadonaki as actress, with actor Hiram Keller, in Fotopoulos' ORESTES (1971).

Greece is full of good singers but the selection of these two was a particularly happy one. There is, however, a popular response to singers who deliver with a kind of emotional monotony. Maria Farandouri and Nana Mouskouri, two of the more successful female vocalists, are gifted with lovely voices but deliver their songs with a curious lack of involvement which fades into early repetitiveness. The composer Dionisis Savopoulos introduces considerable humor into his performances, but his raspy, non-musical voice quickly spells out its limitations. Audiences even love the political cheerleader tonelessness of Mikis Theodorakis, whose love of performing far outstrips his ability.

A touch of nostalgia from THE GREAT LOVE SONGS.

Flery Dadonaki's voice is reminiscent of America's
Salli Terri's, without the academic flavor. She sustains
her phrasing and maintains a lyrical intensity with all her
songs. Psarianos has a natural voice for which no equivalent comes readily to mind. He has a mannerism of occasionally swallowing the tone, producing a sob or crying effect which, if too frequently used, could limit his versatility.
He does this less on other recordings, so it may be assumed
that it was intentional in THE GREAT LOVE SONGS.

The songs themselves are lushly romantic, occasionally verging on soupiness. Versatile and imaginative orches-
tration, utilizing a combination of folk instruments and a
more traditional western orchestra, introduces a sound variety which is important because the songs are somewhat similar in aural mood. Further variance is achieved through the
alternate use of the vocalists as soloists, with duets interspersed. A chorus backs the soloists in a couple of cuts.
The songs are settings of poems by Cavafy and Lorca (among
others).

The record may seem too lush, even sentimental,
while one is experiencing it, but it has an afterglow effect
which encourages an early return to it. In fact, it is rare
to find a piece of music as lush as this that wears as well
as it does.

Though not a soundtrack recording (the record came
before the film), it is available on NOTOS #3901MH, entitled O Megalos Erotikos.

HAPPY DAY

The score for HAPPY DAY is the first full-scale film
score commissioned from a major composer for a Greek film
in the 1970s*, though there have been songs written especially for films, and some very effective use of previously written music. HAPPY DAY is the product of Dionisis Savopoulos, a popular composer and entertainer of the 1970s in
Greece. His songs are primarily leftist political in content;
however, the musical construction is more wide-ranging and
often unexpectedly clever.

---

*The Theodorakis score for IPHIGENIA has already been ex-
cepted.

Director Pandelis Voulgaris and composer Dionisis Savopoulos (Photo by Elliott Landy).

The occasions for music in HAPPY DAY are frequently natural outgrowths of the film. Rehearsals for a staged entertainment, as well as the entertainment itself, provide an excuse for a variety of songs and musical effects. There is much choral work for which the composer has created and arranged with decided facility. Especially memorable is "Exodus, " a choral number occurring toward the end of the "happy day" show. Unfortunately, the soundtrack recording inexplicably abbreviates the number, robbing it of its line of gradual emotional crescendo. The lyrics are based on poems by prisoners whose identities are not known.

The main theme throughout the film is "Comment, " which is used in orchestral form for background. Savopoulos later added words to the melody and premiered the song at a concert in Thessaloniki in 1976. The song was subsequently included on the soundtrack recording, although it is not actually sung in the film. This theme quotes freely from a melody known in the United States as the Christmas carol "Hark, the Herald Angels Sing, " and it has a predictable psychological impact. For the viewer seeped in Christian Christmas tradition, the theme suggests a kind of religious mysticism which is somehow right for the film. But the sudden consciousness that the music is playing "Hark, the Herald Angels Sing" can draw you away from the film; the individual identity of the song is simply overpowering, despite the melodic appropriateness. It is unlikely that Savopoulos anticipated the power of this theme; to have done so would require a very sophisticated awareness of another culture. If he was fully cognizant of the inherent impact of the song, then he simply made a psychologically wrong decision to utilize the theme (at least from an American audience point of view). When an element has assumed an omnipotent identity, it can be utilized and enhanced by setting, but cannot be subordinated to the point where it loses its private impact.

Two other set pieces occur in the score. There is a popular song played for its tacky reality--the kind of indistinguishable pop song which finds its relentless way into all entertainment media. A second popular song is a "pop-folk" blend which Greece has produced in both quantity and quality in its musical history. The style may be loosely compared to that of America's soft-rock performers like Simon & Garfunkel, James Taylor, Don McLean, et al. Program notes on the recording do not make it clear who is responsible for this song or even who sings it. It does not

Composer Savopoulos during HAPPY DAY recording session
(Photo by Elliott Landy).

fit with the rest of the score and makes one wonder whether
Savopoulos wrote the song or just elected to use it.   Michael
Menidiatis receives some credit, but whether he wrote the
music, or the words, or whether he sings is not clear.
"Folk Singer, " "mouthed" by Dimitris Meletis in the film,
is one of the musical highlights of the score.

The soundtrack to HAPPY DAY is available on LYRA
#3294.   The sequence of songs is rearranged from that of
the film, and the shortening of "Exodus" and the addition of
Savopoulos' singing of "Comment" have already been noted.
These elements will not disturb anyone who has not seen the
film.   The musical line of the record, though, seems dis-
jointed and episodic without the memory of the film to smooth
it.   There are highlights within the score, however, which
can be eagerly looked forward to at each playing, making it a
record with potential for repeated enjoyment and fulfillment.

Since HAPPY DAY Voulgaris has directed a revue for the stage (Hellas Youssouroum), but despite his affinity for music his film work suggests no movement toward making an out-and-out musical. His strong suit in relation to music is a tasteful appreciation and use of it to add to the tone of his overall creative work.

HAPPY DAY won a Best Music award at the 1976 Thessaloniki Festival.

ART DIRECTION, SETS AND COSTUMES

These are among the least formulated aspects of film-making in Greece. Set designers and costumers who worked in the commercial cinema have necessarily abandoned the cinema for the more lucrative opportunities in theatre and television. No one has emerged within the new cinema who

THE PROCEEDINGS. Sets by Tonis Ioannou and Thanassis Papayannakos; costumes by Toula Katohianou.

Hiram Keller in ORESTES. Sets, costumes, direction by
Vassilis Fotopoulos.

is known to be actively seeking a career in art direction or costuming.

This doesn't mean that these areas are neglected. Friends and relatives with talent and leanings are pressed into service to fulfill these functions, and they frequently do so with developed success. These areas, in the main, however, present minimal problems in that a large number of the films are contemporary, merely calling for suitable locations for setting, and everyday clothing for costumes. Rules concerning filming on the streets are fairly lax, with the exception of archaeological sites, which are strictly protected against use within a fiction framework. Many of the films are made in villages where permission is obtained by a simple request.

There are notable exceptions to this generalization, however. Theos' THE PROCEEDINGS had an ancient setting, requiring the construction of sets and considerable research into costumes to ensure a faithful reproduction. Toula Katohianou, Theos' sister, successfully made the latter contribution; Tonis Ioannou and Thanassis Papayannakos designed the temple setting. Aristopoulos' CRANIUM LANDSCAPE encountered the problem of costuming Biblical characters, and this was accomplished by his wife, Anastasia Arseni. The Victorian setting for Panayotopoulos' new film THE INDOLENCE OF THE FERTILE VALLEY has been effected by the director and his wife, Marianna, through exhaustive prefilming effort; they spent weeks searching for an adaptable house, then confronted the physical problem of refurbishing and furnishing it as the desired setting.

Manoussakis, in both of his films, has revealed an interest in using costumes as a way of commenting on the absurdities of character and society. Antonis Kyriakoulis was cited at the 1977 New Directors Festival for the outlandish costumes in POWER. Angelopoulos' historical settings require careful attention to detail, which he effects with unusual subtlety. Mitsos Mitsobounis' art direction in Psarras' MAY deserves to be remembered.

Despite the seeming disorganization of these aspects of Greek filmmaking, they do get accomplished with skill and resourcefulness, much as do all other elements of Greek filmmaking--through the commitment and generosity of those who work with little promise of monetary reward.

It would be remiss to discuss Greek art direction without a nod to Vassilis Fotopoulos, despite his minimal participation in 1970s cinema. Fotopoulos was born in Calamata in 1934, and his career as stage designer and decorator has earned him high respect and kudos, including a 1964 American Academy Award (Oscar) for Cacoyannis' ZORBA THE GREEK. Fotopoulos, not immune to the magical pull of directing, made a film in 1971, ORESTES, starring Hiram Keller and singer Flery Dadonaki. Filmed in Mani by Dimitris Papakonstantis, it recreated the classical story as an allegory of modern Greece. Fotopoulos wrote the script, and did the costumes and set decorations, as well as directing. The film has not been widely seen. Fotopoulos spends much time secluded from his former theatrical involvement, but occasionally emerges to restate his mastery of his craft and art. In 1976 he did the sets for the Jules Dassin production of THE THREE PENNY OPERA. His brother, Dionysis, an accomplished costume designer, did the costumes for the production, which starred Melina Mercouri (later replaced by Eva Kotamanidou).

Chapter 19

PRODUCERS, FILM CRITICISM, DISTRIBUTORS

There are no producers in Greece! With the collapse
of the commercial cinema, the supremacy of the two major
film studios in Greece slipped into cinema history, much as
the big Hollywood studios had done in the 1950s in the United
States. Finos Films and Carayannis-Caratzopoulos still exist,
but their function as primary producers of Greek cinema is
a thing of the past. They have been replaced by nobody!

Independent filmmaking in Greece is debilitatingly and
realistically independent. A filmmaker might invest his entire savings in a film, turn to his family and friends, borrow from any source available to him. This is a routine
procedure for the first film. The second film becomes even
more gruellingly difficult because most of the available financial avenues have been exhausted with the first film.

There are occasional individuals who emerge as producers of specific films. They are people who are simply
interested in film and either do not wish actually to make a
film, or may be attracted by the prestige gained for having
financed a film. Several directors expressed their belief
that there may be tax benefits to be gained by producing a
film, in that the venture will surely lose money.

For whatever their reasons, these individuals are welcomed when they do emerge. Businessman Yannis Stefanis
put money into Theos' THE PROCEEDINGS. Millie Delipetrou
produced Costas Ferris' THE MURDERESS and Psarras' ambitious MAY. Ms. Delipetrou reports that she has no interest in further film participation, but on the other hand talks
about the possibilities of a producers' organization which
could form a distribution circuit which might make it possible
to realize some financial return.

George Papalios, a shipowner, has produced Angelopoulos' THE TRAVELLING PLAYERS and Panayotopoulos' THE

COLORS OF IRIS (among others), which together make a major contribution to the qualitative level of Greek films. In 1977 Mr. Papalios produced the award-winning documentary STRUGGLE OF THE BLIND, made by his wife, Maria Hatzimihali-Papaliou, whose interest in film has been rumored to be the guiding force behind Mr. Papalios' film involvement. It is further rumored that Mr. Papalios contemplates becoming more seriously involved in film as a self-sustaining business enterprise, a highly provocative idea.

Obviously the interest and good intentions of these and other individuals cannot be sustained by perpetual loss. It is crucial that the Greek cinema world start thinking in terms of returns, rather than concentrating all of its attention on where the next investment is likely to come from.

The Greek Film Center

The only formal producing organization in existence today is the Greek Film Center, organized during the junta as a kind of clearinghouse for the cinema world (including the function of a watching eye on those involved with cinema to make sure that the film world reflected the position of the then-government). It entered film production in 1971, when it co-produced (with Finos Films and James Paris), PAPAFLESSAS, a film directed by Erricos Andreou which served to commemorate the 50th anniversary of Greek independence. PAPAFLESSAS was a patriotic epic, recounting the life of a legendary priest who was a martyr of the 1821 Revolution against the Turks.

Following the collapse of the junta, the Center was reorganized, changing its name from General Film Enterprises to the current Greek Film Center. George Tsavelas was named director of the Center and it became more actively involved in film production. The Bank of Industrial Development, a government tentacle, provides the money to the Center, which in turn allocates funds to film projects as it elects.

The original intent under the post-junta organization was to produce quality films that had some possibility of bringing a profit which could then be reinvested in more films. This doesn't offer the struggling beginner any assistance or practical encouragement, but were such a system actually to work, there might be some relief for the beginner some time in the dim future. Meanwhile, the Greek Film Center has invested in six films, only one of which shows signs of returning a profit.

In 1975 the Greek Film Center became involved in a situation which harvested ill-will for the Center from the Greek film world. The Center negotiated to produce a script submitted by Nicos Panayotopoulos. Submitting the script to a higher censorship function was viewed as merely a formality, considering that the Greek Film Center is a State-owned and operated organization. It had not occurred to anyone that the State would, in essence, censor what it had already declared permissible. The film was to be made in Germany; Panayotopoulos and crew were ready to leave when the project was cancelled. His DANKESCHON-BITTESCHON remains an unrealized project. The director believes the project was cancelled because the symbolism within the film was viewed as subversive. Many other accounts of the story cast suspicion on an internal power struggle in which the Panayotopoulos project served as pawn. (It is of interest to note that Panayotopoulos' next script was rejected, despite his universal recognition as one of Greece's more knowledgeable and talented directors.) The control of the Center may now be more correctly characterized as representative of the bank and state rather than of the Greek cinema world. *

The Film Center received further criticism when it allocated a considerable portion of its available money to Michael Cacoyannis' IPHIGENIA. This was viewed as another indication of the Center's lack of interest in offering assistance to the struggling new directors. Many of the young directors are political leftists and the government is obviously disinclined to provide financial assistance to an artist who may use it to make an anti-government statement. Thodoros Angelopoulos is the only director since 1970 to acquire international recognition; the Greek Film Center has never participated in an Angelopoulos film.

In fairness to the Film Center, there is no reason to believe that it is not sincere in its desire and intentions to aid the film world. It is simply caught in the commercial-versus-art conflict. IPHIGENIA will surely return a profit which can be reinvested in future film projects. On the oth-

---

*The former director of the Center, George Tsavelas, died in 1976.

er hand, there seems to be an absence of organization or legitimate knowledge about the Center's function as a business enterprise. IPHIGENIA played the Cannes Film Festival, a primary backdrop for promoting and selling a film to the entire world. The film was minimally promoted at Cannes and the Center thus passed up a rare and primary opportunity to invest in an important return potentiality. Perhaps they felt that Cacoyannis' name would insure automatic sales--and there is some truth to that. At this writing the film has been playing for several weeks in New York and shows no indication of running dry at the box office.

Unfortunately the second major undertaking by the Greek Film Center has not paid off. Voulgaris' superior but deceptive HAPPY DAY was produced by the Center, and though money was still a problem, the film is surely an artistic success. It seems to be a film that requires repeated viewing, or time for digestion. This quality doesn't aid its salability, since distributors usually make quick decisions based on a single viewing, and most audiences respond to a single viewing.

The Greek Film Center has also produced or co-produced CLOSED WINDOW (Ermis Vellopoulos), THE OTHER LETTER (Lambros Liaropoulos) and MAKING OF AN HELIOGRAPHY (Dimitris Dimogerontakis) (and possibly others), none of which seems likely to make a financial return. The Center came to the aid of Costas Ferris when he ran out of money near the end of filming PROMETHEUS SECOND PERSON, SINGULAR.

The future and direction of the Greek Film Center is uncertain, but it would be most unfortunate to lose it altogether. Although it is accused of not really helping the new film movement in Greece, this criticism is not totally accurate. HAPPY DAY alone makes it all worthwhile. And though the film is not "new wave," the Center can be earnestly thanked for IPHIGENIA, even though two or three "new wave" films could have been made with the money spent on IPHIGENIA. As a business investment it is a sound decision that IPHIGENIA be a first choice. Perhaps IPHIGENIA will yet parent another two or three films!

FILM CRITICISM

There are eight to ten daily newspapers in Athens,

plus two small English-language papers. Each paper has two or three film critics.

Films normally play for one week. At one time, up to 13 new films opened weekly during the winter season. It is a formidable task for the critics to cover all these films.

Prior to the television drain on the film box office, abundant space was given film in the newspapers. The film audience was large and with so many films from which to select, the audience turned to the reviews as an avenue of selectivity. After TV took its toll, the space devoted to film in the print media was reduced. Film reviews became less evaluative and more informative, in the interest of taking up less space.

This is most specifically the case with evening papers. Morning papers still afford the film enthusiasts a source of more in-depth coverage. The earlier papers found themselves in competition with the late TV news shows, and to avoid meaningless duplication of news coverage, the morning papers have become less succinct in their reporting, leaning toward a more detailed coverage than that given on TV. Film coverage benefits under this umbrella. It is of interest to note that before TV, it was the evening rather than the earlier papers that did this more in-depth reportage.

Newspapers in Athens are more or less voices of political positions, much more openly so than in the United States. The communist papers evaluate film through the sieve of party thinking which means, for example, that Russian films are handled with care and respect, American films are occasions for political proselytizing. The other papers are less reflective of their political positions within the framework of film reviewing, but they are subjected to social and/or economic pressures. A distributor may threaten to withdraw an ad unless his film is greeted with positive reviews. These various forms of blackmail, plus the spatial disregard of film in general, have severely eroded the quality of film criticism.

One other factor which comes into play in the reviewing of local artists' work is the intimacy of the Greek film world. Athens is the center of Greek cinema, which is a tight-knit community of interests within the city. The result is that everyone knows everyone else, with whom they are either friends or enemies. This closeness practically annihilates any attempt at objective criticism.

At least magazines still afford space to film. Two serious film magazines cover the Greek output (as well as international) in detail: Film, edited by filmmaker Thanassis Rentzis, and Contemporary Cinema, which put some money into Costas Sfikas' film MODEL (among other films). An English-language monthly, The Athenian, somewhat akin to New York's Cue with a dash of the New Yorker, also has attended the Greek film scene with sympathetic eyes.

An Additional Comment on Greek Film Critics

The December 1976 issue of The Athenian published an interview with Aglae Mitropoulos, the director of the Athens Cinemathèque, which is Athens' equivalent of New York's Museum of Modern Art or London's British Film Institute. During the interview Mrs. Mitropoulos has this to say of Greek critics:

"The problem here is that the critics have politicized filmgoing--they have tried to 'educate' the public to see films in a political way, and the public has consequently lost confidence in the critics, and in movies altogether.... People must be allowed to discover and learn for themselves. The Greek critics have tried to change people's taste. The general Greek public has always liked entertainment and melodrama, but now they are told that good films must be politically engaged, or avant-garde in some way.... Filmmakers during and just after (the junta) were justly praised for making political statements in their work. Politics was the all-powerful obsession. But we are passing out of that darkness now, and artists can no longer justify agitprop political work. Greek cinema must find itself again ... must begin dealing with the condition of Greek society in human terms, without political prejudice. "

DISTRIBUTION

Greece has a history of being very cinema-conscious. Prior to television there was a network of theaters scattered throughout the country, providing a built-in distribution circuit for a national product. A television set in the local taverna has now replaced the cinema in most villages, and internal distribution can no longer sustain Greek films. They simply must find their way into the international scene if film output is to continue in Greece.

Film is still alive in Athens where the more sophisticated urban dweller spends very little time with Greece's
infantile television. At present, many of the artists and
technicians who would choose film, given a choice, are working in television. This may result in the qualitative uplifting
of Greek television, or it may negatively affect the values of
the artists who view the necessity of TV work as a kind of
"selling out."

Meanwhile, a wealth of international films finds its
way to Athens. The Athens audience has the opportunity to
be as informed about the current film scene as the New Yorker. Commercial theaters play the latest international successes, and two important art theaters provide the more devoted filmgoer with well-rounded fare from other countries:
the Alkyonis theater is politically oriented in its selection of
film-fare, making a specialty of films from Russia; Studio
Cinema, owned by former film director Sokrates Kapsaskis,
is more art-for-art's-sake involved, presenting mini-festivals
of national films or retrospectives of the works of individual
artists. It is interesting to note that Greek audiences like
foreign films in their original languages, preferring subtitles
to dubbing. Dubbing is used only in rare cases, as for instance a film intended for pre-schoolers who cannot read
subtitles (such as a feature-length animated Disney film).

Though not directly related to the problems of distribution, there are other sources of film education which serve
as learning foundations for the filmmaker who must eventually hope for international distribution. The French Institute,
the Goethe Institute, and, less actively, the Hellenic American Union, all provide film programs. But the most important possibility for the film devotee in Athens is the Athens Cinemathèque, located in a crumbling old mansion in the
center of the city. Despite the architectural and historical
interest of the building, it is frightening to contemplate its
fire hazards, considering that it daily attracts the film fa-
natics of Athens, and also serves as storage house for a
permanent collection of over 1,500 films.

Nevertheless, it is a heady experience served up in
this old building, under the enthusiastically watchful eye of
the co-founder and director, Aglae Mitropoulos. The Athens
Cinemathèque has been operating in one form or another
since 1950. Through the tireless lobbying efforts of Mrs.
Mitropoulos and other board members, the Film Club became
an official foundation in 1963, and even continued to function

during the junta, despite considerable chicanery on its part.
During the junta, the club remained a free zone longer than
most cultural institutions. Various foreign embassies cooperated secretly by importing films in diplomatic pouches,
and the club even ran a series of revolutionary films from
Brazil and Cuba during the junta regime. *

Thus, there is ample opportunity for the Greek filmmaker to learn from the international wealth of filmmaking
knowledge, despite the modest sources of technical knowledge
available in Greece. Many Greek films do not even find their
way into Greek cinemas. The films of Angelopoulos and Voulgaris will find theaters and play as long as the market allows. But that doesn't even clear costs--and profit is not
even in question. All of this accentuates the absolute necessity to make quality films which are suitable for foreign distribution. The insulated atmosphere of Greece, and the psychological reflection of that reality, must be dissipated if
Greek films are to become an on-going art in Greece.

---

*See "The House on Kanaris," an interview with Aglae Mitro-
poulos by Gerald Herman, The Athenian, Dec. 1976.

Chapter 20

THESSALONIKI FILM FESTIVAL

The Thessaloniki Film Festival began in 1960, envisioned as part of the International Fair of Thessaloniki. Its stated intentions were to "advance the Greek film industry and promulgate Greek films both inside and outside the country."

Traditionally the festival occurs at the end of September and lasts seven days. Greek feature films and shorts are exhibited in competition; prizes are monetary, presented by the government. Honored films are selected by an all-Greek jury drawn from various professions: academic, film directors, film performers, film critics, producers, painters, writers, producers, film technicians, etc. Vote is by secret ballot.

As of 1972 there also began an International Festival, open competitively to short films. The jury is drawn from the international film world and invited guests add glamor to the event. In 1976 the two festivals were combined, running simultaneously. This seemed to be a particularly agreeable arrangement in that the international guests had an opportunity to view the year's domestic output. Perhaps arrangement logistics were too complex, however; for whatever reason, the 1977 festival arrangements returned the two festivals to exclusive time slots, though with one immediately following the other.

The value and ultimate purpose of the festival have seen dramatic change since its creation. It was originally intended as an opportunity to bestow recognition for quality work in the cinema during the year. Following the collapse of the commercial cinema, annual film output has become minimal. The festival thus becomes a stage not so much for the annual quality work, but for all of the year's work in cinema. (This is a general statement; a few films do get rejected from festival participation, but so few that the festival really can be said to screen very nearly all the films made during the year.) In some cases, a single screening at the festival represents the complete life of a film. Since some films do not get released to theaters nor find any other outlet to an audience, the festival simply becomes the film's life expectancy in Greece (though many films not released in Greece do play festivals outside the country).

A Director's Union exists and is active in its intercourse with the festival authorities. The union represents the filmmakers whose work makes up the festival and thus feel they are in a strong position to participate in the structuring of the festival. Various conflicts arise, during which time the fate of the festival is uncertain. Solutions are found, however, and the festival somehow occurs, despite frequent protests and demonstrations.

A major and unresolvable conflict arose in 1977 which casts some doubt on the future of the festival. The government (represented by the Greek Film Center) attempted an imbalance of representation within the juries adjudging the festival. The union threatened to withdraw their films from the festival and to organize their own. The festival authorities protested their right to set up a second festival and the conflict actually found its way into court. The union was allowed to organize a second festival, and they did; it went on the week after the official festival. A benefit concert was held in Athens at which various musical and cinematic artists contributed time and talent to raise money for the festival. Journalists from Athens remained in Thessaloniki a second week; talent from the Greek cinema world attended.

The official festival was left with a minimal number of films to show; the highlight was Michael Cacoyannis' IPHIGENIA, despite the director's protest. Since the film had played competitively at Cannes (a pinnacle of sorts), Cacoyannis maintained that it was somewhat farcical for IPHIGENIA to play competitively at Thessaloniki. The Greek Film Center, which had produced the film, insisted; the film was played but Mr. Cacoyannis refused to attend the festival.

Meanwhile, amid much internal squabbling, the union managed to organize its festival on short notice, and brought it off with considerable audience support. Much of the festival audience is made up of students; and they supported the rebel festival, absenting themselves from the auditorium of the official festival, which was consequently nearly empty.

Site of Thessaloniki Film Festival.

It can't be concluded that the new directors' festival was particularly creative or revolutionary. It was modeled after the official festival; awards were dispersed to honor conservatism and were given to practically everyone--which meant that no one was slighted or offended, but also that the value of the awards was undermined by excess.

An opportunity seemed to exist for the union to really reach for functional autonomy so that it might organize or create a domestic channel of distribution or even a means by which a package of festival films could find a way to tour the country. It appears, however, that the "rebellion" was not so much against the system as it was a squabble over who was running the system.

What far-reaching effects the 1977 festival split will have is obviously uncertain. Should the government elect to conclude the "official" festival, it will be a challenge to the young directors to continue this most important event. The screens available to their work are so few that the existence of the festival is crucial at this point in Greek cinema history. *

THESSALONIKI FESTIVAL AWARDS

1960

Best Director: Nicos Koundouros for THE RIVER (To Potami).

---

*Variety, Oct. 12, 1977, covers this festival incident from the "official" viewpoint. The Thessaloniki International Fair which organizes the festival with the Ministry of Industry sent a communication to the press explaining the counter-festival was effected for political purposes, motivated by the leftist opposition. This account statedly blames the new directors for the conflict: "The fest regulars and all the people who really are interested in Greece's film production were disappointed seeing such a previously successful event now probably ready to die on account of the union's boycott and intention to stage their own festival." For a less biased account of this conflict, see "The Greek Film Festival--A Fiasco?" by Mirella Georgiadou, Greek World, Sept/Dec. '77.

Best Screenplay: George Roussos for MADALENA.
Best Cinematography: Aristides Carydis Fuchs for CRIME
   OFF STAGE (Englima sta paraskinia).
Best Musical Score: Manos Hatzidakis for THE RIVER.
Best Short Film: Takis Kanellopoulos for MACEDONIAN
   WEDDING.
Best Actor: Dimitris Horn for ONCE A THIEF (Mia tou
   klefti).
Best Actress: Aliki Vouyouklaiki for MADALENA.
Best Supporting Actor: Pandelis Zervos for MADALENA.
Best Supporting Actress: George Sarri for CRIME OFF
   STAGE.

1961

Best Director: Michael Cacoyannis for EROIKA/OUR LAST
   SPRING.
Best Cinematography: Dimos Sakellariou for DREAM FOLK
   (Sinikia to oniro).
Best Musical Score: Argiris Kounadis for ANTIGONE.
Best Actor: Dimitris Horn for ALAS FOR YOUTH (Allimono
   stous neous).
Best Actress: Irene Papas for ANTIGONE.
Best Supporting Actor: Manos Katrakis for DREAM FOLK.
Best Supporting Actress: Athina Mihailidou for NIGHT-
   MARE (Efialtis).
Special Prize to Vassilis Maros for AEGEAN TRAGEDY.

1962

Best Film: ELECTRA (A Finos Film Production).
Best Director: Michael Cacoyannis for ELECTRA.
Best Cinematography: Giovanni Variano & Grigoris Danalis
   for THE SKY (Ouranos).
Best Musical Score: Costas Kapnisis for THE HANDS (Ta
   Heria).
Best Short Film: Lia Karyotou and Dimitri Kollatos for
   ATHENS XYZ.
Best Actor: Titos Vandis for SIEGE (Poliorkia).
Best Actress: Irene Papas for ELECTRA.

1963

Best Film: YOUNG APHRODITES (Mikres Aphrodites), pro-

duced by George Zervos and Nicos Koundouros.
Best Director: Nicos Koundouros for YOUNG APHRODITES.
Best Cinematography: Dimos Sakellariou for A CRETAN
DON JUAN (Enas Delikanis).
Best Musical Score: Yannis Markopoulos for YOUNG APHRO-
DITES.
Best Actor: Petros Fissoun for BROTHER ANNA (Adelfos
Anna).
Best Actress: Ilia Livikou for A CRETAN DON JUAN.

1964

Best Film: PERSECUTION (Diogmos), a James Paris Pro-
duction.
Best Director: Grigoris Grigoriou for PERSECUTION.
Best Screenplay: Panos Kondelis for PERSECUTION.
Best Cinematography: Nicos Gardelis for TREASON (Pro-
dosia).
Best Musical Score: Nicos Mamangakis for MONEMVASSIA.
Best Short Film: Dimitris Kollatos for OLIVE TREES.
Best Actor: Petros Fissoun for TREASON.
Best Actress: Xenia Kalogeropoulou for MARRIAGE GREEK
STYLE (Gamos ala hellinika).

1965

(No awards for film or direction).
Best Screenplay: Michael Grigoriou for NO, MR. JOHNSON
(Ohi kirie Johnson).
Best Cinematography: Dimos Sakellariou and Dinos Katsouri-
dis for THE RUTHLESS (Adistakti).
Best Musical Score. Yannis Markopoulos for FATE OF AN
INNOCENT MAN (Mira enos athoou).
Best Short Film: Rovyros Manthoulis and H. Papadakis for
MEN AND GODS.
Best Actor: Nicos Kourkoulos for THE RUTHLESS.
Best Actress: Elli Fotiou for RETURN (Epistrofi).

1966

Best Film: FORGOTTEN HEROES (Xehasmeni iroes), a
James Paris Production.
Best Director: Rovyros Manthoulis for FACE TO FACE
(Prosopo me prosopo)

Best Screenplay: Panos Glykophridis THE PRICE OF GLORY
(Me ti Lampsi sta Matia).
Best Cinematography: Sirakos Danalis for EXCURSION (Ek-
dromi).
Best Musical Score: Christos Leondis for THE PRICE OF
GLORY.
Best Short Film: Pandelis Voulgaris for JIMMY THE TIGER.
Best Actor: George Foundas for THE PRICE OF GLORY.
Best Actress: Voula Zoumboulaki for BRIEF INTERVAL
(Sintomo Dialima).
Special Awards: Takis Kanellopoulos for EXCURSION; Alexis
Damianos for TO THE SHIP (Mehri to plio); Takis
Hadzopoulos for PRESPES.

1967

Best Artistic Film: SILHOUETTES, produced by Costas Zois.
Best Overall Production: FEVER ON THE ROADS (Piretos
stin Asfalto), produced by Finos Films.
Best Director: Dinos Dimopoulos for FEVER ON THE ROADS.
Best Screenplay: Panos Kondelis for THE THIRTEENTH
MAN (Dekatos Tritos).
Best Cinematography: Stamatis Tripos for SILHOUETTES.
Best Musical Score: Mimis Plessas for BULLETS DON'T
RETURN (I sferes den girizoun piso).
Best Actor: George Foundas for FEVER ON THE ROADS.
Best Actress: Peri Poravou for SILHOUETTES.

1968

Best Artistic Film: PARENTHESIS, produced by Takis Kanel-
lopoulos; and GIRLS IN THE SUN (Koritsia ston ilio)
produced by Klearhos Konitsiotis.
Best Overall Production: ON THE VERGE OF TREASON
(Sta sinora tis prodosias), a James Paris production.
Best Director: Dimis Dadiras for ON THE VERGE OF
TREASON.
Best Screenplay: Iakovos Kambanellis for GUNS AND THE
NIGHTINGALE (To Kanoni ke t'aidoni).
Best Cinematography: Stamatis Tripos and Sirakos Danalis
for PARENTHESIS.
Best Musical Score*:   Stavros Xarhakos for GIRLS IN THE SUN.

---

*Original Soundtrack recording is available on EMI/Columbia
2J062-70044.

Film with Best Plot: THE FUGITIVE, produced and directed by Costas Zois.
Best Documentary: 25,000 YEARS ON THIS EARTH, produced and directed by Nestor Matsas.
Best Actor: Costas Prekas for ON THE VERGE OF TREASON.
Best Actress: Helena Nathanail for APPOINTMENT WITH A STRANGER (Rendezvous me mian agnosti).
Best Supporting Actor: Costas Bakas for GIRLS IN THE SUN.
Best Supporting Actress: Ilia Livikou for ON THE VERGE OF TREASON.

1969

Best Artistic Film: THE GIRL FROM WARD 17 (To Koritsi tou 17).
Best Production: NO (Ohi), a James Paris production.
Best Director: Petros Likas for THE GIRL FROM WARD 17.
Best Screenplay: Petros Likas for THE GIRL FROM WARD 17.
Best Cinematography: Dimitris Papaconstantis for NO.
Best Musical Score: Costas Kapnisis for PANIC (O panikos).
Best Fiction Short: Thodoros Maranghos for his short, TSOUF.
Best Short Documentary: Takis Kanellopoulos for KASTORIA.
Prize for First Work of a New Director: Stavros Hasapis for his short, THE LABYRINTH.
Best Actor: Lambros Constantaras for THE BLUFF (O Blofatzis).
Best Actress: Sofia Roumbou for THE GIRL FROM WARD 17.

1970

Best Artistic Film: RECONSTRUCTION (Anaparastasis), produced by George Samiotis.
Best Production: ASTRAPOYANNOS, produced by Finos Films.
Best Director: Errikos Andreou for MUTINY OF THE TEN (Andarsia ton deka).
Best Cinematography: George Arvanitis for RECONSTRUCTION.
Best First Film Director: Thodoros Angelopoulos for RECONSTRUCTION.
Best Fiction Short: THE LADY AND THE COWBOY, directed by Costas Papadopoulos.

Best Documentary Short: COMMUNICATIONS, directed by
George Lanitis.
Best Actor: Nicos Kourkoulos for ASTRAPOYANNOS.
Best Actress: No Award in 1970.
Best Supporting Actor: Ilias Logothetis for BABYLONIA.
Best Supporting Actress: Toula Stathopoulou for RECON-
STRUCTION.

1971

Best Artistic Film: WHAT DID YOU DO IN THE WAR,
THANASSI? (Ti ekanes sto polemo Thanassi), pro-
duced by Dinos Katsouridis.
Best Production: PAPAFLESSAS, produced by Finos Films-
James Paris-General Film Enterprises.
Best Director: Errikos Andreou for PAPAFLESSAS.
Best Screenplay: Dinos Katsouridis and Asimakis Yalamas
for WHAT DID YOU DO IN THE WAR, THANASSI?
Best Cinematography: Stamatis Tripos for THAT SUMMER
(Ekino to kalokeri).
Best Musical Score: Yannis Spanos for THAT SUMMER.
Best First Feature Director: Dimitris Papaconstantis for
HOLOCAUST (Olokaftoma).
Best Fiction Short: Thodoros Maranghos for SSST.
Best Documentary Short: Basil Maros for THE WORLD OF
THE HOLY PICTURES (O kosmos ton ikonon).
Special Award for Sets and Costumes: Dionisis Fotopoulos
for PAPAFLESSAS.
Best Actor: Thanassis Vengos for WHAT DID YOU DO IN
THE WAR, THANASSI?
Best Actress: Maria Vassiliou for I SEE A SOLDIER
(Evdokia).
Best Supporting Actress: Miranda Kounelaki for DAWN OF
VICTORY (Avgi tis Nikis).
Best Supporting Actor: None Given.

1972

Best Artistic Film: THE ENGAGEMENT OF ANNA, pro-
duced by Dinos Katsouridis.
Best Production: LYSISTRATA, a New Cinema EPE Films
production.
Best Director: Thodoros Angelopoulos for DAYS OF '36
(Meres tou 36).
Best Screenplay: Pavlos Tassios for EVERYTHING IS IN

ORDER, BUT ON THE OTHER HAND... (Nai Men, Alla...).

Best Cinematography: George Arvanitis for DAYS OF '36.

Best Musical Score: None given.

Best First Feature Director: Pandelis Voulgaris for THE ENGAGEMENT OF ANNA.

Best Fiction Short: LETTERS FROM AMERICA (Grammata apo tin Ameriki), directed by Lambros Papastathis.

Best Short Documentary: Vellopoulos and Drakoulakos for MANI.

Best New Director, Short with Plot: Nicos Koutelidakis for LAST REHEARSAL (Ya Lighes monon parastassis).

Best New Director, Documentary Short: M. Kouyoumdzis for COLLECTIONS FROM THE ART THEATER (Sylloghes apo to theatro technis).

Best Actor: Thanassis Vengos for TAKE YOUR GUN, THAN-ASSI (Thanassi, Pare t'oplo sou).

Best Actress: Anna Vagena for THE ENGAGEMENT OF ANNA.

Best Supporting Actor: Costas Rigopoulos for THE ENGAGE-MENT OF ANNA.

Best Supporting Actress: Smaragda Veaki for THE ENGAGE-MENT OF ANNA.

1973

Best Artistic Film: GET ON YOUR MARK (Lavete Thessis), produced by Thodoros Maranghos.

Best Production: MEMORY OF A HERO (Enas Iroas me to mnimoskopio), produced by George Filis and Ilias Pergantis.

Best Director: Tonia Marketaki for VIOLENT JOHN (Ioannis o Vieos).

Best Screenplay: Tonia Marketaki for VIOLENT JOHN.

Best Cinematography: Nicos Petanidis for GET ON YOUR MARK.

Best Musical Score: Vassilis Tenidis for MEMORY OF A HERO.

Best First Film Director: Thodoros Maranghos for GET ON YOUR MARK.

Best Fiction Short: THE LINE (I Grammi), produced and di-rected by Koutsouris & Mirmiridis; and PISSISTRATOS GOURAS, directed by Marinos Kassos.

Best Short Documentary: DEAD END (Adiexodo), produced by Chr. Mangos.

Best Actor: Manolis Logiadis for VIOLENT JOHN.

Best Actress: Not given.
Best Supporting Actor: Minas Christidis for THE VISITOR (Episkeptis).
Best Supporting Actress: George Sarri for THE PROTEC-TORS (I Prostates).
Special Awards: Vangelis Kazan for acting in GET ON' YOUR MARK; George Arvanitis for cinematography for CRAN-IUM LANDSCAPE (Kraniou Topos) and THE GREAT LOVE SONGS (O Megalos Erotikos); and Costas Aris-topoulos for direction of CRANIUM LANDSCAPE.

1974

Best Artistic Film: KIERION, produced by Dimosthenis Theos and George Papalios; and MODEL (Modello), produced by George Papalios, Anna Sfika and Contemporary Cinema magazine.
Best Production: MEGARA, produced by George Tsember-opoulos; and GAZOROS SERRON, produced by "Cinetic" Ap. Papaefstathiou & Co.
Best Director: Costas Ferris for THE MURDERESS (I Fon-issa).
Best Director 1st Film: Dimosthenis Theos for KIERION.
Best Photographer: Nicos Kavoukidis for THE COLORS OF IRIS (Ta Chromata Tis Iridos).
Best Fiction Short: THE ANTIGONE STORY, directed by Thanassis Netas.
Best Short Documentary: GREEK POPULAR PAINTERS, directed by George Dizikirikis.
Best Director, First Short: Nikos Alevrras for MY GRAND-FATHER.
Best Actor: Mihalis Boyaridis for THE REASON WHY (Thi Asimanton Aformin).
Best Actress: Maria Alkeou for THE MURDERESS.
Honorary Mentions: Anestis Vlakos for acting in KIERION, and his work in Greek cinema in general; Nicos Zervos and Magda Zervou for their short, AN AT-TEMPT FOR SOCIAL REVIEW OF MODERN GREECE.

1975

First Prize: THE TRAVELLING PLAYERS (O Thiasos), pro-duced by George Papalios.
Second Prize: STRUGGLE (Agonas), produced and directed by

T. Maranghos, F. Economidis, C. Papanikolaou, D. Yannikopoulos.
Third Prize: BIO-GRAPHY, a Filmogram production (Hristos Mangos and Thanassis Rentzis).
Best Director: Thodoros Angelopoulos for THE TRAVELLING PLAYERS.
Best Screenplay: Thodoros Angelopoulos for THE TRAVELLING PLAYERS.
Best Cinematography: George Arvanitis for THE TRAVELLING PLAYERS.
Best Musical Score: Stamatis Spanoudakis for PROMETHEUS SECOND PERSON, SINGULAR (Promitheas se deftero prosporo).
Best Set Decoration: Marie Louise Vartholomeou for EURIDICE BA-2037 (Evridiki BA-2037).
Best First Feature Director: Nicos Nikolaidis for EURIDICE BA-2037.
Best Short: COINCIDENCES ON A TROLLEY, directed by Takis Davlopoulos.
Best Actor: Vangelis Kazan for THE TRAVELLING PLAYERS and CELL O (To keli milen).
Best Actress: Eva Kotamanidou for THE TRAVELLING PLAYERS.

1976

First Prize: HAPPY DAY, a Greek Cinematography Center production.
Second Prize: THE OTHER LETTER (To allo gramma), produced by Lambros Liaropoulos and the Greek Cinematography Center.
Third Prize: CYPRUS, produced by George Papalios.
Best Director: Pandelis Voulgaris for HAPPY DAY.
Best Cinematography: Stavros Hasapis for THE OTHER LETTER.
Best Musical Score: Dionisis Savopoulos for HAPPY DAY.
Short First Prize: NIGHTS, produced by George Katakounzinos and Athanasios Katakounzinos.
Short Second Prize: THE GREEK COMMUNITY OF HEIDELBERG, directed by Lefteris Xanthopoulos.
Short Third Prize: TSAMIKOS--A HEROIK SHOW, produced and directed by Manos Eustratiadis.
Short Fourth Prize: MINUS--PORTRAIT, produced and directed by Leonidas Papadakis.
Honorary Distinctions: Actors Stathis Yallelis, Stavros Kalaroglou, George Moshidis, George Sarri, Costas

Jury boxes at 1976 Festival. Melina Mercouri in white;
Diane Baker to left of Mercouri; director Philip Saville with
hand to face.

Tzoumas for HAPPY DAY; George Triantafyllou for
editing of CYPRUS; Thanassis Arvanitis, Sound Engineer for HAPPY DAY.

1977 ("OFFICIAL" FESTIVAL)

First Prize: IPHIGENIA, produced by the Greek Film Cen-
  ter, directed by Michael Cacoyannis.
Second Prize: ALEXANDER THE GREAT (Alexandros O
  Megas), produced by Nestor Matsas and Ioannis Syl-
  landavos, directed by Matsas.
Best Photography: Constantine Papayannakis for THE GREAT
  DECISION (Megali Apofasi).
Best Musical Score: Constantine Kapnissis for ALEXANDER
  THE GREAT.

Best Set Design: Mikis Karapiperis for CLOSED WINDOW
(To Klisto Parathyro).
Best Actress: Tatiana Papamoskou for IPHIGENIA.

Shorts

1st Prize: George Belesiotis for ETANA THE FIRST STAR-
SAILOR.
2nd Prize: Yannis Grivas for THE DEATH IN THE ANCIENT
TIMES.
3rd Prize: Dimitris Kapralos and Victoria Fagounaki for
AND WE LIVE BETTER EVER AFTER.
4th Prize: Theodoros Skouras for CARNIVAL IN SKYROS.
(No Other Prizes Given).

1977 ("NEW DIRECTORS" FESTIVAL)

First Prize: THE HEAVY MELON (To Vary Peponi), pro-
duced by Pavlos Tassios.
Second Prize: STRUGGLE OF THE BLIND (O Agonas ton
Tyflon), produced by Positiv, directed by Maria Hazi-
mihali-Papaliou; EDUCATION (Pethia), produced and
directed by Yannis Typaldos.
Third Prize: WOMEN TODAY (Oi Ginekez Simera), pro-
duced by Iason Velisaratos, George Apostolidis and
Cinevision, directed by Popi Alkouli.
Best Director: Pavlos Tassios for THE HEAVY MELON.
Best Screenplay: Pavlos Tassios for THE HEAVY MELON.
Best Photography: Yannis Kaspiris and Thodoros Maranghos
for EVIA--MANTOUDI 76.
Best Sound: Nicos and Andreas Achladis for THE WALL
(O Tihos).
Best Direction, First Film: Antoinetta Angelidi for VARIA-
TIONS ON THE SAME THEME (Parallagez sto Ithio
Thema).
Best Actor: Mimis Chryllomallis & Antonis Antoniou for

Opposite: (above) Melina Mercouri, President of the Domestic Festival Jury; Diane Baker, President of the International
Festival Jury, and actress Eleni Halkousi, President of the
Selection Committee of the Domestic Festival, 1976. (Below) Jury and Award Winners, 1976 Festival. Second from
left, with glasses, Thodoros Angelopoulos; to his right, cinematographer Stavros Hasapis, Melina Mercouri, Pandelis
Voulgaris. Actor Stathis Yallelis, second from right, rear.

THE HEAVY MELON.

Best Actress: Caterina Goghou for THE HEAVY MELON.

Shorts

1st Prize: Vasiliki Iliopoulou for THE TRAGIC DEATH OF GRANDFATHER; and Takis Papayannidis for A HOLIDAY IN DRRAPETHSONA.

2nd Prize: Apostolos Krionas for INSIDE THE WALL; and Frieda Liapa for A WHOLE LIFE YOU ARE LIVING.

3rd Prize: Fivos Konstantiniadis for A USELESS SHORT and GOODNIGHT.

4th Prize: Alida Dimitriou for COAL WORKERS; and Alekos Tsafas for THE WORD.

Honorary Mentions

Kostas Mesaris for acting in A USELESS SHORT.
Nicos Smaragdis for quality of his photography.
Antonis Kyriakoulis for costumes in THE POWER (Aphondez).
George Panousopoulos for photography of THE POWER.

The Panhellinic Union of Critics Awards

Best Film: VARIATIONS ON THE SAME THEME, and THE HEAVY MELON.

Best Documentary: WOMEN TODAY.

Best Short: A WHOLE LIFE YOU ARE LIVING.

Best Short Documentary: A HOLIDAY IN DRRAPETHSONA.

[See Appendix for list of 1978 Festival Awards.]

Chapter 21

A SELECTED FILMOGRAPHY

This selected filmography represents most of the new cinema of the 1970s. A few films are included which do not technically belong to the new movement, especially within the documentary genre; they are listed merely to indicate that a few of the previously established directors have found their way into the new cinematic framework. Films produced by the Greek Film Center are included, despite the fact that a primary quality of the '70s Greek film is independence. The Greek Film Center is a government-supported concern for the film art, created after the collapse of the junta, and thus is technically a distinctive ingredient of the new film movement.

Only reviews in English were actively sought for documentation, but where reviews found in another language they were included.

Most of these films are discussed in greater detail elsewhere, usually within the sections devoted to the individual directors.

ALDEVARAN (1975). Script and Direction: Andreas Thomopoulos. Photography: George Panousopoulos. Editor: Tonia Marketaki. Songs and Music: Dimitris Poulikakos, Rolling Stones, J. S. Bach, Jethro Tull, Chris Tertzis, Wally Shorts, Bob Dylan, Nikos Asimos, Stamatis Spanoudakis. 85 minutes. For Movielab-Hellas. Players: Dimitris Fininis, Helen Maniati, Dimitris Poulikakos, Nikos Glavas, Manolis Logiadis, Despino Tomazani, Achilleas Paniperis. Prizes: Honorary Distinction, 1975 Thessaloniki Festival. Festival Participation: Bologna (Italy) 1976. Reviews: The Athenian, Nov. '75; 1977 International Film Guide; Variety, Nov. 5, 1975.

ATTILA '74 (1975). Script and Direction: Michael Cacoyannis. Photography: Sakis Maniatis. 2nd Unit Phot: Nikos Kavoukidis, Katharine Leroy. Music: Mihalis Hristodoulides. Produced by Michael Cacoyannis. 98 minutes. Cacoyannis' only venture into documentary filmmaking concerns the problems of his home country--Cyprus. Reviews: Monthly Film Bulletin, Oct. '75; Variety, Nov. 19, '75.

BIO-GRAPHY (VIO-GRAFIA) (1975). Director: Thanassis Rentzis. Script by Rentzis based on a book by Chumy Chumez. Photography: Christos Manghos. Music: Stamitis Spanoudakis. Narrator: George Kiritsis. For Filmogram (Manghos and Rentzis). 90 minutes. Prizes: Third Prize, 1975 Thessaloniki Festival. Festival Participation: Rotterdam, 1976; Bologna, 1976; San Sebastian, 1977; Poretta (Italy) 1976; Cannes (Cinemathèque Française manifestation), 1977. Reviews: Athenian, Nov. 1975; Variety, Nov. 5, 1975.

THE BITTERNESS OF THE JEWISH SCAPEGOAT see VIOLENT JOHN

BLACK & WHITE (MAVROS KAI LEVKOS) (1973). Directors: Thanassis Rentzis, Nikos Zervos. Script: Rentzis. Photography: Sakis Maniatis. Music: Manos Loisos and Giorgos Papadakis. 76 minutes. Players: Giorgos Tsemberopoulos, Vicky Potamianou. For Makrofilm. Festival Participation: Thessaloniki, 1973.

BULLETS ARE FLYING LIKE HAIL (PEFTOUI OI SFEPES SAN TO HALAZI) (1977). Written and Directed by Nikos Alevaras. Photography: Lakis Kyrlidis. Edited by Takis Davlopoulos. Sound: Marinos Athanasepoulos. Music: Vangelis Maniatis. For Nikos Alevaras and Kouroz Company. Players: Litsa Gerardou-Alevara, Nikos Alevaras. 150 minutes. Festival Participation: Thessaloniki New Director Festival, 1977 (Out of Competition).

THE CELL ZERO (TO KELLI MIDEN) (1975). Written and Directed by Yannis Smaragdes. Photography: Nikos Smaragdes. Music: Nikos Kanakis. For George Papaleos. 90 minutes. Players: Costas Kazacos, Vangelis Kazan, Sophia Saerle. Festival Participation: Thessaloniki, 1975. Reviews: The Athenian, Nov. '75; Variety, Nov. 5, 1975.

First film by Smaragdes. Political-fiction based on a true
story.   A Communist is arrested and tortured during the junta regime, imprisoned with a veteran officer who, like the
Communist, fought during the Greek Civil War, but on the
opposite side.   Former enemies become allies against common enemy.

CLOSED WINDOW (KLISTO PARATHIRO) (1977).   Script and
Direction: Ermis Vellopoulos. Photography: Dimitris Papaconstantis. Music: Vanghelis Katsolis. Assistant Director:
Angelos Roussos.   Players: Vangelis Kazan, Gogo Anztoletaki, Dinos Avgoustidis, Nina Papazafiropoulou, Giorgos Dimou,
Yannis Himonidis.   For Greek Film Center and Kearhos Konitsiotis.   105 minutes.   Study of the unhappiness of a typical
marriage of convenience and its tragic consequences within
a provincial society with its fear, prejudice and long history
of political oppression.   Festival Participation: 1977 Thessaloniki.

THE COLORS OF IRIS (TA CHROMATA TIS IRIDOS) (1974).
Script and Direction: Nikos Panayotopoulos. Photography:
Nikos Kavoukidis. Sets: Dionisis Fotopoulos. Music:
Stamatis Spanoudakis. Editor: Takis Davlopoulos. Sound:
Thanassis Arvanitis. Production Manager: Lefteris Haron-
itis. Producer: George Papalios. 100 minutes. Players:
Nikitas Tsakiroglou, Vangelis Kazan, George Dialegmenos,
Helena Kirana, Takis Voulalas, Christina, Anghelos Theo-
doropoulos, Flore Darain, George Moshidis, Alecos Deliyan-
nis. Prizes: Best Photography, 1974 Thessaloniki Festival.
Reviews: Athenian, April 1975; International Film Guide 1976;
Variety, Nov. 6, 1974.

CORPUS (1978).   Written and Directed by Thanassis Rentzis.
Photography: Vittorio Pietra.   For Stefi Film and Thanassis
Rentzis.   A study of the effects of environment through his-
tory on the human body.   Also a view of how artists have
depicted man: the Egyptians, the Middle Ages, Modern.
Filming was scheduled for completion in December 1977.

CRANIUM LANDSCAPE (KRANIOU TOPOS) (1973).   Script,
Director, Producer: Konstantinos Aristopoulos. Photography:
George Arvanitis. Editor: Nikos Kanakis. Art Direction
and Costumes: Anastasia Arseni. Music: Dimotika Tra-

goudia. 90 minutes. Players: Takis Kilakos and inhabitants of a small village in Mani. Prizes: Special Awards to Photography and Direction at 1973 Thessaloniki Festival.

CYPRUS (1976). Written and Directed by Thekia Kittou, Lambros Papademetrakis. Photography: Stavros Hasapis. A George Papalios production. 115 minutes. Documentary investigating the difficulties of Cyprus before and after the 1974 Turkish invasion, including a revealing look at the positions of both local and foreign governments in relation to the island's problems. Prize: Third Prize, 1976 Thessaloniki Festival. Review: Variety, Oct. 27, 1976.

THE DARK MAKING OF AN HELIOGRAPHY (I SKOTINI KAT-ASKEVI MIAS ILIOGRAFIAS) (1977). Script and Direction: Dimitris Dimogerontakis. Photography: Stamatis Tripos, George Stavridis. Editor: Kostas Iordanidis. 82 minutes. Produced by Dimogerontakis and Greek Film Centre. Players: Yannis Zavradinos, Irini Kakavouli, Vasilis Tsanglos, Giorgos Grigoriou, Giorgos Tsifos. Metaphysical drama about a solitary young man who sets out on a journey in search of his own identity, leaving behind a catastrophic past and the false values of the establishment.

DAYS OF '36 (MERES TOU 36) (1972). Produced and Directed by Thodoros Angelopoulos. Script: Angelopoulos, Petros Markaris, Stratis Karras. Photography: George Arvanitis. Editor: Takis Davlopoulos. Art Direction: M. Karapiperis. Costumes: Kyriakos Katzourakis. 110 minutes. For Finos Films. Players: Thanos Grammenos, Christos Kalavrouzos, Toula Stathopoulou, Petros Hoidas, C. Himaras, Vassilis Tsanglos, Vangelis Kazan, Costas Sfikas. Prizes: Best Direction, Best Photography, 1972 Thessaloniki Festival; FIPRESCI Prize, Berlin Festival 1972. Additional Festival Participation: Heyres, London, Chicago, Ontario, Barcelona, Venice, Cannes (Director's Fortnightly), New Directors (Museum of Modern Art, New York). Reviews: (In English): Film Comment, Sept. 1974; Films & Filming, Aug. 1973; International Film Guide 1973 and 1974; New York Times, April 3, 1974; Variety, Dec. 12, 1973. See also extensive discussion in Jump Cut, Oct/Dec. 1975. (In French): Cinéma, June 1973; Positif, June 1976; Revue du Cinéma (Image et Son), Oct. 1973, April 1976; Travelling, Sept/Oct. 1973, Jan/Feb. 1974. Additional Reviews: Filmkritik, Aug. 1973 (in German); Cineforum, Sept. 1975 (in Italian).

EDUCATION (PETHIA) (1977). Written, Produced and Directed by Yannis Typaldos. Photography: Andreas Bellis. Editor: Nikos Kanakis. Sound: Panos Panousopoulos. 110 mins. Documentary examining the inadequacies of the educational system in Greece. Prize: 2nd Prize (shared with STRUGGLE OF THE BLIND), 1977 New Directors Festival, Thessaloniki.

THE ENGAGEMENT OF ANNA (TO PROXENIO TIS ANNA) (1972). Director: Pandelis Voulgaris. Script: Voulgaris and Menis Koumantareas. Photography: Nikos Kavoukidis. Editor: Takis Davlopoulos. For Dinos Katsouridis. 87 minutes. Players: Anna Vagena, Costas Rigopoulos, Maria Martika, Smaro Veaki, Alekos Oudinotis, Irini Emirza, Dimitris Malavetas, Stavros Kalaroglou. Prizes: Best Picture; Best First Feature Director; Best Actress (Vagena); Best Supporting Actress (Veaki); Best Supporting Actor (Rigopoulos), 1972 Thessaloniki Festival; FIPRESCI Award, OTTO DIBELIUS Award, OCIC Award, Berlin Festival 1974. Additional Festival Participation: London '74, Beograd '75, Los Angeles Filmex '75, New Directors (Museum of Modern Art, New York) '75. Reviews: Film, Feb '75; New York Times, Apr. 8, 1975; Variety, Dec. 12, 1973; Kosmorama #22 (in Danish). See also extensive discussion in Jump Cut, Oct/Dec. 1975.

EURIDICE BA-2037 (EVRIDIKI B. A. 2037) (1975). Script, Direction, Production: Nikos Nikolaidis. Photography: George Panousopoulos. Editor: George Triantafillou. Assistant Director: A. Tsikifonis. Art Direction and Sets: Marie Louise Vartholomeou. 100 minutes. Players: Vera Tchechova, John Moore, Niki Triantafillidour. Prizes: Best Director First Film; Best Art Direction, 1975 Thessaloniki Festival. Reviews: International Film Guide 1975; Variety, Nov. 5, 1975.

EVERYTHING IS IN ORDER, BUT ON THE OTHER HAND... (NAI MEN ALA...) (1972). Script and Direction: Pavlos Tassios. Photography: Nikos Petanidis. For Finos Films. 85 minutes. Players: Fanis Hinas, Melanie Stanzou, Alexis

Damianos, Anna Metallidou, Manolis Destounis. Prize:
Best Screenplay, 1972 Thessaloniki Festival. Review: International Film Guide 1974.

EVIA-MANTOUDI 76 (1977). Written and Directed and Edited by Yannis Anonopoulos. Photography by Yannis Kaspiris
and Thodoros Maranghos. Sound by Anonopoulos, Kaspiris,
Maranghos and H. Manopoulou. Music by Bakalakos. For
George Aniopoulos and A. Klabatsea. 70 minutes. Documentary about workers' strikes. Prize: Best Photography,
1977 New Directors Festival, Thessaloniki.

EVIDENCE (MARTYRIES) (1975). Directed and Photographed
by Nikos Kavoukides. Produced by Kavoukides and K. Pit-
sios. 100 minutes. Political documentary covering internal
turmoil in recent Greek history: students' demonstrations,
police brutality, the people's resistance, strikes, the Polytechnic uprising, the funeral of poet Costas Varnalis, many
other events. Songs and music of Dionissis Savopoulos are
used. Played the 1975 Thessaloniki Festival. Reviewed in
Variety, Nov. 5, 1975.

EXODUS (EXOTHOS) (1976). Director: Ioannis Lintzeris.
Script: Ioannis and Veronica Lintzeris. Photography: Nikos
Iordanidis. Production: Elissavet Dermentzoglou-Lintzeri,
Ioannis Lintzeris. 90 minutes. Players: Simeon Triantafil-
lidis, Antigone Athanasiou. Played 1976 Thessaloniki Festi-
val.

GAZOROS SERRON (1974). Written and directed by Takis
Hatzopoulos. Photography: Evaguelos Eliopoulos. Music:
George Papadakis. A Cinetic-Ap. Papaefstathiou & Co. production. 77 minutes. "Gazoros is a village, Serron a re-
gion. The film is somewhere between a documentary and fiction, which gives a very personal point of view of how the
lives of these people are. It is the filmmaker's village; the
film is very socially aware. He uses the people of the villages to act their lives. There is minimal dialogue. They
illustrate their worries, their struggles, their concerns.
Hatzopoulos has a great sense of economy of the medium. "
(As quoted in an interview with George Tsemberopoulos regarding documentary filmmaking in Greece.) Prize: Best
Production (shared with MEGARA) at 1974 Thessaloniki Festival. Reviewed in Variety, Oct. 30, 1974.

GET ON YOUR MARK (LEVETE THESIS) (1973). Script, Direction, Production, Editing: Thodoros Maranghos. Photography: Nikos Petanidis. 87 minutes. Players: Vangelis Kazan, Christos Tolios, Costas Tsakonas, Vassilis Tsipidis, Fani Toliou, Costas Alexandrakis. Prizes: Best Picture, Best Cinematography, Best First Picture Director, Special Acting Award to Kazan, 1973 Thessaloniki Festival. Reviewed International Film Guide 1975.

THE GREAT LOVE SONGS (O MEGALOS EROTIKOS) (1973). Script and Direction: Pandelis Voulgaris. Photography: George Arvanitis. Additional Photography: George Panousopoulos. Editor: Panousopoulos. Produced by Voulgaris and Manos Hatzidakis. Music by Hatzidakis. Songs sung by Fleri Dandonaki and Dimitris Psarianos. 75 minutes. Special Award for Arvanitis' Photography at 1973 Thessaloniki Festival. Reviewed International Film Guide 1974.

HAPPY DAY (1976). Directed by Pandelis Voulgaris. Script: Voulgaris, loosely based on a book by Andreas Franghias. Photography: George Panousopoulos. Music: Dionissis Savopoulos. Art Direction: Yannis Kalatzis. Editor: Aristidis Karydis-Fuchs. Sound: Thanassis Arvanitis. Produced by Greek Film Center. 100 minutes. Players: George Sarri, George Moshidis, Stavros Kalaroglou, Nikos Bousdoukos, Costas Tzoumas, Costas Fissoun, Stathis Yallelis, Dimitris Poulikakos, Dimitris Meletis. Prizes: Best Film; Best Director; Best Music; Honorary Distinction for Acting to Yallelis, Kalaroglou, Moshidis, Sarri, Tzoumas; Best Sound Recording, 1976 Thessaloniki Festival. Panhellenic Union of Film Critics Award, Best Picture. Additional Festival Participation: Locarno '76; New Delhi '77; Beograd '77; Rotterdam '77; Los Angeles Filmex '77; Sydney '77; Festival da Figueira da Foz - Portugal '77. Reviews: International Film Guide 1978; The Sunday Times (London), Sept. 5, 1976; Sight & Sound, Winter '76/77; Variety, Oct. 27, 1976.

THE HEAVY MELON (TO VARY PEPONI) (1977). Produced, Directed and Written by Pavlos Tassios. Photography: Costas Nastos. Music: George Papadakis. Editor: Yannis Tsitsopoulos. 95 minutes. Players: Mimis Chryllomallis, Caterina Goghou, Lida Protopsalti, Antonis Antoniou, Costas Messaris, Meropi Ioannidou. Prizes: Best Film; Best Direction; Best Screenplay; Best Actor (Chryllomallis &

Antoniou); Best Actress (Goghou), 1977 New Directors Festival, Thessaloniki. Panhellenic Union of Critics Award: Best Film (shared with VARIATIONS ON THE SAME THEME).

THE HUNTERS (I KYNIGHI) (1977). Written and Directed by Thodoros Angelopoulos. Photography: George Arvanitis. Sound: Thanassis Arvanitis. Music: Loukianos Kilaidonis. Editor: G. Triandafillidis. An Angelopoulos-INA Production. 165 minutes. Players: Mary Hronopoulou, Eva Kotamanidou, Aliki Georgeouli, Betty Valasi, Vangelis Kazan, George Danis, Elias Stamatiou, Stratos Pahis, Nikos Skouris, Christoforos Nezer. Prize: First Prize, Chicago International Festival 1977. Additional Festival Participation: Cannes (in competition) 1977; Thessaloniki New Directors (out of competition) 1977; Montreal Festival of Festivals; London Festival, 1977. Reviews: The Athenian, Oct. 1977 (extensive); Daily News (New York), May 27, 1977; Sight and Sound, Summer 1977; Variety, May 31, 1977. (In French) Cinéma 77, July 1977. See also: "Greek Film Tops Festival," Chicago Sun-Times, Nov. 14, 1977.

I SEE A SOLDIER (TO KORITSI TOU STRATIOTI) (1971). Written and Directed by Alexis Damianos. Photography: Christos Manghos. Music: Manos Loizos. A British-Greek co-production by Catamor-Poria for A. Haliotis. Players: Maria Vassiliou, Giorgos Koutouzis, Christos Zorbas, Koula Agagiotou. A story of love, hate and death by Alexis Damianos, a distinguished figure in the Greek theatre who entered the cinema in 1966 with TO THE SHIP. Prize: Best Actress (Vassiliou), Thessaloniki Festival, 1971.

I STRUGGLE TO LIVE (POLEMONTA) (1975). Director: Dimitris Mavrikios. Photography: Lefteris Pavlopoulos. Music: Helen Karaendrou. A Dimitris Ponticas Production. 70 minutes. "I remember another film which I admire very much. POLEMONTA, roughly translated as I STRUGGLE TO LIVE, was made partially with Greek money, but shot in Sicily where there are two or three villages where people still speak Greek. These people inhabitated Sicily as far back as 300 B. C. Throughout he uses literary, historical commentary within the subtitles. I would have preferred the voice of the people themselves, but that is very personal. This film is really an excellent film; everything he does he complements with the quality of the people. You are very

aware that the essence of the film is the very real human
beings who are in it. " (Quoted from an interview with
George Tsemberopoulos regarding documentary filmmaking in
Greece.) Played 1975 Thessaloniki Festival. Reviewed
Variety, Nov. 5, 1975.

THE INDOLENCE OF THE FERTILE VALLEY (I TEMBE-
LIDES TIS EFORIS KILADAS) (1978). An Alix Film Production. Written and Directed by Nicos Panayotopoulos from the
book by Albert Cossery. Photography: Andreas Bellis. Editor: Yorgos Triantafylou. Players: Olga Karlatos, Nikitas
Tsakiroglou, George Dialegmenos, Dimitris Poulikakos, Vassilis Diamandopoulos, Costas Sfikas, Ivy Mavridis. Won
First Prize at the 1978 Locarno International Film Festival.
Review: Variety, Aug. 23, 1978 (as "The Slothful Ones of
the Fertile Valley"). See also: "A Greek Tops Locarno
Prizings, " Variety, Aug. 23, 1978.

IPHIGENIA (1977). Directed by Michael Cacoyannis. Screen-
play: Cacoyannis based on Iphigenia in Aulis by Euripides.
Photography: George Arvanitis. Music: Mikis Theodorakis.
Editors: Cacoyannis and Takis Yannopoulos. Produced by
Greek Film Center. 130 minutes. Players: Irene Papas,
Costa Kazakos, Costa Carras, Tatiana Papamoskou, Christos
Tsangas, Panos Michalopoulos, Angelos Yannoulis, Dimitri
Aronis, George Vourvahakis, Irene Koumarianou, Georges
Economou. IPHIGENIA played competitively at Cannes and
Chicago International Festivals in 1977; took Best Picture
and Best Actress (Papamoskou) awards at 1977 Thessaloniki
Festival. In general distribution internationally in 1977.
Widely reviewed in general magazines, film specialty maga-
zines, and newspapers.

KARAGHIOZIS (1975). Directed and Produced by Helen Vou-
douri. Photography: Vangelis Iliopoulos. Editor: Spiros
Provis. Historical Advisors: Vangelis Vavanatsos, George
Karanikolas. Music Arrangements: George Papadakis. Nar-
rator: George Karipidis. Shadow Theater Performers:
Savas Glitzanis, Mimis Manos, Manthos Athieneos, Evgenios
Spatharis, Sotiris Spatharis. 90 minutes. Prize: Special
Mention, 1975 Thessaloniki Festival. Additional Festival
Participation: Bologna 1975; Brussels 1976. Reviews: The
Athenian, Nov. '75; International Film Guide 1977; Variety,
Nov. 5, 1975.

KIERION (1968). Produced and Directed by Dimosthenis
Theos. Script: Theos and Costas Sfikas. Photography:
George Panousopoulos. Editor: Vangelis Serdaris. Players: Anestis Vlakos, Dimos Starenios, Stavros Tornes,
Helen Theofilou, Elli Xanthaki, Kiriakos Katsourakis, Titika
Vlahopoulou, Costas Sfikas, Grigoris Masallas, Pandelis Voulgaris, Thodoros Angelopoulos. For George Papalios. 86
minutes. Black & White. Shown at Venice Festival in 1968,
but not premiered in Greece until 1974. Prizes: First
Prize (shared with MODEL); Best First Film Director; Honorary Mention for Acting to Vlakos, 1974 Thessaloniki Festival; Honorary Mention at Venice Festival in 1968. Reviews: International Film Guide 1976; Variety, Oct. 30,
1974.

LETTER TO NAZIM HIKMET (GRAMMA STON NAZIM XIK-
MET) (1976). Screenplay and Direction: Konstantinos Aristopoulos. Production of Positive E. P. E. 70 minutes. The
film consists of photographic material and is a salute to the
people of Turkey, Chile, Spain, and various African countries. Played 1976 Thessaloniki Festival. Review: Variety,
Oct. 27, 1976.

MANI (1975). A Sakis Maniatis production, written, directed
and photographed by Maniatis. 83 minutes. Mani is a particularly unique pocket of Greece which has retained old traditions and customs. Film not only captures the folkloric
quality of Mani, but also questions reasons for retention of
conservative ways, not only in Mani, but also in settlements
of people from Mani who took their traditions with them. A
solitary three-year effort by filmmaker Maniatis. Honorary
Distinction at 1975 Thessaloniki Festival. Reviewed in Variety, Nov. 5, 1975.

MAY (MIAS) (1976). Script and Direction: Tasos Psarras.
Photography: Stavros Hasapis. Sound: Argiris Lazaridis.
Editor: Babis Alepis. Music Selection and Adaptation:
Loukianos Kilaidonis. Art Direction: Mitsos Mitsobounis.
Production Manager: Mihalis Kostopoulos. Production Or-
ganization: Millie Delipetrou. Produced by Sinergatiki
E. P. E. 100 minutes. Players: Vassilis Gopis, Dimitris
Vayas, Stelios Kapatos, Mihalis Boyaridis, Anna Vagena,
George Iordanidis, Helen Karpeta, Costas Constantinidis,
Panos Kaisidis, Helen Mekiosoglou, Thanassis Papadimitriou,

Christos Fitsoris, Kate Mitropoulou, Olympia Tolika, Tho-
doros Rizoudis, Zafiris Katramadas, Thanassis Milonas,
Tasos Pantazis, Roula Pateraki, Mihalis Romanos, Stratos
Tripkos, Dim. Mavromatis, Aspasia Papathanasiou, Vangelis
Kazan. Played 1976 Thessaloniki Festival. Reviewed in
Variety, October 27, 1976.

MEGARA (1974). Script and Direction: Sakis Maniatis,
George Tsemberopoulos. Photography and Editing: Maniatis.
For George Tsemberopoulos. 75 minutes. Documentary
about the last days of a rich rural village evacuated to make
way for an oil refinery. Prizes: Best Production (shared
with GAZOROS SERRON), 1974 Thessaloniki Festival; Special
Distinction, Berlin Festival (Forum of Young Cinema). Additional Festival Participation: Venice, 1975; Rotterdam,
1975; Antwerp, 1975; Cannes (Week of Political Film), 1975;
London (A Month of Greek Films); Poretta (Italy), 1975.
Reviewed in Variety, Oct. 30, 1974.

METROPOLIS (1975). Script and Direction: Costas Sfikas.
Photography: Diamantis Ananidis, Manolis Adamakis, Thanas-
sis Ananidis. Music: Camille Saint-Saens. Excerpts from
Rilke and Proust. For Cinetic. 90 minutes. Played 1975
Thessaloniki Festival. Reviewed in Variety, Nov. 5, 1975.

MODEL (MODELLO) (1974). Script and Direction by Costas
Sfikas. Photography: George Cavayas. Set: Sfikas and
Cavayas. Factory-yard and figure construction: Nikos Papa-
dakis, Yannis Papadakis, Vassilis Spahos. Designers: Zoi
Keramea, Vangelis Chrysovitsiotis, Christos Santamouris.
Art Assistants: Dimitris Mitaras, Yannis Valavanidis. As-
sistant Screenwriter: Thanos Grammenos. Assistants:
Nikos Alevras, Vassilis Vafeas, Manos Efstratiadis, Takis
Davlopoulos, Yannis Smaragdis. Rhythm: Leni Keramea.
Production Manager: Lefteris Haronitis. Produced by George
Papalios, Anna Sfika and Contemporary Cinema. 105 minutes.
Prize: Best Art Feature (Shared with KIERION), 1974 Thes-
saloniki Festival. Festival Participation: Berlin (Forum)
1975; Rotterdam 1975; Toulon 1975; London (Greek Week).
Reviews: International Film Guide 1976; Variety, Oct. 30,
1974.

THE MURDERESS (I FONISSA) (1974). Director: Costas

Ferris. Script: Ferris and Dimosthenis Theos based on the
novel by Alexandros Papadiamantis. Photography: Stavros
Hasapis. Editor: Yanna Spiropoulou. Music: Stavros Logaridis. Art Director: Tasos Zografos. For Semeli Films.
90 minutes. Players: Maria Alkeou, Dimitra Zeza, Fivos
Taxiarhis, Natalia Alkeou, Elpidoforos Gotsis, Costas Dar-
lasis, Helen Ioannou, Anthi Kariofilli. Prizes: Best Director; Best Actress (Alkeou), 1974 Thessaloniki Festival. Reviewed in Variety, Oct. 30, 1974. See also, "Greek Films
vs. Films Made by Greeks, " by Andrew Horton, Pilgrimage,
April 1976.

THE NEW PARTHENON (O NEOS PARTHENONAS) (1975).
Director: Kostas Chronopoulos and G. Chryssovitsianos.
Screenplay: Spyros Zahos. Photography: Thanassis Scrou-
belos. Music: Loukianos Kelaedonis. A George Papaleos-
"Group 4" production. 110 minutes. Documentary: Inves-
tigates the exile of people to the islands of Makronissos and
Yarnos following World War II, and the prevailing conditions
of the time. Constructed of newsreel footage and interviews.
Played 1975 Thessaloniki Festival. Reviewed Variety, Nov.
5, 1975.

THE OTHER LETTER (TO ALLO GRAMMA) (1976). Direction and Screenplay: Lambros Liaropoulos. Photography:
Stavros Hasapis. Production: Lambros Liaropoulos, Greek
Cinematography Center A. B. E. E. 75 minutes. Several
years ago director Liaropoulos did a prize-winning short
called A LETTER FROM CHARLEROIX. Using the short as
a kind of prologue to the feature, he reflects the changes in
Athens as seen by a worker who returns after a long absence. No plot or actors, but not strictly documentary either in that there are fictional elements. Prizes: Second
Prize; Best Photography, 1976 Thessaloniki Festival. Reviewed in Variety, Oct. 27, 1976.

POWER (ARLIONTES) (1977). Produced, Written and Di-
rected by Manoussos Manoussakis. Photographer: George
Panousopoulos. Editor: Takis Davlopoulos. Costumes &
Art Direction: Antonis Kyriakoulis. Music Composed and
Directed by Dimitris Poulikakos. Assistant Director: George
Tsemberopoulos. Players: Minos Argyrakis, Thodoros Dovas,
Max Roman, Irene Dogani, Rita Ban Souzan, Konstantinos
Tzoumas, Spyros Kontoleon, Dimitris Staurakas, Marina

Griva, Tasos Denegris, Nikos Papanikolaou, Manolis Malin-
dretos, Pavlos Patsoukas, Michael Manioudakis, George
Perkikas, Dimitris Meletis, Andreas Liaskos, Tolis Mastro-
kalos, John Pipinis, Thanos Triantifillidis, Dimitris Poulikakos, Nikos Pilavios, Sofia Spyratou, Tasos Prousalis,
Theodor Loukopoulos, Esthir Franko, Stela Geromitsou, Avet
Sfakianaki, Kostas Ziogas, Nick Galiatsos, May Sevastopoulou,
Babis Alatzas, John Bostagoglou, Takis Hristofakis, George
Tzavaras, Sofia Sfiroera, Albert Eskevazy, Alice Throumou-
lopoulou, Nikos Nikolaou, Despina Baboula, Mary Giannako-
poulos, Vaso Boziki, Manolis Logiadis, Moular, Panagiotis
Christopoulos, George Georgis, Mirto Kotzamani, Roi Kat-
sarou, Iris Georgakaki, Natasa, George Tsemberopoulos,
Manoussos Manoussakis. Played 1977 New Directors Festival
at Thessaloniki; cited with Honorary Mention to Costumes
and Photography. Scheduled to play San Remo Festival in
1978, and Cannes Week of Political Cinema, 1978.

THE PROCEEDINGS (I THIATHIKASIA) (1976). Script and
Direction: Dimosthenis Theos. Photography: George Ar-
vanitis, Aris Stavrou. Art Direction: Tonis Ioannou,
Thanassis Papayannakos. Costumes: Toula Katohianou.
Editor: Andreas Andreadakis. Music: Christodoulos Ha-
laris. Producer: Yannis Stefanis. For Cosmovision E. P. E.
110 minutes. Players: Costas Sfikas, Helen Maniati,
Anghelos Sfakianakis, Costas Haralambidis, Yannis Evdemon,
George Balis, Iro Kiriakaki, Costas Mandilas, Nikos Kouros,
Yannis Totsikas, Dimitris Poulikakos, Costas Vrettos. Festival Participation: Thessaloniki, 1976; Pezaro (Italy) (a
week of Ideology and Cinema), 1976; a film seminar in England, "Theory and Movies, " 1976. Reviewed in Variety,
Oct. 27, 1976.

PROMETHEUS SECOND PERSON, SINGULAR (PROMITHEAS
SE THEFTERO PROSOPO) (1975). Produced, Written, Di-
rected by Costas Ferris. Based on Aeschylus' Prometheus
Bound, Hesiod's Theogony and the Bardo Thodol. Text:
Costas Vrettakos. Photography: Stavros Hasapis. Music:
Stamatis Spanoudakis. Choreography and Costume Design:
Myrto Paraschi. A Stefi Film co-produced by the Greek
Film Center. 90 minutes. Players: Yiannis Canoupakis,
Myrto Paraschi, Vangelis Maniatis, George Vouros, Costas
Vrettos, Costas Ferris, and members of the Theatre Re.
Prizes: Best Music, Thessaloniki Festival, 1975; Best Mu-
sic, Cairo Festival, 1976. Reviewed in Variety, Nov. 5,
1975.

THE REASON WHY (THI ASIMANTON AFORMIN) (1974).
Script and Direction: Tasos Psarras. Photography: Stavros Hasapis. Editor: Takis Davlopoulos. Music: Folk-
songs arranged by Domna Samiou. Set Decoration and Costumes: Julia Stavridou. Players: Mihalis Boyaridis, Stelios Kapatos, Byron Tsaboulas, Vana Fitsori, George Four-
niadis, Lazaros Aslanidis, Hristos Fitsoris. For George
Papalios. 120 minutes. Prize: Best Actor Award for Boyaridis at 1974 Thessaloniki Festival. Additional Festival
Participation: Cannes (Director's Fortnightly) 1975. Reviewed in Variety, Nov. 6, 1974.

RECONSTRUCTION (ANAPARASTASIS) (1970). (Alternate
Title: RE-ENACTMENT). Director: Thodoros Angelopoulos.
Script: Angelopoulos, Stratis Karras, Thanassis Valtinos
(based on a true story). Photography: George Arvanitis.
Editor: T. Davlopoulos. Sound: Th. Arvanitis. Producer:
George Samiotis. 100 minutes. Players: Toula Stathopou-
lou, Yannis Totsikas, Thanos Grammenos, Petros Hoedas,
Nikos Alevras, Thodoros Angelopoulos. For Akrololis Films.
Prizes: Best Foreign Film, Hyères Festival 1971. Thessa-
loniki Festival 1970: Best Film; Best First Feature Director;
Best Photography; Best Supporting Actress (Stathopoulou).
Prix Georges Sadoul 1971. FIPRESCI Special Mention, Ber-
lin Festival, 1971. Prix du Bureau Catholique, Mannheim
Festival, 1971. Best Film, Greek Critics, 1971. Additional
Festival Participation: London, Chicago, Ontario, Barcelona,
Venice, 1971. Reviews: International Film Guide 1972; Sun-
day Times (London), Sept. 11, 1975; Variety, Dec. 12, 1973.

THE REHEARSAL (1974). Directed by Jules Dassin. "The
film was made hurriedly in New York on a shoe-string budget of $250,000 but was never released, ironically, because
of the sudden turn of events which overthrew the colonels.
Although it was shown at the Berlin Festival in 1974, it was
not released in Greece until 1975.... [It] is the work of a
Philhellene. Greece has always been fortunate to attract the
love and support of those foreigners who have delighted in
Greece as a tradition and as a country. Dassin ... proves
his ability for social commentary, speaks honestly." (Andy
Horton, The Athenian, Feb. '75). The film is a documentary of sorts, designed to inform those outside of Greece
(specifically in America) about the situation in that country,
then under the junta regime. There are songs, student
meetings, readings of actual letters and documents by such

celebrities as Arthur Miller, Lillian Hellman, Maximilian
Schell, Laurence Olivier. Mr. Dassin and Melina Mercouri
appear. There are songs by Mikis Theodorakis and Yannis
Markopoulos. 90 minutes. (Thanks to Jules Dassin for information regarding this film.)

SONGS OF FIRE (TRAGOUDIA TIS FOTIAS) (1975). Director: Nikos Koundouros. Photography: Nikos Kavoukidis,
Nikos Adamopoulos, Pavlos Filippou, Sirrakos Danalis, Nikos
Gardelis, Sakis Maniatis, Aristidis Karydis Fuchs. Editors:
Fuchs, Koundouros. For Finos Films. "After seven years
of self-exile Koundouros (who directed the well-known YOUNG
APHRODITES) returned to Greece to make his documentary
about the first days of liberation from the junta. Film opens
with two concerts by Theodorakis, Yannis Markopoulos, Stavros Xarhakos and other popular composers and performers
(including Melina Mercouri). Koundouros covers the entire
emotional spectrum in his portrayal of a nation suddenly released from fear and restraint." As quoted in the 1976 International Film Guide. Extensive review in The Athenian,
March 1975.

STRUGGLE (AGONAS) (1975). Produced, Written, Photographed and Directed by Dimitris Yannikopoulos, George
Thanasoulas, Ilias Zafiropoulos, Thodoros Maranghos, Fivos
Ekonomidis, Costas Papanikolaou. Music and songs by Ekonomidis. 180 minutes. Prize: Second Prize, 1975 Thessaloniki Festival. Reviews: Films in Review, April 1976;
International Film Guide 1977; Variety, Oct. 29, 1975. See
also interview with five of the directors regarding the film
in Journal of the Hellenic Diaspora, April 1976.

STRUGGLE OF THE BLIND (O AGONAS TON TYFLON)
(1977). Directed by Maria Hazimihali-Papaliou. Photography: Dimitris Vernikos, Costas Karamanidis. Edited by
Vernikos and Hazimihali-Papaliou. Sound: Yannis Dermi-
zakis and Dim. Athanasopoulos. For Positiv. 90 minutes.
Documentary about the difficult life of the blind, driven to
begging because of no work or help. Prize: Second Prize
at New Directors Festival, Thessaloniki, 1977 (shared with
EDUCATION).

THE TRAVELLING PLAYERS (O THIASSOS) (1975). Script

and Direction: Thodoros Angelopoulos. Photography: George
Arvanitis. Music: Loukianos Kilaidonis. Editor: Takis
Davlopoulos, Georges Trianthaphilou. Art Director: Mike
Karapiperis. Special Effects: Yannis Samiotis. Costumes:
George Patsas. Sound: Thanassis Arvanitis. Producer:
George Samiotis. A George Papalios Production. 230 min-
utes. Players: Eva Kotamanidou, Aliki Georgoulis, Statos
Pachis, Maris Vassiliou, Petros Zarkadis, Kiriakos Katri-
vanos, Yannis Firlos, Nina Papazaphiropoulou, Alekos Bou-
bis, Kosta Stiliaris, Greg Evaghelathos, Vangelis Kazan.
Prizes: First Prize; Best Director; Best Screenplay; Best
Photography; Best Actor (Kazan); Best Actress (Kotamanidou)
1975 Thessaloniki Festival; FIPRESCI Prize, Cannes 1975;
Special Prize, Taormina (Italy) 1975; Interfilm Prize, Berlin
1975; British Film Institute Award for Best Film 1976; Prix
l'age d'or, Brussels; Grand Prize, Figueira da Foz, 1976.
Additional Festival Participation: Barcelona; Montreal; Los
Angeles Expo. Reviews: (In English): The Athenian, Dec.
'75; Cineaste 7:4, '77; The Coffeehouse, Spring, 1976; Film
(London), June '76; Films & Filming, Aug. '75, June '76;
International Film Guide 1976; Journal of the Hellenic Dia-
spora, Aug. 1976; London Observer, Sept. 12, 1976; London
Sunday Times, Sept. 12, 1976; London Times, Sept. 10, 1976;
Millimeter, July/Aug. '75; Monthly Film Bulletin, May '76;
New York Times, Ap. 10, '76; Sight & Sound, Summer 1975;
Variety, June 4, 1975. (In French): Avant-Scène du Ciné-
ma, Dec. '75; Cinéma Pratique, Dec. '75; Ecran, Nov. '75;
Image et Son, June/July '75, Nov. '75; Jeune Cinéma, July/
Aug '75; Positif, Oct '75, July/Aug '75; Télécine, Nov/Dec.
'75; Cinéforum (Italian), Sept. '75. See also: "The Troupe
Battles On, " New Greece, March '75; "The Travelling Play-
ers: A Historical Guide, " by David Wilson, Monthly Film
Bulletin, May '76.

VARIATIONS ON THE SAME THEME (PARALLAGEZ STO
ITHIO THEMA) (1977). Written, Produced, Edited, Directed
by Antoinetta Angelidi. Photography: Pako Perinan. Mu-
sic: Gilbert Artman. 63 minutes. Player: Josie Deleter.
Prizes: Best Directory First Film at 1977 New Directors
Festival, Thessaloniki; Panhellenic Union of Critics Award:
Best Film (shared with THE HEAVY MELON).

VARTHOLOMEOS (1973). Script and Direction: Manoussos
Manoussakis. Photography: George Antonakis. Editor: Ilias
Sgouropoulos. Music and Songs: Yannis Markopoulos (sung

by Xilouris). Players: Giorgos Ballis, Stella Arkadi, Yannis Kafaloukos, Junie Villon, Minas Konstantopoulos, Giorgos Tzerbos, Dimitrios Christopoulos, Christos Kostopoulos, Giorgos Zerigas. Produced by Despina Tataki and Manoussakis. 95 minutes. Prize: Honorary Distinction at San Remo Festival, 1973. Also played 1973 Thessaloniki Festival. Reviews: International Film Guide 1974; Image et Son, Oct. 1973 (in French).

VIOLENT JOHN (IOANNIS O VIEOS) (Also known as THE BITTERNESS OF THE JEWISH SCAPEGOAT) (1973). Script, Direction, Editing: Tonia Marketaki. Photography: George Arvanitis. Produced by Contemporary Cinema-Tonia Marketaki-Finos Films. Players: Manolis Logiadis, Mika Flora, Nikitas Tsakiroglou. Prizes: Best Direction, Best Screenplay, Best Actor (Logiadis), 1973 Thessaloniki Festival. Reviews: The Athenian, April 1975; Variety, Nov. 28, 1973.

THE WALL (O TIHOS) (1977). Director: Stelios Pavlithis. Script by Pavlithis based on the short story by Jean Paul Sartre. Photography: Ariss Stavrou and Tassos Alexakis. Editor: Babis Alepis. Sound: Nikos and Adreas Achladis. Players: Vassilis Diamadopoulos, Christos Tsangas, Andreas Papaspiros. 67 minutes. Produced by Nikos Hatziathanasiou. Prize: Best Sound, New Directors Festival, Thessaloniki, 1977.

WHAT DID YOU DO IN THE WAR, THANASSI? (TI EKANES STO POLEMO, THANASSI?) (1971). Director, Producer, Editor: Dinos Katsouridis. Script: Asimakis Yalamas, Katsouridis. Photography: George Arvanitis. Music: Mimis Pleasas. For Carayannis-Caratzopoulos. 90 minutes. Players: Thanassis Vengos, Efi Roditi, Antonis Papadopoulos, D. Veakis, Ketty Lambropoulou, Katerina Gogou, Nikitas Platis. Prizes: Best Film; Best Actor (Vengos); Best Screenplay, Thessaloniki Festival, 1971. Review: International Film Guide 1973.

WOMEN TODAY (OI GINEKES SIMERA) (1977). Written, Edited, Directed: Popi Alkouli. Photography: Lefteris Pavlopoulos. Sound: George Karavatsis. Music: Haris Vrontos. For Iason Velisaratos, George Apostolidis, Cinevision. 75 minutes. Documentary about women in Greece. Prizes:

Third Prize, New Directors Festival, Thessaloniki, 1977;
Panhellenic Union of Critics Award: Best Documentary,
1977.

USEFUL ADDRESSES

Union of Greek Directors
of Film & Television
Mantzarou 10
Athens, Greece

Greek Film Festival Secretariat
Thessaloniki, Greece

Athens Cinemathèque
Kanaris 1
Athens, Greece

Film Magazine
Zoodohou Pigis 3
Athens, Greece

Contemporary Cinema
Ypatias 5
Athens 118, Greece

The Athenian
Alopekis 20, Kolonaki
Athens, Greece

Additional addresses of more specific nature may be found in the Greek coverage in various issues of International Film Guide.

Greek American Publications of Interest:

The Hellenic Journal
527 Commercial Street
San Francisco, California
94111 U.S.A.

The Coffeehouse
392 San Jose Avenue
San Francisco, California
94110 U.S.A.

Greek World
25 West 45th Street
New York, New York
10036 U.S.A.

Journal of the Hellenic
Diaspora
Pella Publishing Company,
Inc.
461 Eighth Avenue
New York, New York
10001 U.S.A.

1978 THESSALONIKI FESTIVAL AWARDS

Best Films: 1922, produced by The Greek Film Center;
THE INDOLENCE OF THE FERTILE VALLEY (I tem-
belides tis evforis kiladas), an Alix Film Production;
TWO MOONS IN AUGUST (Dio feggaria ton avgousto),
produced by Costas Ferris.

Best Direction: Nicos Koundouros for 1922.

Best Screenplay: Yorgos Scourtis for TWO MOONS IN AU-
GUST.

Best Photography: Nicos Cavoukidis for 1922; Andreas Bellis
for THE INDOLENCE OF THE FERTILE VALLEY
(Award refused).

Best Music: Christodoulos Chalaris for THE AGE OF THE
SEA (I ilikia tis thalassas).

Best Editing: Yorgos Triantafillou for THE INDOLENCE OF
THE FERTILE VALLEY; GOLDEN HAIR (I hrissoma-
loussa); THE AGE OF THE SEA.

Best Art Direction: Dionisis Fotopoulos for THE SUN OF
DEATH (O ilios tou thanatou); THE INDOLENCE OF
THE FERTILE VALLEY; 1922.

Best Sound: Mimis Kassimatis for TWO MOONS IN AUGUST;
Argyris Lazaridis for THE POLK AFFAIR (Ipothesi
Polk).

Best Actor: Vassilis Tsagglos for 1922.

Best Actress: Eleanora Stathopoulos for 1922.

Best First Feature Film: GOLDEN HAIR, produced and directed by Tonis Likouresis.

SHORTS

1st Prize: SKYROS WEDDING (Skyrianos Gamos), produced
& directed by Maria Mavrikou.

2nd Prize: LIVE SHOW (Zontani ekpombi), produced & directed by Fivos Costantinidis.

3rd Prize: THE CARNAGE (To karnagio); produced by Yannis Petropoulakis; directed by Cosmas Panagiotidis.

4th Prize: IT COULD HAVE HAPPENED (Tha borouse nahe
gini), produced and directed by Nicos Zapatinas.

THE CRITICS' CHOICES

Best Films: THE INDOLENCE OF THE FERTILE VALLEY;
THE IRON DOOR (I kallegoporta), produced by D. M.
Film, written & directed by Dimitris Makris.

Best Director: Nicos Panayotopoulos for THE INDOLENCE
OF THE FERTILE VALLEY.

Best Actor: Vangelis Kazan for GOLDEN HAIR; THE POLK
AFFAIR; THE IRON DOOR.

Best Actress: Myrto Parashi for TWO MOONS IN AUGUST.

Best Shorts: GEORGE FROM SOTIRIANIKA (O Yorgos apo
ta Sotirianika), produced by G. Kozombolis, directed
by Lefteris Xanthopoulos; SPATA, SAINT PETER'S
STIFADO (Spata, to Stifado tou Aghiou Petrou), produced by Club Xenophon, directed by Alinda Dimitriou).

Thanks to Pan Bouyoucas for above information. Mr. Bouyoucas covers the festival in detail in the November 1978
issue of The Athenian.

BIBLIOGRAPHY

A limited amount of material on Greek film has been located.
The most important sources are listed below:

Books

Georgiadou, Mirella, in A Concise History of the Cinema,
Vols. 1 & 2, edited by Peter Cowie. London: The
Tantivy Press, 1971.

Georgiadou, Mirella, in International Film Guide, 1971-1978,
edited by Peter Cowie. London: The Tantivy Press.

Mitropoulos, Aglae. Découverte du cinéma Grec. Paris:
Cinema Club Seghers, 1968.

Magazine Articles

Horton, Andrew. "Early Greek Cinema: Karagiozis Un-
chained, " The Athenian, June 21, 1974.

Horton, Andrew. "The Beginnings of a New Wave, " The
Athenian, April 1975.

Schuster, Mel. "A New Vitality in the Struggling Greek
Cinema, " The Hellenic Journal, May 19, 1977. (Re-
printed in the Summer 1977 issue of The Coffeehouse.)

Theos, Dimosthenis. "Film in Griechenland, " Filmkritik,
August, 1973 (in German).

See also: Sight & Sound, July 1945; Winter 1946; Take One,
#7 1967; Variety, May 9, 1973; January 8, 1975; June
11, 1976.

From 1954 through 1958, Films and Filming magazine ran a
column devoted to international news. George Lazarou was
the Greek correspondent. His monthly columns are reflections of the film scene in Greece during the period which
was dominated by the growing international recognition of
Michael Cacoyannis.

Aside from the two film magazines published in Athens, the
most important in-Greek source of information located was:
Iliadis, Frixos. O Ellinikos Kinimatografos. Athens: Fan-
tasia, 1960.